The first edition of this guide was researched and written by **JOHN CURTIN** (right) who lives at the foot of the North Downs Way in Abinger Hammer, Surrey. When not writing, John is busy bird guiding for the RSPB and species surveying for the BTO and Butterfly Conservation.

This second edition was updated by **HENRY STEDMAN**, who was born in Chatham, Kent, and went to school in Rochester, just a mile or so from the North Downs Way. (Indeed, thirty years ago the landlord at the Robin Hood pub, which sits alongside the North Downs Way, was one of several in the area who refused to serve him alcohol because he was under age. Thankfully, he seems to have been forgiven for

the intervening three decades and while researching for this edition enjoyed a pint there without difficulty.) Henry has been writing guidebooks for almost a quarter of a century and is the author of: *Kilimanjaro*, *Coast to Coast Path*, *Hadrian's Wall Path*, *Dales Way* and all three books in the *South-West Coast Path* series. He's also updated *Offa's Dyke*, *Pembrokeshire Coast Path*, *South Downs Way* and *The Ridgeway*.

With him on this trek, as with every walk he does in the UK, was **DAISY** (below), his (mostly) faithful dog. An experienced long-distance walker, Daisy has already completed all the trails above with Henry and her ambition is to walk all 15 National Trails.

North Downs Way
First edition: 2006; this second edition: **2018**

Publisher: Trailblazer Publications
The Old Manse, Tower Rd, Hindhead, Surrey GU26 6SU, UK
www.trailblazer-guides.com

British Library Cataloguing in Publication Data
A catalogue record for this book is available from the British Library

ISBN 978-1-905864-90-4

© **Trailblazer** 2006, 2018: Text and maps

Series editor: Anna Jacomb-Hood
Editor: Anna Jacomb-Hood; **Cartography**: Nick Hill
Layout and index: Anna Jacomb-Hood; **Proof-reading**: Jane Thomas
Illustrations: p60: Nick Hill **Photographs (flora)**: bee orchid opp p64 © John Curtin;
hemp agrimony, C3, © Jane Thomas; all others © Bryn Thomas
All other photographs: © Henry Stedman unless otherwise indicated

The maps in this guide were prepared from out-of-Crown-
copyright Ordnance Survey maps amended and updated by Trailblazer.

Acknowledgements

FROM HENRY: Firstly, thank you to John Curtin for writing the first edition of this guide.
Thanks also to Daisy for accompanying me every step of the way – what a dog! – and to Zoe
for enabling me to complete the trail, and for making each return home such a pleasant one;
and to Henry Jr, of course, for being so brilliant. I'd also like to thank all those readers who
wrote in with comments and suggestions, in particular, Shirley Alexander, George Moberley,
Jeremy Servian, Colin Thompson and Keith Wartnaby. At Trailblazer, thanks to Anna
Jacomb-Hood for her usual forensic approach to editing the text, Nick Hill for the maps, Jane
Thomas for the proofreading and to Bryn Thomas, as always, for keeping me busy.

A request

The authors and publisher have tried to ensure that this guide is as accurate as possible.
Nevertheless things change even on these well-worn routes. If you notice any changes or
omissions please write to Trailblazer (address as above) or email us at ⌨ info@trailblazer-
guides.com. A free copy of the next edition will be sent to persons making a significant con-
tribution.

Warning: long-distance walking can be dangerous

Please read the notes on when to go (pp13-15) and health and safety (pp53-5). Every effort
has been made by the author and publisher to ensure that the information contained herein
is as accurate and up to date as possible. However, they are unable to accept responsibility
for any inconvenience, loss or injury sustained by anyone as a result of the advice and information given in this guide.

PHOTOS – Front cover: Daisy and companion pause to admire the scenery from the
North Downs Way viewpoint (see p152), before Hollingbourne.
This page: Poppies provide a colourful border to many of the fields en route,
such as here just outside Detling.
Overleaf: Strolling through the barley on the way back from Lenham to the trail.

Updated information will be available on: ⌨ **www.trailblazer-guides.com**

Printed in China; print production by D'Print (☎ +65-6581 3832), Singapore

North Downs
WAY

FARNHAM to DOVER via CANTERBURY

84 large-scale maps & guides to 44 towns and villages

PLANNING – PLACES TO STAY – PLACES TO EAT

JOHN CURTIN &
HENRY STEDMAN

TRAILBLAZER PUBLICATIONS

Contents

INTRODUCTION

About the North Downs Way

PART 1: PLANNING YOUR WALK

Practical information for the walker

Budgeting 27

Itineraries

What to take

Getting to and from the North Downs Way

PART 2: MINIMUM IMPACT WALKING & OUTDOOR SAFETY

Minimum impact walking

Outdoor safety

PART 3: THE ENVIRONMENT & NATURE

Conserving the North Downs Way

Flora and fauna

PART 4: ROUTE GUIDE AND MAPS

ABOUT THIS BOOK

This guidebook contains all the information you need. The hard work has been done for you so you can plan your trip without having to consult numerous websites and other books and maps. It contains:

● All standards of places to stay from campsites and hostels to B&Bs, inns, guesthouses and hotels
● Details of walking companies if you'd prefer an organised holiday and baggage-carrying services if you just want your luggage carried
● Varied itineraries for all types of walkers
● Answers to all your questions: when to go, degree of difficulty, what to pack and how much the whole walking holiday will cost

When you're ready to go, there's comprehensive information to get you to and from the North Downs Way and 84 detailed maps and town plans to help you find your way along it. The route guide includes:

● Walking times in both directions
● Reviews of campsites, bunkhouses, hostels, B&Bs, guesthouses and hotels on and near the path
● Cafés, pubs, tea-shops, takeaways and restaurants as well as shops and supermarkets for buying supplies
● Rail, bus and taxi information for the villages & towns along the path
● Street plans of the main towns and villages en route: Farnham, Shalford, Guildford, Shere, Dorking, Redhill, Oxted, Westerham, Otford, Rochester, Aylesford, Lenham, Canterbury and Dover
● Historical, cultural and geographical background information

---

❏ MINIMUM IMPACT FOR MAXIMUM INSIGHT

Nature's peace will flow into you as the sunshine flows into trees. The winds will blow their freshness into you and storms their energy, while cares will drop off like autumn leaves. **John Muir** (one of the world's earliest and most influential environmentalists, born in 1838)

It is no surprise that, since the time of John Muir, walkers and adventurers have been concerned about the natural environment; this book seeks to continue that tradition. There is a detailed, illustrated chapter on wildlife and conservation on the North Downs as well as a chapter devoted to minimum impact walking with ideas on how we can broaden that ethos. By developing a deeper ecological awareness through a better understanding of nature and by supporting rural economies, local businesses, sensitive forms of transport and low-impact methods of farming and land-use we can all do our bit for a brighter future.

As we work harder and live our lives at an ever faster pace a walking holiday is a chance to escape from the daily grind and the natural pace gives us time to think and relax. This can have a positive impact not only on our own well-being but also on that of the area we pass through. There can be few activities as 'environmentally friendly' as walking.

Break clear away, once in awhile, and climb a mountain or spend a week in the woods. Wash your spirit clean. **John Muir**

INTRODUCTION

'I can assure those townsfolk who send forth a cry that wild nature and scenery are becoming difficult to find, that any amount of both still exists, within a short railway ride from London.' **Denham Jordan**, author of *On Surrey Hills*.

Every day tens of thousands of people wend their dreary way along the three of the major transport arteries of South-East England – the M25, M26 & M20. Doubtless many of these same people from time to time turn their gaze from the tarmac to look wistfully up at the gentle grassy slopes that line one side of the motorways and wonder to themselves exactly what lies atop these same hills.

It's probably just as well that they don't know, for if they did they'd probably be tempted to swerve rashly onto the hard shoulder, screech to a halt and run straight up those same verdant slopes – which, if everybody did, would have dire consequences for the smooth running of UK transport network's south-eastern division.

National Trail milestones, such as this one in the woods above the White Horse Stone outside Aylesford, crop up regularly along the path and help you to keep track of your progress.

For hidden amidst the trees that crown the downs is the North Downs Way stretching all the way from Farnham, in Surrey, to Dover, in Kent. Stretching for 131.6 miles (211.6km) – or 124.2 miles (200km) if taking the shorter alternative finish from Boughton Lees to Dover that misses out on Canterbury – it's no coincidence that the North Downs Way is shadowed for much of its length by these major thoroughfares; because for several millennia the North Downs Way was the major transport route between Dover on England's eastern shore and the major trading and population centres of Canterbury, the Medway towns and on into Surrey. Indeed, **Stone Age burial**

The start of the trail at Hinkley Corner (see p71) in Farnham. The sculpture was installed in 2015 and is made from a form of architectural steel called corten that's designed intentionally to rust.

sites and other monoliths in Northern Kent testify to how long the Downs have been inhabited. Given that the trail follows a ridge of chalk hills running across Surrey and Kent, it doesn't take much imagination to see how even Britain's first inhabitants would have followed this trail. Indeed, people in the Stone Age would have doubtless enjoyed how, by following the line of this natural geological phenomenon, they would find it easy to orientate themselves and avoid getting lost – a feature that walkers still appreciate to this day!

If you want to get an idea of just how important this route was, just look at the buildings that you can see along the way. No fewer than **eight castles** and **three cathedrals** lie on or just off the trail, not to mention several **archbishops' palaces** (now, sadly, all in ruins), an assortment of WWII defences and one folly. It is the cathedrals – and, in particular, Canterbury Cathedral, arguably the most important Christian building in

For several millennia the North Downs Way was the major transport route between Dover, Canterbury, the Medway towns and Surrey

England and certainly one of the oldest – that did much to popularise the trail that we now call the North Downs Way, as pilgrims flocked to the cathedral to pray at the tomb of St Thomas à Becket. Indeed, for much of its western half the North Downs Way follows the so-called 'Old Road', also known as the

Pilgrims' Way that worshippers followed from Winchester to Canterbury.

It wasn't only pilgrims and traders who took advantage of this ancient trackway, however. The list of **authors** who found inspiration on the Downs reads like a veritable *Who's Who*. Writers such as Geoffrey Chaucer (who wrote about people on the Pilgrims' Way, of course), John Bunyan, Lewis Carroll, Jonathan Swift, William Cobbett, Charles Dickens, Jane Austen, Rudyard

Kit's Coty (see p146), a 5000-year-old burial site, lies just a few yards off the trail in a beautiful flower-filled meadow.

Kipling, JM Barrie, Henry James, Max Beerbohm, George Meredith, Edmund Spenser, John Keats, Alfred Lord Tennyson and Wilfrid Blunt all found inspiration from both the North Downs and the trail that runs along its length. And throughout this book we have, on occasion, quoted some of them directly.

Science has also benefitted from the Downs, with the home of **Charles Darwin** lying to the north of the trail. Darwin lived with his family for over forty years at the appropriately named Down House and it was here that he would take daily

> **The list of authors who found inspiration on the Downs reads like a veritable *Who's Who*.**

walks around the gardens in order to work on his theories; ideas that would eventually coalesce into *On the Origin of the Species*, the book that not only made his name while simultaneously scandalising Victorian society with its decidedly secular viewpoint but which also completely changed the course of science.

Below: The views from Reigate Hill are amongst the most far-reaching on the trail.

INTRODUCTION

Pilgrim sculpture outside the gates of Chilham Castle (see p169), one of several such statues along the Way.

It's not difficult to see what inspired them. The North Downs is a haven for nature in what was, even in their day, the most populated and developed corner of the British Isles. The trail itself spends most of its time on the top of the chalky ridge, an area of short grazed grass and thick woodland, stooping only to cross five rivers that bisect the Downs at various points. It's a path that is a veritable haven for wildflowers, as well as several mammals and insects which have been eradicated from much of the rest of the south-east.

But has this natural beauty of the North Downs Way been compromised by the proximity of the motorways? Not to any great degree, in this author's opinion at least. For one thing, the path actually takes you through two sizeable Areas of Outstanding Natural Beauty – the Surrey Hills and the North Kent AONBs. Furthermore, the roads, where they are visible, are usually far enough away to render the noise of the traffic to a barely audible hum – a hum that serves to emphasise rather than detract from the sense of tranquillity at the top of the Downs. Plus, of course, the proximity of such major roads means that transport along the way is, by the standards of the fifteen National Trails of England and Wales, fairly plentiful – allowing you a lot of flexibility when planning your trail.

So there you have it: a splendid two-week jaunt along the course of a spectacular geological feature, following a trail that's replete with history, ancient buildings and beautiful scenery – and all within a short train ride from London. What, as the phrase goes, is not to like?

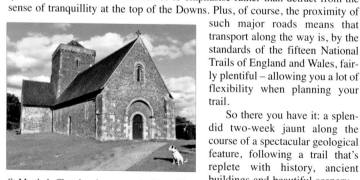

St Martha's Church enjoys a wonderful position at the top of St Martha's Hill (see p86). Also known as the Pilgrims' Church, it is one of the landmarks of the North Downs Way.

History

The North Downs Way was officially opened as a national trail in 1978 by the then Archbishop of Canterbury, Dr Donald Coggan. The route follows the chalk ridge that forms the North Downs between Farnham and Dover. It also follows, in parts, the Pilgrims' Way, reputedly taken by pilgrims to the shrine of St Thomas à Becket at Canterbury Cathedral, though its existence on maps only appeared from the late 19th century. In all likelihood prehistoric man used trackways along the North Downs which were also later used by drovers and traders keen to avoid toll roads. It is a natural route east to the Continent.

A highlight of this walk, **Canterbury Cathedral** (see p173) was founded in 597. After the murder of Archbishop Thomas à Becket in 1170 the cathedral became one of the most important pilgrimage centres in the medieval world. Following the Pilgrims' Way from London people came to make offerings at his tomb and the journey of one group and the stories they told became the subject of Chaucer's classic, *The Canterbury Tales*. The impressive Perpendicular nave was completed in 1405. (Photo © Bryn Thomas).

How difficult is the path?

The North Downs Way is a well-signposted 131.6-miles (211.6km) or 124.2 miles (200km) if completing the alternative walk via Canterbury; and it's 155.9 miles (250.9km) if you manage somehow to combine both without missing any part of either trail, and without going over any of the trail twice. It is also one of the less taxing trails, as you walk over generally level and firm ground with very few steep ascents or descents. You do not need previous experience of long-distance path walking. What you do need is suitable clothing, money, time, a half-decent pair of leg muscles and a realistic assessment of your fitness. Remember you don't have to do it all in one go and because transport options are so good you can tackle it in bite-sized stages. The main thing is not to push yourself beyond your ability.

If you don't have the time or want to skip the less interesting parts where motorways intrude, there are excellent transport links to most parts of the North Downs Way from London and the south coast making day and weekend trips easy (see Highlights box pp32-3).

How long do you need?

You can have an invigorating holiday easily completing the walk in 10 days, or 14 if you prefer a more relaxed pace.

You can do it in a week if you are determined to crack off the miles day after day and provided you are fit. But that really feels like a race against

Marbled White
(*Melanargia galathea*)

Large Skipper
(*Ochlodes sylvanus*)

time. You can have an invigorating holiday easily completing the walk in 10 days, or 14 if you prefer a more relaxed pace. Bear in mind that if you are camping, carrying a heavier pack will slow you down and many of the official camp-sites are well off the trail. You may also want to take a day off – you'll probably be tempted by Canterbury. Both Guildford and Rochester are worth at least half a day each and this will add to the time needed. Then again there are superb **day** and **weekend walks** (see pp32-3) with easy access and excellent transport links.

See p31 for some suggested itineraries covering different walking speeds

INTRODUCTION

When to go

SEASONS

The old joke is Britain doesn't have a climate; it has weather and if you don't like it just wait five minutes. Walking the North Downs Way can be enjoyed year-round as long as you dress suitably and take it for granted that even in summer there may be parts of the trail that are muddy. However, severe conditions of heat, cold or rain seldom last for long.

You may get wet on the North Downs but you're unlikely to perish. Temperatures seldom dip below 0°C in winter or above 32°C in summer and the south-east tends to have the highest temperatures and the greatest number of sunshine hours in Britain. In summer it tends to be slightly cooler by the coast because the sea takes longer to heat up. Conversely in winter it takes longer for the sea to cool so it's milder by the coast because of the warming effect of the sea.

Spring

This is a great time of year for stands of bluebells and spring wild flowers along the Surrey sections of the North Downs Way. With the first leaf growth coming

Below: Butterfly-filled meadows such as here, near Titsey Plantation, are a feature of the Downs.

INTRODUCTION

❏ FESTIVALS & ANNUAL EVENTS

There are numerous village fêtes and events during the summer months and it's fun to go along if you happen to be there on the day. There are also annual events you should be aware of because they may make finding accommodation difficult.

March
● **Guildford International Music Festival** (🖳 surrey.ac.uk/arts/festivals) is a biennial classical music festival.

May
● **Surrey County Show** (🖳 surreycountyshow.co.uk; Stoke Park, Guildford; end of May Bank Holiday Monday) is the biggest one-day agricultural show in the UK.
● **Chatham Maritime Food and Drink Festival** (🖳 cmtrust.co.uk/play/food-and-drink-festival) takes place over the last bank holiday weekend in May.

June
● **Dickens Festival** (🖳 rochesterdickensfestival.org.uk and 🖳 enjoymedway.org/events/festivals) Dickens' characters in period costumes flock to the streets of Rochester over the first weekend of June.

July
● **Kent County Show** (🖳 kentshowground.co.uk) Held over three days in early July at the showground near Detling.
● Rochester, quite the party place, has regular **concerts** at the castle (🖳 thecastleconcerts.co.uk).

September and October
● **Always the Sun Festival** (🖳 alwaysthesunfestival.co.uk), Guildford, early Sep.
● **Guildford Book Festival** (🖳 guildfordbookfestival.co.uk) is in early Oct.
● **Guildford Jazz Festival** (🖳 guildfordjazzfestival.co.uk) is held in late Oct.
● **Canterbury Festival** (🖳 canterburyfestival.co.uk) – celebration of the arts in the city and around Kent; three weeks in Oct.

December
● Dickens' characters in period costumes are out again in Rochester for a **Dickensian Christmas Festival**, (bah humbug!), first weekend of December.

on there is a tapestry of green before the views become obscured later in the year. It's difficult to predict the weather from year to year but there's often a settled period of fine weather around mid May. The trail is generally quiet but gets busier around the Easter and May holidays. Days are getting longer and temperatures are rising, pubs open beer gardens and a few brave souls turn their minds to BBQs.

Summer

June can start unsettled and blustery but later in the season it can get very hot on the Downs. Fortunately much of the Surrey section is wooded so while you may miss the views the worst of the heat is taken by the trees. The open fields of Kent can be like outdoor ovens so bring plenty of water with you. Expect the trail to be busier and you'll be competing for accommodation with other holidaymakers and those on their way across the Channel. With early dawns and long days there's little need to rush on the trail though you may find it dusty across the Kent arable fields as the farmers gather in the harvest.

Autumn

The weather is generally settled early in the season and everything seems to slow down after the August Bank Holiday. Children are back at school, holidays are over and it's easier to find accommodation. September is a wonderful time to walk. There can be crisp bright days with a slight chill in the air and later the vivid autumn colours emerge as the leaves begin to change and the nights start to draw in. Farmers will be ploughing so you can expect some tough going over recently ploughed fields, especially if it's been raining.

Winter

There is nothing like a bright, clear, frosty day to admire the views from the North Downs' ridgeline and we often get a spell of weather like that early in the New Year. But it's wet, relatively mild, damp days that are the norm. With good waterproofs there is nothing to hold you back from walking the North Downs even if it's a bit dispiriting. With the leaves off the trees the views on a clear day are uninterrupted. Most pubs and B&Bs remain open as their business here is year-round so it will be easier to find accommodation but do make sure you get an early start each day as the nights draw in quickly.

TEMPERATURE

Temperatures are pleasantly warm during the summer and generally seldom drop below 0°C in the south-east in winter.

RAINFALL

Rain falls in every month of the year and is highest in winter as expected. England is affected by weather systems coming from the south-west containing a lot of rain.

DAYLIGHT HOURS

If walking in autumn, winter or early spring, you must take account of how far you can walk in the available light.

Crossing the River Medway alongside the thunderous M2 is perhaps the least pleasant part of the entire trail. Distract yourself from the motorway by looking north towards Rochester.

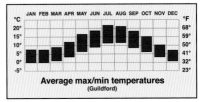

Average max/min temperatures
(Guildford)

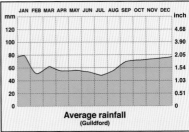

Average rainfall
(Guildford)

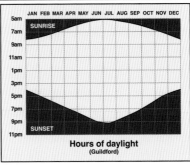

Hours of daylight
(Guildford)

PLANNING YOUR WALK

1

Practical information for the walker

ROUTE FINDING

There is little chance of becoming lost for long on the trail. Not only are you following the top of a natural – and obvious – chalk ridge but you're following in the footsteps of tens of thousands of people who have walked this way before you, from neolithic settlers to pilgrims and trekkers, so it's fair to say the path is pretty well established. There's also plenty of signage with signposts and waymark posts positioned at very frequent intervals. Indeed, such is their regularity that you actually start to doubt you're on the right path if, after a few hundred metres, you *don't* see one; and if you haven't seen a North Downs Way sign or waymark for 15 minutes or more, it's pretty safe to say that you really have come off the trail. And if and when the signage does fail you, the aim of this book is to keep you on the correct path with detailed instructions on the maps at key points.

Any slightly tricky directions not immediately obvious on the ground are noted on the appropriate **trail guide** maps in **Part 4** of this book. In most cases the path is obvious and well trodden and certainly on weekends, in particular, there are bound to be other walkers about to point you in the right direction. A compass is not necessary.

Do remember that summer foliage may obscure signs or they may go missing so it's best to read ahead in the trail guide and refer to the maps occasionally to confirm your location.

Using GPS with this book

Given the above, modern Wainwrights may scoff at those who use GPS technology, but more open-minded walkers will accept that it can be an inexpensive, well-established if non-essential, navigational aid. In no time at all a GPS receiver with a clear view of the sky will

---

(Opposite) Left: Crossing the River Mole on the stepping stones before the 275 steps leading up Box Hill (see p100), the steepest section on the whole trail. **Top**: Despite its location, squashed between the M25 and A23, the church of St Katharine's near Merstham remains a relatively peaceful spot. **Bottom**: A fox enjoys the afternoon sun in a meadow by St Peter's & St Paul's Church, Charing.

❏ **Alternative route**
The 'official' North Downs Way divides at Boughton Lees (see p154 & p162) and this guide takes the longer northern route through Canterbury, across Kent country and hop country and on to Dover. However, we do also cover the alternative route, which we found to be just as interesting and which takes you via Wye and the out-skirts of Folkestone before culminating in an exhilarating stroll along the White Cliffs of Dover. This alternative route is described in Appendix A on pp195-201.

establish your position and altitude in a variety of formats, including the British OS grid system, to within a few metres.

The maps in the route guide include numbered waypoints; these correlate to the list on pp203-5, which gives the latitude/longitude position in a decimal minute format as well as a description. Where the path is vague, or there are several options, you will find more waypoints. You can download the complete list of these waypoints for free as a GPS-readable file (that doesn't include the text descriptions) from the Trailblazer website: 🖳 trailblazer-guides.com (click on GPS waypoints).

It's also possible to buy state-of-the-art digital mapping to import into your GPS unit, assuming that you have sufficient memory capacity, but it's not the most reliable way of navigating and the small screen on your pocket-sized unit will invariably fail to put places into context or give you the 'big picture'.

Bear in mind that the vast majority of people who tackle this path do so per-fectly well without a GPS unit. Instead of rushing out to invest in one, consider putting the money towards good-quality footwear or waterproofs instead.

ACCOMMODATION

The **route guide** (Part 4) lists a comprehensive selection of places to stay along the full length of the trail and often in each town or village there are a number of options. The three main types are camping, staying in hostels/bunkhouses, or using B&Bs/hotels. In the ever-more populated and prosperous south-east low-cost accommodation is increasingly hard to find. Proximity to London, soaring property values and a healthy demand for rooms from business travellers drives prices up.

Camping
Official campsites are few and far between on the North Downs Way. The sit-uation is particularly grim along the western half of the trail, where there are large sections completely empty of campsites. One option is to look at the web-site 🖳 **campinmygarden.com**, where homeowners advertise the possibility of pitching a tent on their property in return for a small fee. A quick look at their website shows that there are camping opportunities just outside Puttenham, north of Guildford and south of Oxted – and presumably others will be added in the months and years to come. All of which is useful, of course, but again there still aren't really enough to make camping every night a viable option unless you wild camp (see opposite).

It's a rare trekker who would want to camp every night anyway – there is always the temptation to have a hot bath in a cosy B&B and rest your head on a feather pillow. You will be carrying a heavier pack and this can slow you down and could add an extra day and additional costs to your walk. You'll have to buy breakfast and won't have the fuel which a full English breakfast provides and you might buy more snacks and energy boosters as a result.

What's more, while on other trails you could expect to pay anywhere from £6 per camper, on the North Downs Way organised sites can cost as much as £13pp. A number of sites are a fair distance from the trail too. Some sites have no facilities, others have coin-operated showers and laundry facilities, whilst others are swish holiday parks with some tent spaces.

Wild camping Camping on land that is not a recognised campsite is possible along the route – though do note that it's also, officially, illegal. You must try to obtain the landowner's permission first but this is often impossible as you won't know who the landowner is, or even if you do you may not be able to find the relevant person. The amount of cultivated arable land in Kent reduces the number of potential sites and Surrey is very wooded; the most versatile set up is a bivvy bag or lightweight tarp.

Wild camping is not permitted on National Trust (NT) land. Expect wardens to be particularly alert to campers in Surrey where there have been problems with raves in the past. Elsewhere, wild camping is not for the fainthearted and you'll be carrying extra gear but it does add a sense of freedom and adventure. See also p53.

Camping barns/bunkhouses and hostels

There is only one **camping barn** along the North Downs Way, at Puttenham (see p74), just a few miles from the start of the walk at Farnham. This provides comfortable accommodation on foam-lined wooden sleeping platforms and has a basic kitchen facility. Both a sleeping bag and booking in advance are essential.

Youth hostels have come a long way since the days of crowded dorms and chores. Sadly only two **Youth Hostel Association** (YHA; ☎ 0800 0191 700 or ☎ 01629 592700, 🖵 yha.org.uk) hostels on this trail remain open: Tanners Hatch (see p94) and Canterbury (see p175). YHA Holmbury St Mary (see p91) lies a good distance off the trail but you can get to it by bus.

The downsides of YHA hostels are that opening hours are often limited and the chances are you'll end up next to a Vesuvial snorer so bring ear plugs. You don't have to be a member of the YHA to stay at their hostels but you will pay an additional £3 per night.

Membership costs from £5/15/25 (under-26/adult/household) if paying by direct debit; pay by credit or debit card and you'll need to add on a fiver. You can book hostels online on the YHA website (see above) or by either calling the central reservations number or the hostel direct.

Note that **dogs are not allowed in a YHA hostel** though they can stay in campsites and cabins – so Tanners Hatch Campsite at Ranmore Common (see p94) will be available to you.

There are also a few independent hostels that bookend the walk at Farnham (The Mulberry pub; see p68) and Backpacker in Dover, as well as Kipps (see p178) in Canterbury.

B&Bs

The B&B is a British institution. Although normally a reserved nation, you're welcomed into people's homes as a guest, provided with a comfortable bed (usually) and sent on your way the next morning with an enormous full English breakfast – often bacon, sausages, eggs, sometimes baked beans, maybe black pudding, all fried and washed down with lashings of tea or coffee and of course accompanied by buttered toast and marmalade. It's great but two weeks of this and you're ready for the cardiac unit.

More and more B&Bs offer a lighter, kinder on the arteries, help yourself buffet breakfast of cereals, fruits, pastries and breads which comes as a welcome relief. Alternatively, and particularly if you are planning an early start, it may be worth asking if you can have a (free) packed lunch instead of breakfast.

Some B&Bs are charming, some luxurious, others are modest. Rates (based on two sharing) vary from about £25 per person (pp), though £30pp or above is more common. Often the solo walker will pay a supplement to occupy a double or twin room when a single isn't available; this may mean paying £10-15 less than the room rate, or even the full room rate at peak times.

The listings in this book concentrate on establishments close to the trail but you should be prepared to walk for up to a mile, sometimes more, descending off the North Downs ridge to the villages and towns below at the end of the day. Some B&Bs proudly display four stars, others no stars, some are vetted by Tourist Boards, for others it is a low-key sideline business. In my experience the number of stars is not a sure guide to quality and it'll all depend on how enthusiastic the owner is.

Rooms vary but in general you'll find few **single rooms (S)**. **Twin rooms (Tw)** usually have two single beds with a gap between the beds and a **double room (D)** has a double bed but sometimes two single beds put together. **Triple/ quad rooms** sleep up to three/four people but most of these have a double bed

---

❏ **Booking accommodation in advance**

Always book your accommodation and I suggest doing so several weeks before departure. Because the trail is close to London and major business arteries, a busy port, as well as two of the country's busiest airports and top tourist attractions it means that demand for rooms is always high. Furthermore there has been quite a serious decline in B&Bs and pubs offering accommodation over the past decade or so. It doesn't take long for all beds to go if one of the major motorways is forced to close, either. The M25 shut down twice in the course of researching the first edition of this book and within hours there was no room in any manger.

Booking in advance means you risk losing your deposit and tie yourself to a schedule, but you'll be assured of a bed and have an idea of what to expect and know the price. If you do have to cancel a booking let the owners know as soon as possible so they can re-let the room.

and one/two single beds or bunk beds; thus two people in a group of three or four, may have to share the double bed. The room can also be used as a double or twin.

More and more B&Bs offer en suite facilities; these are often squeezed into the corner of an already tight room. It can take Houdini-like contortions to shower in a tiny cubicle fighting back a clinging shower curtain.

Owners may offer to collect walkers from the trail but do check when booking. It's an added service, so an offer to pay the petrol money will be appreciated. Your offer will probably be refused but it's a courtesy that doesn't cost much.

Pubs/inns
Many walkers write off pubs as noisy and perhaps not offering the best in the way of B&B. That's not been my experience. True they're sometimes less personal, but no worse for that and often a great deal less precious about muddy boots. I've got to confess the Devil's at my elbow and it's difficult to resist the sybaritic pleasure of bed, bath, booze and board under one roof at the end of a long day's walk. Prices start at £25 per person (pp). If you want to get an early start the next day, do check that this is possible – landlords tend to keep late hours.

Hotels
Generally not considered the first choice of billet for walkers but if you want a touch of luxury at the end of the day and you can afford it there's no harm in spoiling yourself. There are several hotel options along the North Downs Way, some very upmarket. Quite a number of business travellers use hotels during the week so you'll probably find some discounted rates at the weekend at several hotels on the trail.

Airbnb
The rise and rise of Airbnb (🖥 airbnb.co.uk) has seen private homes and apartments opened up to overnight travellers on an informal basis. While accommodation is primarily based in cities, the concept is spreading to tourist hotspots in more rural areas, but do check thoroughly what you are getting and the precise location. While the first couple of options listed may be in the area you're after, others may be far too far afield for walkers. At its best, this is a great way to meet local people in a relatively unstructured environment, but do be aware that these places are not registered B&Bs, so standards may vary, yet prices may not necessarily be any lower than the norm.

FOOD AND DRINK

Breakfast and lunch
Breakfast is usually included when staying at B&Bs though some owners and pubs offer bed-only rates in larger towns where there are breakfast options nearby. Hosts can usually provide a packed **lunch** for an additional cost but let them know in advance. That said, there is really no hardship in preparing your own

lunch. If you buy local produce (see box below) so much the better. Details of lunch places, tea shops, pubs and eateries are in Part 4 but for an overview look at the Village and Town Facilities table on pp28-9.

Always bring some food with you and don't rely on making it to a pub for lunch – country pubs usually finish food service by 3pm at the latest and frequently close for the afternoon, especially during the week.

Evening meals

There is nothing like a pint at the end of a day's walking and many of the **pubs** on the North Downs Way can trace their origins back to the 15th and 16th centuries. Most are now owned by one or other of the drinks conglomerates but by and large retain their individual character thanks to a resident landlord. Some have à la carte restaurants as well as a bar menu, which is usually cheaper, and some have become 'gastropubs' serving restaurant quality food in a pub environment, but often at near restaurant prices.

There is a wide choice of **restaurants and takeaways** in the larger villages and towns from Italian to Indian, burger joints to modern British, Asian fusion to fast food. Of course the Great British culinary institution, the fish 'n' chip shop, can also be found along the route.

Finally, some B&Bs offer a evening meal, though often you need to book this in advance and there will be an additional charge.

Camping supplies

There are plenty of shops along the North Downs Way for you to buy food and there are outdoor shops in Farnham, Guildford, Shere, Dorking, Redhill and Canterbury where you can get gas and other essential camping supplies.

Drinking water

There are next to no drinking-water taps along the North Downs Way – the only one we found was at Box Hill by the toilets there – so take plenty of water with you each day. There are five rivers on this walk and drinking water from those

---

❏ **Markets**

Britain's food reputation has come a long way since the days of warm beer, surly service and chips with everything. More and more people are looking for fresh quality produce, locally grown. **Farmers' markets** give local producers a chance to showcase their products and in a recent survey 70% of shoppers said they would buy local produce if they could identify it. These markets are also a fun way to fill the larder while at the same time cutting down the food miles travelled and getting tastier, fresher produce. Markets along the North Downs Way are held at:

• **Farnham** (🖥 www.farnham.gov.uk) (see p67)
• **Guildford** (🖥 www.guildford.gov.uk/visitguildford/markets) (see p82)
• **Dorking** (🖥 www.surreymarkets.co.uk/dorking-traditional-market) (see p96)
• **Redhill** (🖥 www.reigate-banstead.gov.uk) (see p104)
• **Rochester** (🖥 kfma.org.uk/Rochester) (see p142)
• **Lenham** (🖥 kfma.org.uk/Lenham) (see p156)
• **Canterbury** (🖥 www.canterbury.co.uk/things-to-see-and-do/Markets) (see p175)

PLANNING YOUR WALK

☐ **Beer, wine and other local drinks**

Farnham had five breweries and Guildford had nine during the heyday of brewing in the 19th century. But now most pubs and brewers are owned by one of the international conglomerates. **The Hogs Back Brewery** (🖳 hogsback.co.uk) survives as a small independent brewery and has a thriving mail-order service for its bottle-conditioned ales. Particular favourites are the classic TEA (Traditional English Ale) at 4.2% and Hogs Back Bitter at 3.7% but after a bottle or two of Old Tongham Tasty at 6.9% it's difficult to put one foot in front of the other.

If you stop by the **Percy Arms** in Chilworth, or the **Drummond** (see p86 for both) in Albury, it's worth asking if Shere Drop is a guest beer; this local brew has the nice tartness of an India Pale Ale. The beer is produced by **Surrey Hills Brewery**, who are based on the **Denbies Wine Estate** (see p94), the largest vineyard in Britain. Their winery tour and tasting is highly recommended. Their Surrey Gold is a delicate 11.5% white aperitif wine, perfect on a summer evening.

When you reach Kent, sample Shepherd Neame (🖳 shepherdneame.co.uk) beers from Britain's oldest brewer and still a family company.

You'll also find fine apple juices at **Godstone Vineyards** (see p112).

is not recommended. Even if you do purify the water using a filter or iodine tables you will not succeed in removing heavy metals or pesticides present from run-off from roads and agricultural use.

Luckily there are many tea shops, pubs and refreshment kiosks within easy access of the North Downs Way so buying bottles of water should not be a problem. Alternatively you could always just ask the owner if they'd mind filling up your water bottle from the tap.

MONEY

There are several **banks** and many **post offices** on or close to the trail, some of which have **ATMs** (cash machines). ATMs can also be found in local shops and at petrol stations but they may charge for withdrawals (about £1.85), though they have to inform you of this before you take your money out.

A large number of UK banks have an arrangement with the Post Office enabling you to withdraw cash from branches by debit card (with a PIN number); a few permit withdrawals using a chequebook and card. You can also get money in a shop by using '**cashback**' where the retailer advances cash against your debit card. Usually shops require a minimum purchase of £5 though some also charge a fee of up to £1.50.

Not everybody accepts **debit** or **credit cards** as payment and that includes many B&Bs but you'll find that many restaurants and shops now do. As a result, you should always carry a fair amount of cash with you just in case.

OTHER SERVICES

Some villages and towns have a **post office** (from where you can mail back unnecessary items if your pack is too heavy). Thanks to the rise of smartphones, internet cafés seem to be a thing of the past, but you'll still find **public internet access** in the libraries along the trail. Most pubs, cafés and B&Bs also have **free wi-fi** for customers who have their own devices.

Towns have at least one **supermarket** and most villages have a **grocery store**. You'll sometimes find a **phone box** near these shops, though you will

---

❏ Information for foreign visitors

● **Currency** The British pound (£) comes in notes of £100, £50, £20, £10 and £5, and coins of £2 and £1. The pound is divided into 100 pence (usually referred to as 'p', pronounced 'pee') which comes in silver coins of 50p, 20p, 10p and 5p, and copper coins of 2p and 1p.

● **Money** Up-to-date **rates of exchange** can be found on ▢ xe.com/currencyconverter, at some post offices, or at any bank or travel agent.

● **Business hours** Most **village shops** are open Monday to Friday 9am-5pm and Saturday 9am-12.30pm, though some open as early as 7.30/8am; many also open on Sundays but not usually for the whole day. Occasionally you'll come across a local shop that closes at lunchtime on one day during the week, usually a Wednesday or Thursday; this is a throwback to the days when all towns and villages had an 'early closing day'. **Supermarkets** are open Monday to Saturday 8am-8pm (often longer) and on Sunday from about 9am to 5 or 6pm, though main branches of supermarkets generally open 10am-4pm or 11am-5pm.

Main **post offices** generally open Monday to Friday 9am-5pm and Saturday 9am-12.30pm though where the branch is in a shop PO services are sometimes available whenever the shop is open; **banks** typically open at 9.30/10am Monday to Friday and close at 3.30/4pm, though in some places both post offices and banks may open only two or three days a week and/or in the morning, or limited hours, only. **ATMs (cash machines)** located outside a bank, shop, post office or petrol station are open all the time, but any that are inside will be accessible only when that place is open. However, ones that charge, such as Link machines, may not accept foreign-issued cards.

Pub hours are less predictable as each pub may have different opening hours. However, most pubs on the North Downs Way continue to follow the traditional Monday to Saturday 11am to 11pm, Sunday to 10.30pm, but some still close in the afternoon.

The last entry time to most **museums and galleries** is usually half an hour, or an hour, before the official closing time.

● **National (Bank) holidays** Most businesses are shut on 1 January, Good Friday and Easter Monday (March/April), the first and last Monday in May, the last Monday in August, 25 December and 26 December.

● **School holidays** State-school holidays in England are generally as follows: a one-week break late October, two weeks over Christmas and the New Year, a week mid February, two weeks around Easter, one week at the end of May/early June (to coincide with the bank holiday at the end of May) and five to six weeks from late July to early September. Private-school holidays fall at the same time, but tend to be slightly longer.

● **Documents** If you are a member of a National Trust organisation in your country bring your membership card as you should be entitled to free entry to National Trust properties and sites in the UK (see box p57).

● **Travel/medical insurance** Although Britain's National Health Service (NHS) is free at the point of use, that is only the case for residents. All visitors to Britain should

almost definitely need a card (credit, debit, BT or prepaid) as many phone boxes no longer accept coins. Calls from a phone box cost a minimum of 60p (including a 40p connection charge; thereafter 10p a minute).

There is a snapshot of **services and facilities** in towns and villages en route on pp28-9 and further details in Part 4.

be properly insured, including comprehensive health coverage. The **European Health Insurance Card (EHIC)** entitles EU nationals (on production of the EHIC card so ensure you bring it with you) to necessary medical treatment under the NHS while on a temporary visit here (probably until Brexit is complete, that is). For details, contact your national social security institution. However, this is not a substitute for proper medical cover on your travel insurance for unforeseen bills and for getting you home should that be necessary.

Also consider cover for loss and theft of personal belongings, especially if you are camping or staying in hostels, as there may be times when you'll have to leave your luggage unattended.

● **Weights and measures** In Britain milk is sold in pints (1 pint = 568ml), as is beer in pubs, though most other liquid including petrol (gasoline) and diesel is sold in litres. Distances on road and path signs are given in miles (1 mile = 1.6km) rather than kilometres, and yards (1yd = 0.9m) rather than metres.

The population remains divided between those who still use inches (1 inch = 2.5cm), feet (1ft = 0.3m) and yards and those who are happy with millimetres, centimetres and metres; you'll often be told that 'it's only a hundred yards or so' to somewhere, rather than a hundred metres or so.

Most food is sold in metric weights (g and kg) but the imperial weights of pounds (lb: 1lb = 453g) and ounces (oz: 1oz = 28g) are frequently displayed too. The weather – a frequent topic of conversation – is also an issue: while most forecasts predict temperatures in Celsius (C), many people continue to think in terms of Fahrenheit (F; see the temperature chart on p15 for conversions).

● **Time** During the winter the whole of Britain is on Greenwich Meantime (GMT). The clocks move one hour forward on the last Sunday in March, remaining on British Summer Time (BST) until the last Sunday in October.

● **Smoking** Smoking in enclosed public places is banned. The ban relates not only to pubs and restaurants, but also to B&Bs, hostels and hotels. These latter have the right to designate one or more bedrooms where the occupants can smoke, but the ban is in force in all enclosed areas open to the public – even in a private home such as a B&B. Should you be foolhardy enough to light up in a no-smoking area, which includes pretty well any indoor public place, you could be fined, but it's the owners of the premises who suffer most if they fail to stop you, with a potential fine of £2500.

● **Telephones** The international code for Britain is +44, followed by the area code minus the first 0, and then the number you require. To call a number with the same area code as the landline phone you are calling from you can omit the area code. From a landline it's cheaper to phone at weekends and after 7pm and before 7am on weekdays. If you're using a mobile (cell) phone that is registered overseas, consider buying a local SIM card to keep costs down. See also opposite and above.

● **Internet access** and wi-fi See opposite.

● **Emergency services** For police, ambulance, fire and mountain rescue dial ☎ 999 (or the EU standard number ☎ 112).

PLANNING YOUR WALK

WALKING COMPANIES

If all you want to carry is a day pack consider one of the following companies as they'll transport your bags, book your accommodation and generally keep an eye on your progress along the way. It's a good idea to call each of the companies and study their brochures and websites to get a feel for their style.

None of the companies currently offers a guided walk on the North Downs Way though Walk Awhile does for The Pilgrims' Way.

● **British & Irish Walks** (☎ 01242-254353, ▢ britishandirishwalks.com; Cheltenham) Offer itineraries from Rochester to Canterbury in 5 nights, and also offer the complete North Downs Way.
● **Contours Walking Holidays** (☎ 01629-821900, ▢ contours.co.uk; Derbyshire) Offers self-guided 11-, 12- and 13-night itineraries on both the Canterbury and Folkestone routes, including luggage transfer (one suitcase per person). They also have 7- and 8-night itineraries from Farnham to Rochester and 5- to 6-night sections from Rochester to Dover via either Folkestone or Canterbury for those who want to do it in two stages, as well as a 3-night 'taster' from Canterbury to Dover.
● **Explore Britain** (☎ 01740-650900, ▢ explorebritain.com; Durham) Offer Rochester to Canterbury in 5-, 6- or 7-day trips.
● **Freedom Walking Holidays** (☎ 07733-885390, ▢ freedomwalkingholidays .co.uk; Goring-on-Thames) Offer the whole North Downs Way.
● **Let's Go Walking** (☎ 01837-880075, ▢ letsgowalking.com; Devon) Offer the whole North Downs Way and The Pilgrims' Way.
● **Responsible Travel** (☎ 01273-823700, ▢ www.responsibletravel.com; Brighton) Offer both the North Downs Way and The Pilgrims' Way.
● **The Walking Holiday Company** (☎ 01600-713008, ▢ thewalkingholiday company.co.uk; Monmouth, Wales) Offer the whole North Downs Way.
● **Walk Awhile** (☎ 01227-752762, ▢ walkawhile.co.uk; Kent) Offer a 5-night itinerary on The Pilgrims' Way from Rochester to Canterbury, either guided or self-guided, as well as a 14-night itinerary covering the whole of the trail.

> ❏ **Disabled access**
> Unfortunately most of the North Downs Way is inaccessible to disabled people but there are some areas where roads provide access to good views and stretches of the trail that can be followed, particularly at **Newlands Corner** (see p88) and **Blue Bell Hill** picnic site (see p146).
> **Disabled Ramblers** (▢ disabledramblers.co.uk) is a national charity of like-minded disabled people who enjoy being in the countryside and get about using a variety of mobility aids. They have a busy calendar of events including rambles along the North Downs near Guildford. Resisting being ghettoised and confined to areas catering to every conceivable need their rambles take them nationwide.
> At Newlands Corner there are designated paths for the use of an electric off-road **Tramper buggy** specially designed for countryside use. This is available for hire free from the Countryside Centre most Sundays; pre-booking is essential (☎ 01483-795440).

TAKING DOGS ALONG THE NORTH DOWNS WAY

The North Downs Way is dog-friendly but owners must behave in a responsible way; see pp201-3. The first thing to decide is whether you think your dog will actually enjoy the walk. Dogs should always be kept under close control to avoid disturbing wildlife, livestock and other walkers. Man's best friend is not everyone's best friend and being territorial he or she may be uneasy and unwelcome in the presence of farm dogs.

Budgeting

England is not a cheap place to go travelling at the best of times and the North Downs Way, with its proximity to London, is in one of the most affluent areas in the UK. Add to this the demand from other tourists and business travellers and it is easy to understand why prices are high. Budget accommodation is at a premium, camping opportunities are at a minimum and hostel prices are at the higher end of the scale. After you've allowed for accommodation and food and the cost of getting to and from the start of the trail you'll have to allow for incidentals and unexpected expenditure: beer, snacks, bus and taxi fares, admission tickets and so on. It all adds up.

CAMPING

With some sites costing more than a tenner per person and the cost of food and the effort involved in carrying all the gear, camping might not be the attractive option it is elsewhere. It's also unlikely you'll be able to camp all the way so you'll have to budget for some nights in a hostel or bunkhouse. In all, reckon on needing a minimum of £20 per person (pp) per day.

HOSTELS AND CAMPING BARNS

The least expensive YHA hostel on the route costs from £12pp for members. Add a £3 supplement for non-members, or fork out for a year's membership (see p19). You'll get a bunk at Puttenham camping barn for £15pp which is good value for the area; the private hostels charge from £25pp in Farnham, from £14.50pp in Canterbury and from £15pp in Dover. You'll have to buy breakfast, lunch and dinner and just getting by will set you back a minimum of £30pp a day. Buy a couple of beers as well and you're looking at £35-40pp.

B&Bs

The cheapest B&B on this walk charges around £25pp (based on two sharing) and breakfast isn't included though you have the use of the kitchen; most cost around £30-35pp but expect to pay more for single occupancy of a room. Add on the cost of lunch, dinner and a couple of pints in the evening and you should reckon on about £50pp minimum per day.

VILLAGE AND

Place name (Places in **bold** are directly on the NDW)	Distance from previous place approx miles	km	Cash Machine (ATM)/Bank	Post Office	Tourist Information Centre (TIC)
Farnham	0	0	✔	✔	
Seale	4.0 (0.25)	6.4 (0.4)			
Puttenham	2.9	4.6			
Compton	2.7	4.3			
Shalford	2.4 (1.5)	3.9 (2.25)	✔	✔	
Guildford	(0.5)	(0.8)	✔	✔	TIC
Chilworth	1.8 (1.25)	2.9 (2)			
Albury	1 (1.25)	1.6 (2)		✔	
Newlands Corner	0.6	1			
Shere	2.1 (0.75)	3.4 (1.2)		✔	
Holmbury St Mary	3 (2)	4.8 (3.2)			
Ranmore Common	2.3 (0.85)	3.7 (1.4)			
Denbies Wine Estate	1.7	2.7			
Dorking	0.4 (1.6)	0.6 (2.5)	✔	✔	
Box Hill	1.4 (1)	2.3 (1.6)			
Box Hill Village	1.4 (1)	2.3 (1.6)		✔	
Reigate Hill	5	8			
Redhill	(1.8)	(2.9)	✔	✔	
Merstham	2.1	3.4	✔		
Oxted	8.3 (1.5)	13.4 (2.25)	✔	✔	
Westerham	4.1 (1.4)	6.6 (2.2)	✔	✔	TIP
Knockholt Pound	3.1 (0.25)	5 (0.4)			
Dunton Green	2.7 (1)	4.3 (1.6)			
Otford	1.7	2.7	✔	✔	
Kemsing	2.1 (0.5)	3.4 (0.8)			
Wrotham	4	6.4	✔		
Borough Green	(1.6)	(2.5)			
Ryarsh	4.3 (1.5)	6.9 (2.25)			
Cuxton	4.8	7.7			
Rochester	2.6 (1.6)	4.2 (2.5)	✔	✔	TIC
Aylesford	4.7 (1.7)	7.6 (2.7)			
Detling	4.5	7.2			
Thurnham	1.3	2.1			
Hollingbourne	4.3	6.9		✔	
Harrietsham	2.3 (1)	3.7 (1.6)		✔	
Lenham	1.5 (0.6)	2.4 (1)	✔	✔	
Charing	4.2 (0.25)	6.8 (0.4)		✔	
Westwell	2.6	4.2			
Eastwell	1.2	1.9			
Boughton Lees	0.8	1.3			
Chilham	5.9	9.5		✔	
Chartham Hatch/Chartham	3.3 (1.25)	5.3 (2)			
Canterbury	3.1	5	✔	✔	TIC
Bridge	3.7(0.5)	6 (0.8)	✔	✔	
Shepherdswell	7.1	11.4	✔		
Dover	8.6	13.8	✔	✔	TIC
TOTAL DISTANCE	**131.6 miles/211.6km**				

Note: Places not in bold are a short distance from the path. Distances are given to the place on the path nearest to the village/town with the distance from that point to the village/town in brackets

PLANNING YOUR WALK

TOWN FACILITIES

Eating Place	Food Store	Campsite	Hostels YHA or H (ind hostel)/ Camping barn (B)	B&B-style accommodation	Place name (places in bold are directly on the NDW)
✓✓✓	✓		H	✓✓✓	**Farnham**
✓					Seale
✓✓✓			B		**Puttenham**
✓✓✓					**Compton**
✓✓✓	✓			✓✓	Shalford
✓✓✓	✓			✓✓✓	Guildford
✓				✓	Chilworth
✓✓	✓			✓	Albury
✓✓				✓	**Newlands Corner**
✓✓✓	✓			✓✓✓	Shere
✓		✓	YHA		Holmbury St Mary
		✓	YHA		**Ranmore Common**
✓✓✓				✓✓	**Denbies Wine Estate**
✓✓✓	✓			✓✓✓	Dorking
					Box Hill
✓	✓				Box Hill Village
✓✓				✓	**Reigate Hill**
✓✓✓	✓			✓✓✓	Redhill
✓✓✓	✓				**Merstham**
✓✓✓	✓			✓✓	Oxted
✓✓✓	✓			✓✓	Westerham
✓✓					Knockholt Pound
✓✓✓	✓			✓ (+1 in Chevening)	**Dunton Green**
✓✓✓	✓				Otford
✓✓	✓			✓	Kemsing
✓✓	✓	✓		✓	**Wrotham**
	✓				Borough Green
✓				✓	Ryarsh
✓✓	✓			✓	**Cuxton**
✓✓✓	✓			✓✓✓	Rochester
✓✓✓	✓			✓✓	Aylesford
✓				✓	**Detling**
✓		✓ (15 mins)		✓✓	Thurnham
✓✓✓	✓				Hollingbourne
✓	✓			✓	Harrietsham
✓✓✓	✓			✓	Lenham
✓✓	✓				Charing
✓		✓			**Westwell**
✓				✓	Eastwell
✓		✓		✓	**Boughton Lees**
✓✓✓	✓			✓	**Chilham**
✓				✓✓✓	Chartham Hatch/Chartham
✓✓✓	✓	✓	YHA/H	✓✓✓	**Canterbury**
✓✓	✓			✓	Bridge
✓✓	✓				**Shepherdswell**
✓✓✓	✓	✓*	H	✓✓✓	**Dover**

Note: * at Hawthorn Farm, nr Martin Mill Railway Station

Eating place/B&B-style accommodation: ✓ = one place, ✓✓ = two, ✓✓✓ = three or more

PLANNING YOUR WALK

Itineraries

Most people tackle the North Downs Way west to east and Part 4 has been written that way. It's perfectly possible to walk it in the opposite direction (the way-marking is in place) but there are advantages in doing it west to east (see below).

To help you plan your walk there is a **planning map** (see map opposite inside back cover) and a **table of village/town facilities** (see pp28-9); the latter gives a snap shot of the essential information you will need regarding accommodation possibilities and services. You could follow or adapt one of the suggested itineraries (see below) which are based on preferred type of accommodation and walking speeds. There is also a list of recommended linear **day** and **weekend walks** on pp32-3 which cover the best of the North Downs Way, all of which are well served by public transport. The public transport map and table are on pp45-8.

Once you have an idea of your approach turn to **Part 4** for detailed information on accommodation, places to eat and other services in each village and town on the route. Also in Part 4 you will find summaries of the route to accompany the detailed trail maps.

SUGGESTED ITINERARIES

The itineraries in the boxes opposite are based on different accommodation types (camping, hostels/bunkhouses and B&Bs), with each one divided into three alternatives depending on your walking speed. They are only suggestions so you can adapt them to suit your circumstances. Some accommodation and public transport options may be a considerable distance off the trail and where this is the case it is noted in Part 4 and on the maps where appropriate. Be sure to add travelling time before and after the walk. This is especially important in winter when there are fewer hours of daylight.

WHICH DIRECTION?

Most walkers tackle the path west to east. There are a few advantages. The prevailing wind tends to be at your back as is the sun if you get a later start. As most others are going this direction, if you are walking alone but want some company you can fall in step with them. Also it's worth having a destination to look forward to and Canterbury, though not at the end, is a worthy penultimate goal. And like a river on its journey it seems natural to follow the route to the sea.

SIDE TRIPS

The North Downs Way is plenty long enough to satisfy energetic walkers. Yet the path cuts through a part of Britain that's packed with castles, grand country

CAMPING OR STAYING IN HOSTELS/CAMPING BARN

	Relaxed			Medium			Fast		
Night	**Place**	**Approx Distance**		**Place**	**Approx Distance**		**Place**	**Approx Distance**	
		miles	km		miles	km		miles	km
0	Farnham			Farnham			Farnham		
1	Puttenham	6.9	11.1	Holmbury St Mary (SM)	20.5	33	Ranmore Common	22.8	36.7
2	Holmbury SM	13.6	21.9	Merstham*	14.3	23	Oxted*	20.3	32.7
3	Redhill*	12.2	19.6	Westerham*	12.4	20	Wrotham	17.7	28.4
4	Oxted*	10.4	16.8	Wrotham	13.6	21.8	H'bourne*	26.5	42.6
5	Otford*	11.6	18.6	Rochester*	11.7	18.8	Canterbury	24.9	40.1
6	Ryarsh*	10.4	16.7	H'bourne*	14.8	23.8	Dover	19.4	31.2
7	Aylesford*	12.1	19.5	Westwell	10.6	17.1			
8	H'bourne*	10.1	16.2	Canterbury	14.3	23			
9	Westwell	10.6	17.1	Dover	19.4	31.2			
10	Chilham*	7.9	12.7						
11	Bridge*	10.1	16.3	* No campsites or hostels/bunkhouses but other					
12	Dover	15.7	25.2	accommodation is available					

Note distances given are to nearest point on the trail to the campsite only. Please refer to the Route Guide (Part 4) to see how far you have to walk from there to the campsite.

STAYING IN B&B-STYLE ACCOMMODATION

	Relaxed			Medium			Fast		
Night	**Place**	**Approx Distance**		**Place**	**Approx Distance**		**Place**	**Approx Distance**	
		miles	km		miles	km		miles	km
0	Farnham			Farnham			Farnham		
1	Guildford	12	19.3	Newlands Corner	15.4	24.8	Shere	17.5	28.2
2	Dorking	12.9	20.7	Reigate Hill	17.3	27.8	Oxted	25.6	41.2
3	Reigate Hill	7.8	12.6	Dunton Green	20.3	32.7	Ryarsh	22	35.3
4	Westerham	14.5	23.4	Rochester	19.5	31.3	Harrietsham	24.5	39.4
5	Wrotham	13.6	21.8	Lenham	18.6	29.9	Chilham	16.2	26.7
6	Rochester	11.7	18.8	Chilham	14.7	23.7	Dover	25.8	41.5
7	Thurnham	10.5	16.9	Bridge	10.1	16.3			
8	Boughton Lees	16.9	25.9	Dover	15.7	25.2			
9	Canterbury	12.3	19.8						
10	Dover	19.4	31.2						

houses and sites of great antiquity. A glance at the Ordnance Survey map will give you some idea for side trips and possible walking trails to them as well as other long-distance paths such as the Greensand Way (Haslemere, Surrey, to

❏ HIGHLIGHTS – DAY WALKS & WEEKEND WALKS

There is nothing like walking the entire length of a long-distance path in one go but some people don't have the time and others want to experience only the best of what the trail has to offer. For details of public transport to and from the start and finish of each walk see pp45-8. The weekend walks can be split in two to suit day walkers, or combined and completed in a day by those who want a challenge. That would, however, leave little time for sightseeing which is a pity on this culturally rich route.

Day walks

● **Farnham to Guildford** 12 miles/19.3km (see pp70-80) Walk through farmland, woodland and along sandy bridleways to Guildford where there is plenty of sightseeing. Visit the ancient burial tumulus at Puttenham Heath, itself geologically unusual in this area of chalk, and stop at the excellent Watts Gallery and the Cemetery Chapel, Compton (see p78), where you can rest up for awhile at café.

● **Guildford to Shere** 5½ miles/8.9km (see pp84-90) A relaxed pace crossing the River Wey, the path climbs through woods (bluebell-filled in spring) to the top of St Martha's and Newlands Corner from where there are great views on a clear day. You can then detour to Shere, Surrey's prettiest village.

● **Otford to Rochester** 17.8 miles/28.6km (see pp127-140) Not the prettiest or quietest of sections and one of the longest but it passes through Kemsing Downs, a significant chalk grassland habitat, the woods of Trosley Country Park, with a short detour to see one of Kent's best-known megaliths, Coldrum Barrow. Much of the walk is in woodland and surprisingly isolated from the industrial Medway valley towns and emerges by pretty Upper Bush into Cuxton before crossing the M2 and Channel Tunnel Rail link.

The lonely, enigmatic stones of Coldrum Barrow lie just off the trail and are one of several Neolithic structures along the Way.

Rochester is 35-40 minutes off the trail from where there are fast train connections to London, Canterbury and Dover. Consider an overnight stay there – the Norman Castle, England's second oldest cathedral, and Restoration House are well worth visiting.

● **Charing to Chilham** 10½ miles/16.9km (see pp158-167) A stroll through a quintessential Kentish landscape, with oast-houses and orchards abounding, and finishing at the prettiest village on the trail. Great fun.

Hamstreet, near Ashford in Kent) and Weald Way (Gravesend in Kent to Eastbourne in East Sussex). A detailed description is beyond the scope of this book but you can find information online.

Those inspired to try more Downs walking may want to tackle the South Downs Way for which there is a Trailblazer guide (see p208). The Downs Link, a 32-mile bridleway utilising a disused railway line links the North Downs Way at St Martha's (see Map 7, p85) with the South Downs Way, near Steyning.

PLANNING YOUR WALK

● **Chilham to Canterbury** 6.4 miles/10.3km (see pp168-173) Starting at the loveliest little settlement on the trail and finishing at the most important city, this tranquil stroll is untaxing but filled with some lovely walking, including a visit to No Man's Orchard and some lengthy sections through even more of Kent's idyllic agrarian landscape.

● **Folkestone outskirts to Dover** 5 miles/8km (see p201) You'll need to hike a couple of miles (3km) uphill from Folkestone's Central Station to join this, the ultimate section of the North

Chilham, the prettiest village on the North Downs Way, makes the perfect start or end to a day's walk.

Downs Way's Alternative Route (see Appendix pp195-201). Once on the trail, however, you can enjoy some fantastic cliff-top walking, with the Battle of Britain Memorial, Norman encampments, Napoleonic forts, sonar mirrors and WW2 pillboxes en route and the sound of the sea a constant accompaniment.

Weekend (two-day) walks

● **Farnham to Dorking** 24.9 miles/40km (see pp67-96) This is easy walking through farmland, heath and woodland to overnight in Guildford (12 miles/19.3km).

After a climb to St Martha's – the Pilgrims' Church – with wonderful views and a further climb across Albury Downs the path gains the ridgeline at Newlands Corner, and follows a mostly wooded drove road to descend through England's largest vineyard, Denbies Wine Estate, with views to Box Hill on the outskirts of Dorking. Two castles, one cathedral, a gallery to eminent Victorian artist, George Frederic Watts, a Gilbert Scott church, WWII fortifications, good wine, and views that stretch for miles on a clear day – not bad for two days' walking.

● **Charing to Canterbury** 16.9 miles/27.2km (see pp158-173) Follow in the footsteps of pilgrims passing the ruined archbishop's palace in Charing to follow the Pilgrims' Way emerging from dense woodland into the tranquil landscape of Eastwell. Climb to Soakham Downs with extensive views over the Stour valley and emerge from the King's Wood to overnight in Chilham with its remarkably preserved medieval square (10½ miles/16.9km).

The following day's walk is through Kent's orchard country before arriving at Canterbury, worth at least a day's exploration (6.4 miles/10.3km).

What to take

What you take depends on personal preference and experience. As many walking the North Downs Way may be new to long-distance walking the suggestions below are a guide. What you must ensure is that you have all the equipment necessary to make the trip safe and comfortable.

KEEP YOUR LUGGAGE LIGHT

There are a few ways to do this. Buy the lightest equipment you can afford. Choose the smaller of pack sizes so you don't overpack (see below). Before packing lay out only what you deem essential. With the exception of the first-aid kit (see p37) ask whether or not you will use the item every day. If not, consider very carefully whether or not to pack it. Remember on the North Downs Way you are not so far away from a town or village that you can't get something you've forgotten even if it does mean interrupting your walk. If you have booked a self-guided holiday (see p26) your main luggage is likely to be transferred to your next accommodation stop and you can instead head off onto the trail with just the essentials you need for the day.

HOW TO CARRY IT

The size and type of **backpack** you carry will depend on how you plan to walk the North Downs Way. If you are day hiking, or booked a self-guided holiday, at a minimum you should have a small **daypack** filled with those items that you will need during the day: water bottle, this book, a map, sun screen, hat, gloves, wet-weather gear, some food, camera, money, first-aid kit and so on.

If you are hiking the route end to end with no baggage service you will have to consider carefully the type of backpack you use. Its size will depend largely on where you plan to stay but do try to err on the smaller of sizes as it's so easy to overpack – and thus overburden – yourself.

With all backpacks make sure it is adjustable so you can fit it to your back length and body shape – there are both men- and women-specific fits now – and it should have adjustable chest and hip belts to distribute the weight and improve stability. Some shops allow you to take a pack home so you can try it out by filling it with what you intend to take; if it's not right you can then try a different model.

Campers bringing a tent, cooking equipment and food will probably need a 65- to 75-litre pack while if you plan on staying at B&B-style accommodation you should need no more than a 30- to 40-litre pack. A small daypack is useful so you can carry essentials on a day off around town or when leaving the main pack at your lodgings. Don't rely on manufacturers' claims to water resistance – it doesn't take a long shower to soak through most packs. Pack everything inside in **waterproof liners** or **canoe bags** or save weight and money by using strong plastic bags or bin liners.

FOOTWEAR

Boots

Quality is remembered long after the price is forgotten; invest in a pair of **suitable** boots. The North Downs Way has few sustained ascents or descents, is on a generally firm track with little rough or stony ground but it can be muddy. Therefore you do not need high, stiff-as-a-board boots that make you feel as if you're walking in a diving bell. Look for boots that are waterproof (Gore-Tex lined), provide sufficient ankle support but retain residual flexibility for comfort and don't require much breaking in. If you are camping you may need to consider a boot with greater ankle support to cope with carrying a heavier pack; it is money well spent. When you go to try boots do so later in the day when your feet have swelled a little so you get a proper fit and also try on several brands.

Some people like to bring a change of shoes for the evening. If you are carrying all your own gear consider something lightweight such as flip flops or **sports sandals** – or just make do with the one pair.

Socks

Modern hi-tech socks are very comfortable if you choose a high-quality pair designed for walking. Again don't stint on money. Many swear by a liner sock under a thicker wool sock – each to their own but the modern fibres dry quicker. Two pairs are fine, three are ample. You can wash socks each evening leaving them to dry overnight.

CLOTHES

British weather is notoriously changeable and you should bring clothes that can cope with the sun, rain and cold. But you needn't bankrupt yourself. Wear clothes that are lightweight, durable, quick drying and that can keep you warm, cool and dry depending on the weather conditions. While you can get away with hiking in ordinary cotton-based clothes, provided you have a waterproof outer layer, you will feel more comfortable in specialised outdoor clothes – indeed they are even becoming street fashion. The number of retailers also means they have to work hard to keep prices keen.

On this trail you will encounter cyclists and horse riders and in the short sections which are by-ways you may encounter off-road vehicles, though the state of the tracks suggests that this is not so common. You will also need to cross country lanes and roads at times so you may want to opt for bright colours, though this is a matter of personal preference. Personally, I think it's more important that you can be seen in the dark, just in case you end up walking outside after the sun's gone down. Many trekking clothes have reflecting strips or glow-in-the-dark features on them which could be life-savers if you're walking along a road after dark.

Modern hi-tech outdoor clothes still follow the basic two- or three-layer principle, with an inner base layer to transport sweat away from your skin, a mid-layer for warmth and an outer layer to protect you from the wind and rain. A thin lightweight **thermal top** of a synthetic material is ideal as the base layer as it draws sweat away from your body keeping you cool in hot weather and warm when worn under other clothes in cold weather. Some walkers like to bring a **shirt** of synthetic material, giving coverage to the neck, and somewhere to pack small items in the pockets and they may want to smarten up in the evening. A light- to mid-weight **polyester fleece** over this will help keep you warm in cold weather. Fleeces are ideal trekking gear being light, fairly water-resistant, quick drying, remain warm when wet and pack down small in backpacks.

A **waterproof jacket**, preferably with Gore-Tex, is essential and 'breathable' jackets help to cut down the build up of condensation. In dry weather this layer can be worn to keep the wind out.

Leg wear
Most modern **trekking trousers** are a good investment providing a light, durable and quick-drying trouser. Go for a dark colour in trousers as this hides trail dirt much better. Jeans should never be worn as they are heavy and, when wet, cold and binding on the legs. On really hot sunny days you may wish you had brought **shorts**. Some trekking trousers zip off and convert to shorts, which we think is the best compromise, weight-wise, and you can also convert them back to trousers again when walking if you're cold or where the path is lined with stinging nettles. Thermal **longjohns** are useful if camping and could come in handy in winter.

On wet or particularly cold days you may want to bring a pair of **waterproof trousers**. A cheaper (usually), less bulky and lighter solution, at least for the lower half of the leg, is **gaiters**. They provide extra protection when walking through muddy ground and when the vegetation around the trail is dripping wet after bad weather or early morning dew. They also help keep you looking presentable when you pitch up at the pub.

Underwear
Three changes of underwear are plenty and you may want to invest in the kind made from modern wickable fabrics that can be washed and dried overnight. Because backpacks can cause bra straps to dig painfully into the skin, women may find a **sports bra** more comfortable.

Other clothes
In winter don't leave home without a warm **hat** as you never know when you might need one (a sun hat is useful in summer). Many people bring **gloves** too in the winter.

TOILETRIES
Once again, take the minimum. **Soap**, **towel**, a **toothbrush** and **toothpaste** are pretty much essential (although those staying in B&Bs will find that most provide soap and towels anyway). Some **toilet paper** could also prove vital on the trail, particularly if using public toilets (which occasionally run out of it). If defecating outdoors use a **lighter** for burning the paper and a **plastic trowel** to bury the evidence. Other items to consider taking are: **razor**; **deodorant**; **tampons/sanitary towels** and a high-factor **sun-screen** (especially if you are walking in the summer.

FIRST-AID KIT

A small first-aid kit packed in a waterproof container could prove useful for those emergencies that occur along the trail. Carry some **aspirin** or **paracetamol** (in a small tupperware box) for relief from mild pain; **plasters/Band Aids** for minor cuts; **'Second Skin'** or **'Compeed'** for blisters; a **bandage** for holding dressings, splints, or limbs in place and for supporting a sprained ankle; **an elastic support** for a weak knee, ankle or arches; a small selection of different-sized **sterile dressings** for wounds; **porous adhesive tape**; **antiseptic wipes**; **antiseptic cream**; **tweezers**; **scissors** and **safety pins** – useful also for attaching wet clothes to your backpack so they can dry as you walk. If you develop heat rash or suffer chafing, **nappy cream** works wonders. For information on outdoor safety, avoidance of hazards and dealing with emergencies see pp53-5.

GENERAL ITEMS

Essentials

Many people find a **smartphone** pretty much essential these days, enabling you to look up bus timetables, accommodation details, the nearest town (and how to get to it). You can also download a map of the entire route (see Maps p39), and download apps to see how far you've walked, check your heart rate, find out how many calories you've burned etc etc. Most, of course, also have a decent torch on them. You can also use it as a phone(!), confirming accommodation bookings or letting them know what time you're hoping to arrive. There is reception throughout most of the North Downs Way. Just as essential as the phone itself is its charger and a battery pack for when it dies on the trail (as they always do). Battery packs for smartphones are cheap, small and lightweight these days and could prove to be a lifesaver.

Most people like to carry a separate **torch** too (I find a headtorch more useful, so you can keep both hands free), at least a one-litre **water bottle or pouch**, **spare batteries** and a **penknife**. Carry a **plastic bag** for your litter. A **whistle** (see p54 for details of the international distress signal) can fit in a shirt pocket and carries further than any amount of shouting if attention is needed.

Carry some **emergency food** such as raisins, prunes or dried apricots which will give an instant energy boost (see p54) and a **watch** with an alarm to get you up in the morning. Many people also find a **walking pole** or **sticks** essential. You may want to protect your eyes from the sun by wearing **sunglasses** (or clip-on shades if you wear glasses).

Usefuls

Some will think a **camera** is essential but a **notebook** may be a better way of recording your impressions; with a camera you often get too busy composing the picture and rarely appreciate the view. A **map** (see pp39-40) is a good idea if you are planning to explore off the North Downs Way.

A **book** may pass the time on days off, or on train and bus journeys, but you'll have to consider how much extra weight you want to carry. Often a period of reflection as you write up your notes is time well spent.

PLANNING YOUR WALK

With **binoculars** you'll get a closer look at wildlife and trees but these would also add extra weight.

CAMPING GEAR

Campers and those intending to stay in the camping barns en route will need a sleeping bag. A two- to three-season bag should suffice for summer. In addition, campers will need: a decent bivvy bag or tarp, if travelling light, or a tent; a sleeping mat; fuel and stove; cutlery/pans; a cup; and a scrubber for washing up if you intend doing any cooking.

MONEY

ATMs (cash machines) are common along the North Downs Way; many post offices and shops along the trail have installed them. There are also plenty of banks with ATMs in the larger towns. Many restaurants and shops accept **debit and credit cards** but not all do, including many B&Bs. As a result, you should always have a fair amount of **cash** (at least £100) with you just in case and a **cheque book** from a British bank could be a useful back up. See also p23.

❏ **SOURCES OF FURTHER INFORMATION**

Trail information The latest trail information including any diversions to the route can be found on 🖳 nationaltrail.co.uk/north-downs-way.

Tourist information centres (TICs) Many towns around Britain have a TIC which provides all manner of locally specific information for visitors and most can help with accommodation. The TICs along or near the North Downs Way are at Guildford (see p82), Rochester (p142), Canterbury (p174) and Dover (p192). Farnham (p67) and Dorking (p96) now have websites with tourist information rather than TICs.

Tourism South East (🖳 visitsoutheastengland.com) There is a whole host of information on its website about accommodation, things to do and see, and upcoming festivals and events. **Surrey** (🖳 visitsurrey.com) and **Kent** (🖳 visitkent.co.uk) also have lots of information on their respective websites.

Organisations for walkers
● **The Long Distance Walkers' Association** (🖳 ldwa.org.uk) An association for people with the common interest of long-distance walking in rural, mountainous and moorland areas. Membership includes a journal, *Strider*, three times per year giving details of challenge events and local group walks as well as articles on the subject. Membership costs £13 per year.
● **Ramblers** (formerly Ramblers' Association; 🖳 ramblers.org.uk) Looks after the interests of walkers. They publish a large amount of useful information including their quarterly *Walk* magazine. Individual/joint membership costs £34.50/45/50.
● **The Backpackers' Club** (🖳 backpackersclub.co.uk) A club aimed at people who are involved or interested in lightweight camping through walking, cycling, skiing, canoeing, etc. They produce a quarterly magazine, provide members with a comprehensive advisory and information service on all aspects of backpacking, organise weekend trips and also publish a farm-pitch directory. Membership costs £15 per year.

❏ **Digital mapping**
There are several software packages on the market today that provide Ordnance Survey maps for a PC or smartphone. The two best known are Memory Map and Anquet. Maps are supplied electronically, on DVD, USB media, or by direct download over the internet. The maps are then loaded into an application, also available by download, from where you can view them, print them and create routes on them.

The real value of digital maps, though, is the ability to draw a route directly onto the map from your computer or smartphone. The map, or the appropriate sections of it, can then be printed with the route marked on it, so you no longer need the full versions of the OS maps (though the *North Downs Way AZ Adventure Atlas*, see below, provides the same thing). Additionally, the route can be viewed directly on the smartphone or uploaded to a GPS device. Most modern smartphones have a GPS chip so you will be able to see your position overlaid onto the digital map on your phone. Almost every device with built-in GPS functionality now has some mapping software available for it. One of the most popular manufacturers of dedicated handheld GPS devices is Garmin, who have an extensive range. Prices vary from around £100 to £600.

Smartphones and GPS devices should complement, not replace, the traditional method of navigation (a map and compass) as any electronic device can break or, if nothing else, run out of battery. Remember that the battery life of your phone will be significantly reduced, compared to normal usage, when you are using the built-in GPS and running the screen for long periods.   **Stuart Greig**

MAPS

The hand-drawn maps in this book cover the trail at a scale of 1:20,000, better than any other scale currently available for the whole route; notes, tips and comments are written on the maps so you should not need any others if you are walking just the North Downs Way. But if you want to explore further afield it is a good idea to have **Ordnance Survey** (🖳 ordnancesurvey.co.uk) maps. The OS Landranger series (1:50,000) for this area are 178 (The Thames Estuary); 179 (Canterbury & East Kent); 186 (Aldershot & Guildford); 187 (Dorking & Reigate); 188 (Maidstone & Royal Tunbridge Wells); 189 (Ashford & Romney Marsh). The larger-scale OS Explorer series (1:25,000) are Nos 137 (Ashford); 138 (Dover, Folkestone & Hythe); 145 (Guildford & Farnham); 146 (Dorking, Box Hill & Reigate); 147 (Sevenoaks & Tonbridge); 148 (Maidstone & the Medway Towns); 149 (Sittingbourne & Faversham); 150 (Canterbury & the Isle of Thanet).

Members of **Ramblers'** (see box opposite) can borrow up to 10 Ordnance Survey maps for a period of six weeks at 30p per map from their library. Many **public libraries** in Britain also have maps that members can borrow.

Cheaper and lighter than buying the whole set of maps, **Harveys** (🖳 harvey maps.co.uk) produce strip maps (1:40,000) covering the whole of the North Downs Way as well as an app for smartphones covering the entire route.

Also worth considering is *North Downs Way AZ Adventure Atlas* (🖳 www.az .co.uk); this booklet contains the relevant part of the OS maps, each to a scale of 1:25,000, for the whole walk and there is also an index.

PLANNING YOUR WALK

RECOMMENDED READING

Some of the following books can be found in the tourist information centres and they may also have a number of books about the towns and villages en route, usually printed by small, local publishers.

For a thematic treatment of the North Downs through the eyes of painters, poets and novelists Kent County Council produced a richly illustrated guide, *North Downs Way: An Inspirational Journey* by Gillian Duff, which you can still find on Abebooks and other second-hand retailers.

The North Downs Way by Belinda Knox (publisher Kneading) is a photographic guide to the Way.

The Pilgrims' Way: Fact and fiction of an ancient trackway by Derek Bright is about the various origins of The Pilgrims' Way and provides a great background resource for anyone walking this path.

If you are inspired to try out other long-distance walks, check out the other titles in the Trailblazer series; see p208.

Flora and fauna field guides

Collins *Bird Guide* with its beautiful illustrations of British and European birds continues to be the favourite field guide of both ornithologists and laymen alike. For a guide to the flora you'll encounter on the North Downs Way, *The Wild Flower Key* (Warne) by Francis Rose and Clare O'Reilly, is arranged to make it easy to identify unfamiliar flowers. Another in the Collins Gem series, *Wild Flowers*, is more pocket-sized and thus more suitable for walkers.

There are also several field guide apps for smart phones and tablets, including those that can aid in identifying birds by their song as well as by their appearance.

Getting to and from the North Downs Way

Surrey and Kent have excellent transport services and with its proximity to London the North Downs Way is one of the most easily accessible national trails. Travelling to it by public transport is convenient, reasonably inexpensive and makes sense.

NATIONAL TRANSPORT

Train

You are only ever an hour or two from London on the North Downs Way with convenient and frequent train services to Farnham, Guildford, Dorking, Redhill, Merstham, Oxted, Otford, Rochester, Hollingbourne, Harrietsham, Lenham, Charing, Chilham, Canterbury, Bekesbourne, Shepherds Well (for Shepherdswell) and Dover amongst other places.

❑ GETTING TO BRITAIN

Air

There are plenty of cheap flights to London's airports. The most convenient for the trail are **Heathrow** (🖥 heathrowairport.com) – from where you can take National Express's 701 service to Woking (see p44), or London Underground to Waterloo and onwards to Farnham – and **Gatwick Airport** (🖥 gatwickairport.com), with train and bus services to Redhill. **London City Airport** (🖥 londoncityairport.com) has good transport links on the Docklands Light Railway to Bank station on the London Underground with easy connections to London Waterloo and onwards to Farnham.

Far less convenient is **Luton** (🖥 london-luton.co.uk); there is a shuttle (£2) from the airport to Luton Airport Parkway railway station and Thameslink trains to London St Pancras International, from where you can catch the London Underground to Waterloo. Thameslink also stops at Redhill from where there are train connections to stations on the North Downs Way. Easybus, National Express and Greenline coaches go to London Victoria from Luton. The quickest way from **Stansted** (🖥 stanstedair port.com) is to take the Stansted Express rail service to London Liverpool St and then London Underground to Waterloo and onwards to the start of the trail.

From Europe by train

Eurostar (🖥 eurostar.com), the high-speed rail link, travels between Paris and Brussels to London via Ashford International from where there are easy connections to stations along the North Downs Way.

The Eurostar terminal in London is at St Pancras International, from where there are connections to the London Underground and to all other main railway stations in London. Two of those underground stations are Waterloo and Victoria, from where you can catch trains to Farnham/Dover at the start/end of the walk respectively. For more information about rail services to the UK contact Railteam (🖥 railteam.eu).

From Europe by coach (bus)

Eurolines (🖥 eurolines.com) have a huge network of long-distance coach (bus) services connecting over 600 destinations in 36 European countries to London. But when compared to the prices of some of the budget airlines and once expenses such as food for the journey are taken into account; the time it takes and the condition you're in on arrival having sat like a pretzel for hours, the rock-bottom prices may not be such a bargain after all.

From Europe by ferry and car

The shortest sea crossing from Europe is Calais–Dover and regular services are run by **DFDS Seaways** (🖥 dfdsseaways.co.uk) and **P&O Ferries** (🖥 poferries.com); the journey takes about 40 minutes. There are also ferry services from Bilbao and Santander and ports in western France to Portsmouth, as well as Santander and Roscoff to Plymouth, and Cherbourg to Poole. Look at 🖥 ferrysavers.com or 🖥 www .directferries.com for a full list of companies and services.

Eurotunnel (🖥 www.eurotunnel.com) operates 'le shuttle' train service for vehicles via the Channel Tunnel between Calais and Folkestone.

PLANNING YOUR WALK

At a minimum you can expect at least one train an hour operating these routes and from some mainline stations up to four an hour. Trains to stations on or close to the North Downs Way depart from London Waterloo, London Victoria, London Charing Cross and London Bridge.

All timetable and fare information can be found at **National Rail Enquiries** (☎ 0345-748 4950, 24hrs, 🖳 nationalrail.co.uk), or through the relevant operator (see box below).

Tickets can be bought online through the relevant operator, or at 🖳 thetrain line.com and 🖳 qjump.co.uk. For the cheapest fares book well in advance.

PLANNING YOUR WALK

❏ RAIL SERVICES

Note: not all stops are listed

South Western Railway (🖳 southwesternrailway.com)
- London Waterloo to Alton via Clapham Junction, Woking, Aldershot & **Farnham**, Mon-Sat 1/hr, Sun 1/hr
- London Waterloo to **Guildford** via Clapham Junction, Epsom & Leatherhead, Mon-Sat 2/hr, Sun 1/hr
- London Waterloo to Portsmouth via Woking & **Guildford**, daily 4/hr
- London Waterloo to **Guildford** via Clapham Junction & Effingham Junction, Mon-Sat 4/hr, Sun 2/hr
- London Waterloo to **Dorking** via Clapham Junction, Epsom & Leatherhead, Mon-Sat 2/hr, Sun 1/hr (note that on Sundays and bank holidays services also stop at **Box Hill & Westhumble**)
- Ascot to **Guildford** via Aldershot, Mon-Sat 2/hr, Sun 1/hr

Southern Railway (🖳 southernrailway.com)
Note: on Monday to Friday some of these services are operated by Thameslink
- London Victoria to Horsham via Clapham Junction, Sutton, Epsom, Leatherhead, **Box Hill & Westhumble** & **Dorking**, Mon-Sat 1/hr plus 1/hr to Dorking, Sun 2/hr to Dorking only
- London Victoria to East Grinstead via Clapham Junction, East Croydon, **Oxted** & Hurst Green, daily 2/hr
- London Victoria to Reigate via Clapham Junction & **Redhill**, Mon-Sat 1hr
- London Bridge to Edenbridge Town via East Croydon & **Oxted**, daily 1/hr
- London Bridge to Uckfield via East Croydon, **Oxted**, Hurst Green, Edenbridge Town & Crowborough, Mon-Sat 1/hr, Oxted to Uckfield Sun 1/hr
- London Bridge to Horsham via East Croydon, **Merstham**, **Redhill** & Gatwick Airport, Mon-Sat 2/hr, Sun 1/hr plus 1/hr to Redhill
- Brighton to Ashford International via Hastings, daily 1/hr

GWR (🖳 gwr.com)
- Gatwick Airport to Reading via **Redhill**, Reigate, **Dorking Deepdene** & **Guildford**, Mon-Sat 15/day, Sun 10/day
- **Redhill** to Reading via Reigate, Betchworth, **Dorking Deepdene**, **Dorking West**, **Chilworth**, **Shalford** & **Guildford**, Mon-Sat 10/day (plus additional services that call at some, but not all, of these stops), Sun 8/day inc from Gatwick Airport

South Eastern Railway (🖳 southeasternrailway.co.uk)
- London Charing Cross to **Dover Priory** via Waterloo East, London Bridge, Tonbridge, Ashford International & Folkestone (West & Central), daily 1/hr
- London Charing Cross to **Canterbury West** via Waterloo East, London Bridge, Tonbridge, Ashford International, Wye, **Chilham & Chartham**, daily 1/hr (some services continue to Ramsgate)

It is possible to buy a train ticket that includes bus travel at your destination: for further information visit the **Plusbus** website (▢ www.plusbus.info). If you think you'll want a **taxi** when you arrive consult the town guides included in this book, many of which have taxi numbers in their transport sections. Alternatively, visit ▢ www.traintaxi.co.uk.

South Eastern Railway (*cont'd*)

- London Charing Cross to Gillingham via Waterloo East, London Bridge, Dartford, Gravesend, Strood, **Rochester** & Chatham, daily 1/hr
- London Charing Cross to Sevenoaks via Waterloo East, London Bridge, Orpington, **Knockholt** & **Dunton Green**, Mon-Sat 1-2/hr

Note: the evening and Sunday (2/hr) services depart from London Cannon St.

- London Victoria to **Canterbury West** via Bromley South, **Otford**, **Borough Green** & **Wrotham**, Maidstone East, Bearsted (for Leeds Castle), **Hollingbourne**, **Harrietsham**, **Lenham**, **Charing**, Ashford International, Wye, **Chilham** & Chartham, daily 1/hr but note that services end at Ashford International on weekday evenings

Note: the Victoria and Charing Cross services connect at Ashford International for services to Wye, **Chilham** & **Chartham**

- London Victoria to Ashford International via Bromley South, **Otford**, **Kemsing**, **Borough Green** & **Wrotham**, Maidstone East & Bearsted (for Leeds Castle), Mon-Sat 1/hr
- London Victoria to Ramsgate via Bromley South, **Rochester**, Chatham, Gillingham & Faversham, daily1/hr
- London Victoria to Dover Priory via Sole Street, **Rochester**, Chatham, Gillingham, Sittingbourne, Faversham, **Canterbury East**, **Bekesbourne** & **Shepherds Well**, daily1/hr
- St Pancras International to Ramsgate via **Rochester**, Chatham, Gillingham, Sittingbourne & Faversham, daily 1/hr
- St Pancras International to Margate via Ebbsfleet International, Ashford International, **Canterbury West** & Ramsgate (high-speed service), daily 1/hr
- St Pancras International to Gravesend via Ebbsfleet International, Ashford International, Folkestone West, **Dover Priory**, Martin Mill, Ramsgate, Faversham, Sittingbourne, Gillingham, Chatham, **Rochester** & Strood (high-speed service), daily 1/hr
- Strood to Paddock Wood/Tonbridge via **Cuxton**, **Aylesford** & Maidstone West, Mon-Fri 1/hr plus 1/hr to Maidstone West, Sat & Sun 1/hr (for some Monday to Friday services it is necessary to change at Paddock Wood)

Thameslink Railway (▢ thameslinkrailway.com)

Note: Until the work at London Bridge station is complete in 2018 services between Bedford and Brighton will go via London Blackfriars

- West Hampstead Thameslink to Sevenoaks via St Pancras International, London Blackfriars, Bromley South, Swanley & **Otford**, Mon-Fri 2/hr, Sat & Sun 2/hr but from London Blackfriars only
- Bedford to Three Bridges via Luton Airport, London St Pancras International, East Croydon, Purley, **Merstham**, **Redhill** & Gatwick Airport, daily 2/hr

Coach

National Express (☎ 0871 781 8181, daily 10am-6pm, 🖳 nationalexpress .com) is the principal coach (long-distance bus) operator in Britain. Coach travel is generally cheaper but longer than travel by train.

Whilst there are excellent services between London, Dover and Canterbury (London to Dover/Deal via Canterbury NX007; & London to Ramsgate via Canterbury NX022), only one service a day calls at Farnham (London to Portsmouth via Farnham; NX031) for the start of the walk; the service from London reaches Farnham in the late afternoon so you would then have the cost of an extra night's accommodation but if coming from Portsmouth the service arrives around 9.15am. However, if starting at Guildford (London to Southsea; NX030) there are eight departures a day from London.

National Express also operates a service (NX701; approx 1/hr) from Heathrow Central Bus Station to Woking Railway Station via Terminal 5.

Car

The south-east of England is criss-crossed by roads and motorways and the North Downs Way itself crosses the M25, M20, M23 and M2 on its journey east to Dover. You can, of course, drive to the start of the trail but then you have the problem of safe parking and getting back to it at the end of the walk. With so many train services and the roads so busy, do your bit for the environment and don't bother to drive.

LOCAL TRANSPORT

The number of railway stations and bus services on or close to the route opens up the possibility of linear walks throughout the length of the North Downs Way lasting several hours or days without having to park a car, worry about it and then figure out a way of getting back to it.

The map on pp46-7 gives an overview of the principal direct routes of use to walkers and an indication of the frequency of services in both directions and who you should contact for further information.

For general information about bus links, for this edition we found the website with the most up-to-date and accurate information was 🖳 bustimes.org.uk. To double-check the information you find there, it may be a good idea to look at the operator's website, or the information service **traveline** (☎ 0871-200 2233, 🖳 traveline.info), which has public transport information for the whole of the UK though note that the phone calls cost at least 12p a minute. Tourist information centres along the North Downs Way can also answer questions about local public transport. **Check the services** you might use before you plan to travel as bus services, in particular, may be cancelled. Note that on many bus routes there is no Sunday service, or a limited one. Train services are better, Kemsing being the only station not to have any trains on a Sunday.

One-way rural bus fares can be expensive and services sometimes infrequent so you may find it cheaper and more convenient to take a **taxi** for short hops, especially if there are two or more of you. Fares generally cost a few pounds minimum charge with a per-mile charge thereafter.

❏ PUBLIC TRANSPORT TABLE

Note Not all stops are listed and check all services before travel in case of cancellation.

Stagecoach in Hants and Surrey (🖳 stagecoachbus.com)
KITE Aldershot to Guildford, Mon-Sat 4/hr, Sun 2/hr
4/5 Aldershot to Farnham, Mon-Sat 3/hr, Sun 6/day
18 Aldershot to Haslemere via Farnham & Whitehill, Mon-Sat 1/hr, Sun 5/day but to Whitehill only
19 Aldershot to Haslemere via Farnham, Mon-Sat 1/hr
46 Farnham to Guildford via Elstead, Godalming & Compton, Mon-Sat 10/day
65 Alton to Guildford via Farnham, Seale & Puttenham, Mon-Sat 12/day

Stagecoach in East Kent (🖳 stagecoachbus.com)
1/1A/1X Ashford to Canterbury via Wye, Chilham & Chartham, Mon-Sat 11/day, plus 6/day Chartham to Canterbury only
10X Maidstone to Ashford via Hollingbourne, Harrietsham, Lenham & Charing, Mon-Sat 9/day, Sun 4/day
15 Canterbury to Dover, Mon-Sat 3/hr, Sun 1/hr
16 Canterbury to Folkestone & Hythe, daily 2/hr (plus Mon-Sat 2/hr to Folkestone)
17 Canterbury to Folkestone via Bridge, Mon-Sat 1/hr, Sun 6/day
89/89A Canterbury to Dover via Bridge, Aylesham, Elvington, Shepherdswell (2/day), Coldred (2/day) & Lydden (2/day), Mon-Fri 7/day
Canterbury to Dover via Bridge, Aylesham, Shepherdswell & Coldred, Sat 4/day plus Canterbury to Aylesham via Bridge, Sat 5/day inc one to Coldred
666 Ashford to Faversham via Boughton Lees, Mon-Fri 9/day, Sat 6/day

Quality Line (🖳 ratpdevlondon.co.uk)
465 Kingston-upon-Thames to Dorking via Denbies Estate, Mon-Sat 2/hr, Sun 1/hr

Buses Excetera (☎ 01737-642225, 🖳 busesetc.com)
32 Guildford to Dorking via Shalford, Chilworth, Albury, Shere, Gomshall, Abinger Hammer & Westcott, Sun 5/day (see Compass Travel for Mon-Sat)
489 Leatherhead to Merstham via Dorking & Redhill, Mon-Sat 1/hr

Southdown PSV (🖳 southdownpsv.co.uk)
236 East Grinstead to Oxted via Lingfield & Westerham, Mon-Fri 4/day
357 Selsdon to Reigate via Caterham, Merstham & Redhill, Mon-Fri 8/day
410 Redhill to Hurst Green via Oxted, Mon-Fri 2/hr, Sat 1/hr, Sun 3/day
424 Redhill to Crawley via Reigate & Three Bridges, Mon-Fri 12/day, Sat 8/day
594/595 Oxted to Westerham, Mon-Fri 13/day, Sat 9/day

Compass Travel (🖳 compass-travel.co.uk)
24 Cranleigh to Guildford via Shalford, Mon-Fri 7/day, Sat 5/day
25 Cranleigh to Guildford via Shere & Newlands Corner, Mon-Fri 4/day
32 Guildford to Redhill via Shalford, Chilworth, Albury, Shere, Gomshall, Abinger Hammer, Westcott, Dorking, Betchworth & Reigate, Mon-Sat 10/day (for Sun see Buses Excetera)

London General (🖳 goaheadlondon.com)
246 Bromley to Westerham via Hayes & Biggin Hill, Mon-Sat 2/hr, Sun 1/hr; the Sunday service continues to Chartwell (Mar-Oct; see box p118)
405 Redhill to West Croydon via Merstham & Purley, Mon-Sat, 3-4/hr, Sun 2/hr

(cont'd on p48)

PLANNING YOUR WALK

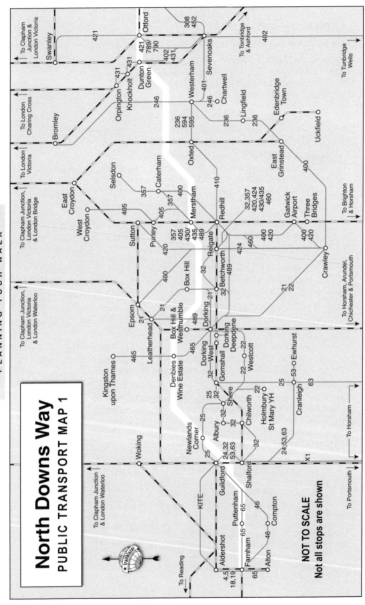

North Downs Way
PUBLIC TRANSPORT MAP 1

NOT TO SCALE
Not all stops are shown

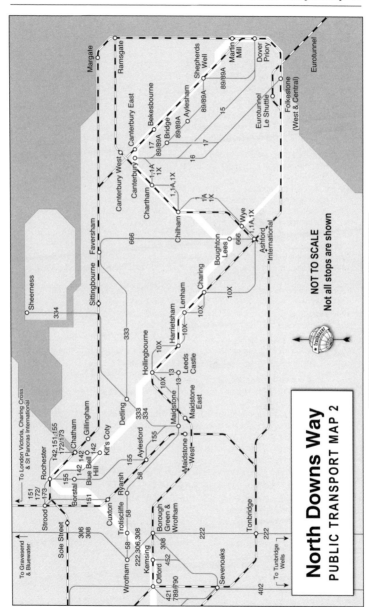

North Downs Way
PUBLIC TRANSPORT MAP 2

NOT TO SCALE
Not all stops are shown

PLANNING YOUR WALK

PLANNING YOUR WALK

PUBLIC TRANSPORT TABLE *(cont'd from p45)*

Go Bus (🖥 go-coach.co.uk)
401 Sevenoaks to Westerham, Mon-Sat 1/hr, Sun 5/day
421 Swanley to Sevenoaks via Otford, Mon-Sat 4/day
431 Sevenoaks to Orpington via Dunton Green, Knockholt Pound & Knockholt
   station, Mon-Fri 5/day

Centaur Travel (🖥 centaurtravel.co.uk)
789/790 Farmingham to London via Otford & Sevenoaks, Mon-Fri 2/day early
   morning and 4/day evening (a commuter service)

Arriva (🖥 arrivabus.co.uk/kent-and-surrey)
13 Hollingbourne to Maidstone via Leeds Castle, Sat 4-5/day (see NuVenture for
   Mon-Fri service)
53 Cranleigh to Guildford via Shalford, Mon-Sat 2/hr, Sun 1/hr
   note: one service an hour starts from/continues to Ewhurst
63 Horsham to Guildford via Cranleigh & Shalford, Mon-Sat 1/hr
X1 Horsham to Guildford via Shalford, Mon-Fri 1/hr
155 Chatham to Maidstone via Rochester, Borstal & Aylesford, Mon-Sat 11/day,
   Sun 5/day
306 Bluewater to Borough Green via Wrotham, Mon-Sat evening service only 4/day
308 Gravesend to Sevenoaks via Trosley Country Park (Vigo Village), Wrotham &
   Borough Green, Mon-Sat 1/hr
333 Faversham to Maidstone via Detling, Mon-Sat 1/hr, Sun 3/day
334 Sheerness to Maidstone via Detling, Mon-Sat 1/hr
402 Tunbridge Wells to Dunton Green via Sevenoaks, Mon-Sat 3/hr, Sun 1/hr
452 Sevenoaks to Kemsing, Mon-Fri 2/hr, Sat 7/day

Autocar Bus & Coach Services
222 Tonbridge to Borough Green, Mon-Fri 8/day – 3/day start/end at Tunbridge
   Wells and 3-/2-day continue to/start from Wrotham

Nu-Venture (☎ 01622-882288, 🖥 nu-venture.co.uk)
13 Maidstone to Hollingbourne via Leeds Castle, Mon-Fri 5/day (see Arriva for
   Sat service)
58 Maidstone to Wrotham Heath via Ryarsh & Trottiscliffe, Mon-Fri 6/day, Sat 3/day
142 Chatham circular route via Rochester, Kit's Coty & Blue Bell Hill, Mon-Fri
   6/day, Sat 4/day
151 Chatham to West Malling via Rochester, Strood & Cuxton, Mon-Fri 12/day,
   Sat 10/day, Sun 5/day
172/173 Chatham to Strood via Rochester, Mon-Fri 6/day, Sat 9/day

Metrobus (☎ 01293-449191, 🖥 metrobus.co.uk)
21 Crawley to Epsom via Dorking, Box Hill & Leatherhead, Mon-Sat 5/day
   plus 1/day to Leatherhead
22 Crawley to Holmbury St Mary via Dorking, Westcott, Shere (1/day term-time
   only), Abinger Hammer & Abinger Common, Mon-Fri 5/day
400 East Grinstead to Caterham via Crawley, Gatwick Airport & Redhill, Mon-Sat
   12-13/day, Sun 4/day
420 Redhill to Sutton via Reigate, Mon-Sat 13/day
   Crawley to Sutton via Gatwick Airport, Redhill & Reigate, Sun 5/day
430/435 Merstham circular route via Redhill & Reigate, Mon-Sat 2/hr, Sun 1/hr
460 Crawley to Epsom via Redhill & Reigate, Mon-Sat 13/day, Sun 6/day

MINIMUM IMPACT & OUTDOOR SAFETY

Minimum impact walking

The south-east of England is a congested place and having protected landscapes such as the North Downs to get away to is a valuable resource. The countryside is becoming ever more popular for recreation and walkers should be aware of their responsibilities to help protect the countryside and minimise their impact on it.

By following a few simple guidelines while walking the North Downs Way you can have a positive impact, not just on your own well-being but also on local communities and the environment, thereby becoming part of the solution.

ACCESS

The right of access to open land under the **Countryside and Rights of Way Act 2000** (CRoW), dubbed 'freedom or right to roam' by the press and walkers alike, was first rolled out in the south-east in September 2004 and came into effect in full throughout England and Wales on 31 October 2005. Walkers have the legal right to access on foot to defined areas of uncultivated open country, basically mountain, moorland, downland and heathland. What the act does not do is give walkers the right to wander willy nilly over private farmland, woodland, paddock or gardens.

So when you are on the North Downs Way keep to designated footpaths and follow the 'acorn' signs. There are, however, areas of open access land adjacent to the trail, notably land managed by the National Trust, the Forestry Commission and the Woodland Trust and areas of registered common land such as St Martha's Hill (Map 7, p85) and Newlands Corner (Map 8, p87).

Rights of access have also recently been created over areas such as the open land north of Hollingbourne (see Map 42, p153). But the effect of the Act on the North Downs is not so significant when compared to the large tracts of land now accessible in the Peak District, or the opening up of land on the South Downs between Poynings and Upper Beeding which now have permanent access rights rather than permissive access which could be withdrawn at any time.

❏ THE COUNTRYSIDE CODE

The Countryside Code, originally described in the 1950s as the Country Code, was revised and relaunched in 2004, in part because of the changes brought about by the CRoW Act (see p49); it was updated again in 2012, 2014 and also 2016. The Code seems like common sense but sadly some people still appear to have no understanding of how to treat the countryside they walk in. An adapted version of the 2016 Code, launched under the logo 'Respect. Protect. Enjoy.', is given below:

Respect other people

● **Consider the local community and other people enjoying the outdoors** Be sensitive to the needs and wishes of those who live and work there. If, for example, farm animals are being moved or gathered, keep out of the way and follow the farmer's directions. Being courteous and friendly to those you meet will ensure a healthy future for all based on partnership and co-operation.

● **Leave gates and property as you find them and follow paths unless wider access is available** A farmer normally closes gates to keep farm animals in, but may sometimes leave them open so the animals can reach food and water. Leave gates as you find them or follow instructions on signs. When in a group, make sure the last person knows how to leave the gate. Follow paths unless wider access is available, such as on open country or registered common land (known as 'open access land'). Leave machinery and farm animals alone – if you think an animal is in distress try to alert the farmer instead. Use gates, stiles or gaps in field boundaries if you can – climbing over walls, hedges and fences can damage them and increase the risk of farm animals escaping. If you have to climb over a gate because you can't open it always do so at the hinged end. Also be careful not to disturb ruins and historic sites.

Stick to the official path across arable/pasture land. Minimise erosion by not cutting corners or widening the path.

Protect the natural environment

● **Leave no trace of your visit and take your litter home** Take special care not to damage, destroy or remove features such as rocks, plants and trees. Take your litter with you (see opposite); litter and leftover food don't just spoil the beauty of the countryside, they can be dangerous to wildlife and farm animals.

Fires can be as devastating to wildlife and habitats as they are to people and property – so be careful with naked flames and cigarettes at any time of the year.

● **Keep dogs under effective control** This means that you should keep your dog on a lead or keep it in sight at all times, be aware of what it's doing and be confident it will return to you promptly on command.

Across farmland dogs should always be kept on a short lead. During lambing time they should not be taken with you at all. Always clean up after your dog and get rid of the mess responsibly – 'bag it and bin it'. (See also pp201-3).

Enjoy the outdoors

● **Plan ahead and be prepared** You're responsible for your own safety: be prepared for natural hazards, changes in weather and other events. Wild animals, farm animals and horses can behave unpredictably if you get too close, especially if they're with their young – so give them plenty of space.

● **Follow advice and local signs** In some areas there may be temporary diversions in place. Take notice of these and other local trail advice. Walking on the North Downs Way is pretty much hazard-free but you're responsible for your own safety so follow the simple guidelines outlined on pp53-5.

ECONOMIC IMPACT

Buy local

Rural businesses and communities in Britain have been hit hard in recent years by a seemingly endless series of crises. Most people are aware of the country-side code – not dropping litter and closing the gate behind you are still as per-tinent as ever – but in light of the economic pressures that local countryside businesses are under, there is something else you can do: buy local.

Look and **ask for local produce** (see box p22) to buy and eat. Not only does this cut down on the amount of pollution and congestion that the trans-portation of food creates – so-called 'food miles' – but also ensures that you are supporting local farmers and producers, the very people who have moulded the countryside you have come to see and who are in the best position to protect it. If you can find local food which is also organic so much the better.

Money spent at local level – perhaps in a market, or at the greengrocer, or in an independent pub – has a far greater impact for good in that community than the equivalent spent in a branch of a national chain store or restaurant. It would be going too far advocate that walkers boycott the larger supermarkets, which after all do provide local employment, but it's worth remembering that smaller businesses in rural communities rely heavily on visitors for their very existence. If we want to keep these local shops and post offices, we need to use them.

ENVIRONMENTAL IMPACT

By choosing a walking holiday you are taking a positive step towards minimis-ing your impact on the environment. The following are some ideas on how you can go a few steps further while walking the North Downs Way.

Use public transport whenever possible

Public transport to and along the North Downs Way is generally excellent with just about everywhere served by at least one bus or train; see pp45-8 for more details. Public transport is always preferable to using private cars as it benefits everyone: visitors, locals and the environment.

Never leave litter

Leaving litter shows disrespect for the natural world and others coming after you. As well as being unsightly litter pollutes the environment and can be dan-gerous to farm animals. **Please** carry a plastic bag so you can dispose of your rubbish in a bin in the next village. It would be very helpful if you could pick up litter left by other people too.

● **Is it OK if it's biodegradable?** No. Would you like to see litter at your picnic spot? When was the last time you saw a citrus grove on the North Downs Way? It spoils the natural beauty of the trail. Apple cores, banana skins, orange peel and the like are unsightly, encourage flies, ants and wasps and ruin a picnic spot.

● **The lasting impact of litter** A piece of orange peel left on the ground takes six months to decompose; silver foil 18 months; a plastic bag 10 years; clothes 15 years; and an aluminium can 85 years.

Erosion

● **Stay on the main trail** The effect of your footsteps may seem minuscule but when they are multiplied by several thousand walkers each year they become rather more significant.

Avoid taking shortcuts, widening the trail or taking more than one path; your boots will be followed by many others. This is particularly true on the North Downs Way which is heavily used by local day walkers.

● **Consider walking out of season** It's possible to walk the North Downs Way at any time of year but it's particularly popular in spring and summer. Consider walking at less busy times – autumn and mid-winter can be just as enjoyable and sometimes afford better views. And it may be a more relaxing experience with fewer people on the path and less competition for accommodation.

● **Respect all wildlife** Care for all wildlife you come across along the path; it has as much right to be there as you. Tempting as it may be to pick wild flowers leave them so the next people who pass can enjoy them too. If you want to identify them make a note or photograph them. Don't break branches off or damage trees in any way.

If you come across wildlife keep your distance and don't watch for too long. Your presence can cause considerable stress, particularly if the adults are with young, or in winter when the weather is harsh and food is scarce.

Young birds and animals aren't usually abandoned – just leave them alone and their mothers will return.

The code of the outdoor loo

You're never far from a proper toilet on the North Downs Way be it in a village or at a café or refreshment kiosk but the chances are you will need to 'go' outdoors at some point. Judging by the scraps of toilet paper you see about so have many others. In some parts of the world walkers and climbers are required to pack out their excrement. We haven't reached that stage but you need to be as sensitive as possible towards others.

● **Where to go** Wherever possible **use a toilet**. Where there are public toilets on the trail they are marked on the trail maps in this guide and you will also find facilities in pubs, cafés and campsites along the North Downs Way.

If you do have to go outdoors choose a site at least 30 metres away from running water and 200 metres away from the trail. Use a trowel or stick to **dig a small hole** about 15cm (6 inches) deep to bury your excrement in. It decomposes quicker when in contact with the top layer of soil or leaf mould. Do not squash it under rocks as this slows down the composting process.

● **Toilet paper and sanitary towels** These take a long time to decompose whether buried or not and may be dug up by animals and then blow into water sources or onto the path. To avoid this **pack them out**: put the used items in a paper bag which you then place inside a plastic bag (or two). Then simply empty the contents of the paper bag at the next toilet you come across and throw the bag away.

Wild camping

There is no general right to camp on land in England. You must first obtain the permission of the landowner and in the absence of this you may be trespassing. Camping outside official sites on National Trust land is against its bye-laws. Much of the North Downs Way is heavily wooded and most open land is private farmland and much of this is arable cropland. The opportunities for wild camping are therefore limited. But wild camping provides the walker with a uniquely fulfilling experience of living in a simple and sustainable way in which the habitual activities of cooking, eating, washing and sleeping take on greater importance.

Follow these suggestions for minimising your impact and encourage others to do likewise:

● **Be discreet** Camp alone or in small groups, spend only one night in each place and pitch your tent, tarp or bivvy late and move off early.

● **Never light a fire** The deep burn caused by camp fires, no matter how small, damages the turf which can take years to recover. Cook on a camp stove instead.

● **Don't use soap or detergent** There's no need to use soap; even biodegradable soaps and detergents pollute streams. You won't be away from a shower for more than a day or so. Wash up without detergent; use a plastic or metal scourer, or failing that, a handful of fine pebbles or some bracken or grass.

● **Leave no trace** Learn the skill of moving on without leaving any sign of having been there: no moved rocks, ripped up vegetation or dug drainage ditches. Make a final check of your campsite before departing; pick up any litter that you or anyone else has left, so leaving the place in a better state than you found it.

Outdoor safety

AVOIDANCE OF HAZARDS

The North Downs Way is not a difficult or dangerous walk and with common sense as well as good planning and preparation most hazards can be avoided. This information is just as important for those out on a day walk as for those walking the entire trail. To ensure a safe and stress-free trip **follow the countryside code** (see box p50) and:

● Before going out **get information** about where and when you can go;

● Check **weather forecasts** before you leave by listening to the radio or TV, or visit one of the online forecasts such as 🖳 bbc.co.uk/weather or 🖳 metoffice .gov.uk;

● Make sure that **somebody knows your plans** for every day you are on the trail. This could be a friend or relative whom you have promised to call every night, or the owners of the B&Bs that you plan to stay in at the end of each day's walk. That way, if you fail to turn up or call that evening, they can raise the alarm;

● **Stick to the path** and avoid old quarries or taking shortcuts on steep sections of the escarpment;

● **Check your location** regularly on the map; it's unlikely that you'll lose your way on the Downs but it'll save you missing a turning to a village and the frustration of retracing your steps at the end of a long day;

● Always fill your **water** bottles/pouches at every available opportunity and drink regularly;

● Make sure you have some **high-energy snacks** – fruit, nuts, or chocolate – to keep you going on the last few miles of a long day or in an emergency;

● Always carry a **torch** and **whistle** (the international distress signal is six blasts on the whistle or six flashes on a torch); a compass is not vital on this trail;

● Wear strong **boots** with good ankle support and a good grip, not trainers, and have **suitable clothes** including wet-weather gear (see pp35-6).

● Be extra vigilant with **children** and dogs (see pp201-3);

● Take a **first-aid kit** (see p37). If there is a casualty use basic first aid to treat the injury to the best of your ability. Work out exactly where you are. If possible leave someone with the casualty while others go to get help if you are not able to summon help via a mobile. If there are only two people, you have a dilemma. If you decide to get help leave all spare clothing and food with the casualty. On this trail you are never far from a road, village or farmhouse where you can summon help;

● In an emergency dial ☎ 999.

BLISTERS

It is important to break in new boots before embarking on a long trek. Make sure the boots are comfortable and try to avoid getting them wet on the inside. Air your feet at lunchtime, keep them clean and change your socks regularly. If you feel any hot spots stop immediately and apply Compeed or Second Skin before the blister develops. Applied at the right time it's magic stuff. If you've left it too late, do not burst the blister as this can lead to infection; dress it with any blister kit to protect it from abrasion. If the skin is broken keep the area clean with antiseptic and cover with a non-adhesive dressing material held in place with tape.

HYPOTHERMIA, HYPERTHERMIA & SUNBURN

Also known as exposure, **hypothermia** occurs when the body can't generate enough heat to maintain its normal temperature, usually as a result of being wet, cold, unprotected from the wind, tired and hungry. It is usually more of a problem in upland areas such as in the Lakes and on the moors than on the North Downs Way. Hypothermia is easily avoided by wearing suitable clothing, carrying and eating enough food and drink, being aware of the weather conditions and checking the morale of your companions.

Early signs to watch for are feeling cold and tired with involuntary shivering. Find some shelter as soon as possible and warm the victim up with a hot drink and some chocolate or other high-energy food. If possible give them another warm layer of clothing and allow them to rest until feeling better. If allowed to worsen, strange behaviour, slurring of speech and poor co-ordination will become apparent and the victim can quickly progress into unconsciousness, followed by coma and death. Quickly get the victim out of wind and rain, improvising a shelter if necessary. Rapid restoration of bodily warmth is essential and best achieved by bare-skin contact: someone should get into the same sleeping bag as the patient, both having stripped to their underwear, placing any spare clothing under or over them to build up heat. Send urgently for help.

Hyperthermia is the general name given to a variety of heat-related ailments. Not something you would normally associate with England, heatstroke and heat exhaustion are serious problems nonetheless. Symptoms of **heat exhaustion** include thirst, fatigue, giddiness, a rapid pulse, raised body temperature, low urine output and, if not treated, delirium and finally a coma. The best cure is to drink plenty of water. **Heatstroke** is another matter altogether and even more serious. A high body temperature and an absence of sweating are early indications, followed by symptoms similar to hypothermia (see opposite), such as a lack of coordination, convulsions and coma. Death will follow if treatment is not instantly given. Sponge the victim down, wrap them in wet towels, fan them, and get help immediately.

Sunburn can easily happen even on overcast days and especially if you have a fair complexion. The only surefire way to avoid it is to stay wrapped up, but that's not really an option. What you must do, therefore, is to smother yourself in sunscreen (with a minimum factor of 15) and apply it regularly throughout the day. Don't forget your lips, nose, ears, the back of your neck if wearing a T shirt, and even under your chin to protect against rays reflected up off the ground.

PERSONAL SAFETY

This is an issue usually raised by women walking or travelling on their own. The North Downs Way is much safer than any city and you are more likely to twist an ankle and have to hobble painfully to the nearest village, than become a crime victim. However, if you do walk on your own it's all the more important to make sure someone knows your plans for the day (see p53), and take all the usual precautions such as keeping an eye on your belongings at all times.

OTHER USERS

Just under 20% of the North Downs Way is bridleway, almost the same amount is metalled road, and about 14% is classed as a byway. So you may encounter off-road vehicles. Most of the byways are in Kent. The petrolheads I've met, and luckily it's not many, have stopped their engines and let me pass. Whatever you think about them in the countryside, and I don't like it, those I've met have been courteous and they were riding where they were allowed. When it comes to horses I've had many encounters with riders who are clearly over-mounted as they grimly try to control the equine equivalent of an F1 racing car. Give them a wide berth. Mountain-bikers are allowed to use bridleways and you just have to keep an eye out for the fast youthful types – usually their girlfriends following behind sheepishly apologise. Most though are a decent bunch. Hot spots are Newlands Corner through to Dorking.

3

THE ENVIRONMENT & NATURE

Conserving the North Downs Way

Britain is an overcrowded island, and England is the most densely populated part of it. The south-east has suffered a great deal of pressure from both over-population and competition for land use. The landscape of the North Downs in Surrey and Kent is the levee holding back London's sprawl.

Thankfully there are several bodies at local and national level whose job it is to protect and conserve that landscape for future generations.

NATURAL ENGLAND

The official responsibilities of Natural England (🖥 gov.uk/govern ment/organisations/natural-england) are to 'enhance biodiversity and our landscapes and wildlife in rural, urban, coastal and marine areas; promote access, recreation and public well-being, and contribute to the way natural resources are managed, so they can be enjoyed now and for future generations'. Essentially this organisation gives advice and information, designates Sites of Special Scientific Interest, National Parks, Areas of Outstanding Natural Beauty, manages some of the National Nature Reserves and enforces existing regulations. Natural England also manages England's National Trails.

There are 37 **Areas of Outstanding Natural Beauty** (**AONBs**) in England, covering some 15% of the country. Their primary objective is conservation of the natural beauty of a landscape and responsibility for this falls to the local authority within whose boundary they fall. The North Downs Way passes through two: **Surrey Hills AONB** (🖥 surreyhills.org) and **Kent Downs AONB** (🖥 kentdowns .org.uk).

None of the 224 **national nature reserves** (**NNRs**) in England is actually on the route, though Wye Downs is on the alternative loop. **Local nature reserves** (**LNRs**) are designated and managed by local councils. The main wildlife sites/local nature reserves along the North Downs Way are Colekitchen Down (off Map 10, p92), Ranmore Common, White Downs and Denbies Hillside (Map 11, p93 and Map 12, p95), Box Hill (Map 13, p97), Kemsing Downs

(Map 28, p129), Shoulder of Mutton Wood (Map 36, p139) and Blue Bell Hill (Map 38, p145). Wye Downs (p196) is on the alternative route to Dover.

The route also passes through other areas of protected land designated as **Sites of Special Scientific Interest** (**SSSI**); see for example Box Hill (p97) and Oxted Downs (Map 21, p113). There are over 4000 SSSIs in England (including 62 in Surrey and 98 in Kent), ranging in size from little pockets protecting wild-flower meadows, important nesting sites or special geological features, to vast swathes of upland, moorland and wetland. SSSIs are managed by Natural England in cooperation with their owners who are prevented from doing any work that is likely to damage the special features of the site. Many SSSIs are also either a NNR or a LNR.

Special Areas of Conservation (**SAC**) is an international designation which came into being as a result of the 1992 Earth Summit in Rio de Janeiro, Brazil. This European-wide network of sites is designed to promote the conservation of habitats, wild animals and plants, both on land and at sea. At the time of writing 235 land sites in England had been designated as SACs. Almost all UK SACs are based on SSSIs (although SSSIs cannot extend beyond low tide whereas SACs can).

❏ Campaigning/conservation organisations and charities

A number of voluntary organisations started the conservation movement in the mid 19th century. They rely on public support and can concentrate their resources either on acquiring land, which can then be managed purely for conservation purposes, or on influencing political decision-makers by lobbying and campaigning.

● **National Trust** (🖥 nationaltrust.org.uk) A charity with over two million members which aims to protect, through ownership, threatened coastline, countryside, historic houses, castles and gardens, and archaeological remains for everybody to enjoy. Box Hill (see p97) is managed by the National Trust as is much of the land through which the NDW passes from Brockham (Map 14, p101) to Reigate Hill (Map 16, p105).

● **Royal Society for the Protection of Birds** (RSPB; 🖥 rspb.org.uk) The largest voluntary conservation body in Europe with 150 reserves and over a million members.

● The umbrella organisation for the 47 wildlife trusts in the UK is **The Wildlife Trusts** (🖥 wildlifetrusts.org); two relevant to the North Downs Way are: **Surrey Wildlife Trust** (🖥 surreywildlifetrust.com; looks after 82 sites in Surrey), and **Kent Wildlife Trust** (🖥 kentwildlifetrust.org.uk).

● **Campaign to Protect Rural England** (CPRE; 🖥 cpre.org.uk) A charity which exists to promote the beauty and diversity of rural England by encouraging the sustainable use of land and other natural resources in town and country and whose members care about the countryside and campaign for it to be protected and enhanced.

● **Woodland Trust** (🖥 woodland-trust.org.uk) The trust aims to conserve, restore and re-establish native woodlands throughout the UK.

● **The Conservation Volunteers** (TCV; 🖥 tcv.org.uk) Encourages people to value their environment and take practical action to improve it.

● **Common Ground** (🖥 commonground.org.uk) Organises arts and environmental events believing that celebrations are the starting point for actions to improve localities.

● **World Wide Fund for Nature** (WWF; 🖥 wwf.org.uk) One of the world's largest conservation organisations, protecting endangered species and threatened habitats.

● **Friends of the Earth** (🖥 foe.co.uk) Campaigns for a better environment worldwide.

THE ENVIRONMENT & NATURE

THE ENVIRONMENT & NATURE

The **Environmental Stewardship Scheme** provides financial incentives to farmers to adopt low-impact agricultural practices. Particular priority is given to applications by farmers which will help conserve and restore chalk grassland along the scarp of the North Downs Way (NDW) and between the NDW and the so-called Pilgrims' Way. Farmers are also encouraged (financially) to establish grass margins, protect historic field boundaries and create and enhance bird habitats with the assistance of the RSPB (see box p57).

There is no doubt that these designations play a vital role in safeguarding the land they cover for future generations. However, the very fact that we rely on these labels for protecting limited areas begs the question: what are we doing to the vast majority of land that remains relatively unprotected? Surely we should be aiming to protect the natural environment outside protected areas just as much as within them.

Natural England also oversees the **National Trails** (🖥 nationaltrail.co.uk) staff who are responsible for the day-to-day management and running of the North Downs Way. They employ wardens and conservation officers – many of them volunteers – to maintain the trail and they also organise guided events and publish information about the North Downs Way for the public. Natural England provides most of the funding and resources for path maintenance.

General maintenance of the trail includes such things as surface repairs, signpost and waymark installation and replacement, converting stiles to gates and installing water taps and troughs. They are also responsible for the protection of endemic species and habitats, as well as geological features, along the North Downs Way. If necessary this may involve access restrictions, especially for motorised vehicles. However, promoting public access and the appreciation of the North Downs Way's natural heritage is also of importance, as is educating locals and visitors about the significance of the environment.

Flora and fauna

MAMMALS

Mammals in Britain tend to be nocturnal or crepuscular (ie emerging to feed at twilight and dawn) and/or just very shy so you may only see evidence of their existence from their tracks or scat. Nevertheless, it would be very strange not to see a **rabbit** (*Oryctolagus cuniculus*) especially as the trail crosses several warrens. You may see a **hare** (*Lepus europaeus*) which is bigger, has erect black-tipped ears, and is capable of running at speeds of up to 40mph/64km to escape its predator the **fox** (*Vulpes vulpes*), one of the more adaptable of Britain's native species. Generally nocturnal you may see them during the day. Now they are also common in urban areas feeding well on our leftovers and scraps.

The **badger** (*Meles meles*) with its distinctive black and white markings is fairly common judging by the numbers killed crossing roads on their habitual routes called runs. They live in underground setts often dug next to a tree in the side of a bank. The **hedgehog** (*Erinaceus europaeus*), alas, is fast disappearing from the British countryside and when you do see one, it will most commonly be as roadkill. Of the 18 species of **bat** in the UK, 17 actually breed here too (the 18th, the greater mouse-eared bat, was only discovered in 1958 and officially declared extinct in 1990, but one individual has been hibernating in southern England since 2002).

The **pipistrelle** (*Pipistrellus pipistrellus*) is the most common and easy to spot flitting at speed over water and hedgerows picking off insects just after dusk. There are signs that the **otter** (*Lutra lutra*) is making something of a comeback in Surrey and this is a good indication of a healthy environment. Now even Kent, the last county to see the otter reappear within its borders, has reported otters building holts on the rivers Medway and Eden.

The North American **grey squirrel** (*Sciurus carolinensis*) is constantly rustling about in the woodlands along the trail but sadly the **red squirrel** (*Sciurus vulgaris*) has lost its habitat to the grey squirrel and you won't see it on the North Downs Way. There are also some species of mice, voles and shrew.

With all the woodland along the trail there's a good chance of seeing **roe deer** (*Capreolus capreolus*), a small native species that likes to inhabit woodland and sometimes can also be seen grazing in fields. Early mornings are best.

FISH

In rivers such as the Wey (Map 1, p71 & Map 6, p79), the Mole (Map 13, p97) and the Darent (Map 26, p125) you may see fish feeding. The waters along the trail are home to **trout** (*Salmo trutta*), **pike** (*Esox lucius*) and **roach** (*Rutilus rutilus*).

BIRDS

The landscape of the North Downs is ideal for a variety of birds – the woodlands are an obvious habitat but there are also species at home on the open downs.

In woodland areas on the trail, look out for **treecreepers** (*Certhia familiaris*), **tits** (family *Paridae*, including blue, great, coal and long tailed), **nuthatches** (*Sitta europaea*) and **goldcrests** (*Regulus regulus*). These are tiny and you'll probably hear their high-pitched 'see see' call in the conifers, a habitat also popular with **siskins** (*Carduelis spinus*). They'll be joined by **spotted flycatcher** (*Muscicapa striata*) in summer and **chiffchaffs** (*Phylloscopus collybita*).

You'll see a lot of **pheasant** (*Phasianus colchicus*), many of which are bred by gamekeepers for shooting; you may see the feeding hoppers or bins deep in the woods. This encourages the bird to stay in an area and come the season (it starts in October and continues until the beginning of February) the birds are driven from the woods by 'beaters' to fly over guns. The plumage of the male is beautiful, with distinctive red head-sides and often a glossy green-black head. The female is a dull brown.

The **woodcock** (*Scolopax rusticola*) with its long straight beak and plump body frequents damp woodland where it can lie hidden thanks to its leafy brown plumage. It is most easily sighted in the spring at dusk and dawn. This is when the males perform their courtship flight known as 'roding' which involves two distinct calls, one a low grunting noise, the other a sharp 'k-wik k-wik' call.

The most frequently seen birds of prey are the **kestrel** (*Falco tinnunculus*) and the **sparrowhawk** (*Accipiter nisus*), small and agile, well able to pursue prey through forests. If you hear a loud hooting and a sharp 'ke-wick' after dark the **tawny owl** (*Strix aluco*) is responsible and you may see a **barn owl** (*Tyto alba*) with its pale plumage, white breast and heart-shaped face, glide silently by as it hunts open country along the woodland edge.

SKYLARK
L: 185MM/7.25"

The sight and sound of a **skylark** (*Alauda arvensis*) with its warbling song pouring out, getting higher pitched the further it spirals upwards specking out against a blue sky is a joy. A good place to see and hear skylarks is crossing Reigate Hill Golf Club (see Map 17, p108) but they are common along the open land of the North Downs Way.

Although it's more common on the downland of the South Downs Way you may catch sight of the **stonechat** (*Saxicola torquata*), a colourful little bird with a deep orange breast and a black head. They are easily identified by their habit of flitting from the top of one bush to another, only pausing to call out across the fields. The call sounds much like the sound of two stones being struck together, hence the name.

LAPWING/PEEWIT
L: 320MM/12.5"

One of the most attractive birds the Downs walker might spot, usually seen feeding on open arable farmland, is the **lapwing** (*Vanellus vanellus*), which is also known as the peewit after its characteristic call. It has long legs, a short bill and a distinctive long head crest. Sadly, this attractive bird is declining in numbers. The name comes from its lilting flight, frequently changing direction with its large rounded wings. It is also identified by a white belly, black and white head, black throat patch and distinctive dark green wings that look black from a distance.

YELLOWHAMMER
L: 160MM/6.25"

The **yellowhammer** (*Emberiza citrinella*), also known as the yellow bunting, can sometimes be seen perched on the top of gorse bushes. Most field guides to birds along with most old romantic country folk will claim that the distinctive song of the yellowhammer sounds like 'a little bit of bread and no cheese'. At a push they are right but the yellowhammer is certainly no talking parrot.

If you see a **kingfisher** (*Alcedo atthis*) you are in for a treat. Likely places are along the river Wey and the Mole but don't blink – these vivid blue birds with a long spiked beak streak past just above the water when disturbed.

The **green woodpecker** (*Picus viridis*) is not all green, sporting a bright red and black head. Green woodpeckers are sometimes spotted clinging to a vertical tree trunk or feeding on the ground in open fields. The most common view, however, is as the bird flies away when disturbed. The undulating flight pattern of the woodpecker is characterised by rapid wing beats as the bird rises followed by a pause when the bird slowly drops. This is accompanied by a loud laughing call that has earned the bird its old English name of yaffle.

REPTILES

Reptiles have had a bad rap ever since slithering into the Garden of Eden. Britain's only poisonous snake, the **adder** (*Vipera berus*) is recognised by its zig-zag body pattern. They pose very little risk to walkers but dogs can get bitten when snakes come out of hibernation to warm themselves, often on a sunny path. They only bite when provoked, preferring to hide instead, and the venom is designed to kill small mammals such as mice, voles and shrews, so deaths in humans are very rare (10 attributed to adder bites in the last hundred years) but a bite can be extremely unpleasant and occasionally dangerous for children or the elderly. Adders are a measure of the health of an environment and Kent Reptile & Amphibian Group (🖥 wkentarg.org) has projects in Kent along the Medway paths recording their distribution. The **common lizard** (*Lacerta vivipara*) may sometimes be seen basking in the sun and is harmless.

BUTTERFLIES

Two species that are dependant on the chalk grassland for their survival are the **Adonis blue** (*Polyommatus bellargus*) and the **Chalk hill blue** (*Polyommatus coridon*). Both feed on horseshoe vetch and August is a good time to spot them. The best butterfly spotting is on Box Hill where over two-thirds of the British butterfly species have been recorded.

❑ **Unusual insects**
Perhaps the most unusual insect on the North Downs Way is the **glow worm** (*Lampyris noctiluca*). It's not actually a worm but a beetle and related to the firefly. The best time to see these creatures is at night (10pm to midnight), between mid June and mid July, when the vivid glow of the female is used by her to attract males. The light glows like a luminous watch dial and is caused by a chemical reaction on the underside of the adult female. Unlike fireflies the glow can't be switched on and off instantly but takes minutes to turn on and off. A good place to see them is Box Hill (Map 13, p97); visit 🖥 glowworms.org.uk for lots more information.

Two species you may see are the **Brimstone** (*Gonepteryx rhamni*) and the less common **White Admiral** (*Limenitis camilla*) which is in fact predominantly black with white banded wings. Look for it on woodland edges and in brambles where it feeds on honeysuckle. The male brimstone is easy to identify – it's bright yellow. The name butterfly may have come from this and it's said the brighter the brimstone the better the summer will be. Expect to see it along Albury Downs (see Map 8, p87).

Chances are you'll see, at some point on the walk, the familiar orange-winged **Small Tortoiseshell** (*Aglais urticae*) common in many gardens and urban parks.

TREES

The number of trees and the amount of woodland along the North Downs Way are a striking feature of this walk. Surrey is England's most wooded county but since 1600 much of its ancient woodland has been felled for fuel and building material or cleared for agriculture.

In the last 50 years 88% of coppiced woodland has disappeared. But coppicing and old woodland skills are making a comeback and the north slopes of the North Downs Way remain heavily wooded.

Much of the woodland is mixed deciduous made up largely of **oak** (*Quercus petraea*) and **ash** (*Fraxinus excelsior*). The **beech** (*Fagus sylvatica*) with its thick, silvery trunk is one of the most attractive native trees. It can grow to a height of forty metres with the high canopies blocking out much of the light. As a result the floors of beech woodlands tend to be fairly bare of vegetation. They favour well-drained soil, hence their liking for the steep scarp slope. In autumn the colours of the turning leaves can be quite spectacular.

Other trees that flourish include **silver birch** (*Betula pendula*) and **hazel** (*Corylus avellana*) which has traditionally been used for coppicing. There is frequent coppicing carried out in King's Wood (see Map 51, p167). The trees are cut off at ground level every few years yielding many slender, straight and pliable branches used for making charcoal, fences, hurdles, bean poles, barrels and by some as dowsing rods for water divining.

The **alder** (*Alnus glutinosa*) is a tree which thrives near reliable sources of water and thus is often found along riverbanks. The River Mole is known for its picturesque stands of alders. The **whitebeam** (*Sorbus aria*), though not a common tree, can be seen in parts of Surrey along the trail. It gets its name from the white mealy down which covers the undersides of the leaves; beam is Saxon for 'tree'.

Famous for its life expectancy, lasting for well over 1000 years in some cases, the **common yew** (*Taxus baccata*) is abundant in churchyards but there are also natural stands among beech woodland. The dark glossy needles are quite distinctive as is the flaky red bark of the often gnarled and twisted old trunks and branches. Do not be tempted to eat the bright red berries as they are poisonous. Taxine, this natural poison, has been used to make a drug for cancer treatment.

Hawthorn (*Crataegus monogyna*) is common in hedgerows and a valuable supply of berries for birds as is **holly** (*Ilex aquifolium*). Solitary hawthorn trees are also associated with spirits and fairies.

At Box Hill there are fine stands of **box** (*Buxus sempervirens*) after which it is named. This is one of the few places in Britain where the box grows wild: it's usually seen in a neatly clipped state in a garden. Box is the hardest and heaviest of all European woods, the only one which does not float in water.

Many of the woods are owned and cared for by the National Trust, the most significant being Denbies Hillside (see Map 12, p95) and Box Hill (Map 13, p97). Kemsing Parish Council owns Kemsing Down Nature Reserve where in addition to woodland there are important chalk grassland and scrub habitats.

FLOWERS

Woodland and hedgerows

Spring is the time to come and see the rich displays of colour on the North Downs Way. From March to May **bluebells** (*Hyacinthoides non-scripta*) proliferate on the woodland floor along the North Downs Way forming large carpets of bright blue, bell-shaped flowers.

Other common spring woodland flowers are the pink-tinged **wood anemone** (*Anemone nemorosa*) and the yellow clump-forming **primrose** (*Primula vulgaris*). The feathery **Travellers' Joy** (*Clematis vitalba*) has pale-cream fluffy blooms in autumn – hence its other name **old man's beard** – twists through hedgerow and trees. Another climber is the **honeysuckle** (*Lonicera periclymemum*), a valuable butterfly food plant. A member of the carrot family, but not edible is **Queen Anne's Lace** or **cow parsley**, with its white flowers covering banks and verges from early summer. **Red campion** (*Silene dioica*) is a decorative pinkish red flower with five petals and is common on the path edge between March and October. The pretty pink geranium **herb robert** flowers through to September.

At the woodland edge and in scrubland you will also find **bramble** (*Rubus fruticosus*), a common vigorous shrub; edible **blackberry** fruits ripen from late summer into autumn. They can be quite tart and very pippy with a free-running and staining purple juice. Fairly common in scrubland and on woodland edges is the **dog rose** (*Rosa canina*) which has a large pink flower, the fruits or 'hips' of which are rich in Vitamin C and can be used to make the delicious rose-hip syrup.

Other flowering plants to look for in wooded areas and in hedgerows include the tall **foxglove** (*Digitalis purpurea*) with its trumpet-like flowers and **forget-me-not** (*Myosotis arvensis*) with tiny, delicate blue flowers.

Perhaps the most aromatic plant is **wild garlic** (*Allium ursinum*) whose broad pointed leaves release an onion bouquet when crushed. This plant carpets the verge of War Coppice Rd (see Map 19, p110) and is abundant in Marden Park and Church Woods (see Map 20, p111). Its early summer white, star-like flowers, held high on a stem, add a splash of colour to the woodland floor.

THE ENVIRONMENT & NATURE

THE ENVIRONMENT & NATURE

The chalk grassland

The flowers of the chalk grassland are a hardy group. A farmer tells me that to grow anything well there you'd need rain every day and a dose of manure on Sundays. Battered by wind and grazed by sheep and rabbits, they eke out an existence in a poor, thin chalk soil. The best way to look at them is up close and personal so drop to your knees at the top of Box Hill (see Map 13, p97) or on Oxted Downs (see Map 21, p113). They've all adapted to the poor soil and a relatively harsh environment. The dominant grass, **sheep's fescue** (*Festuca ovina*), has folded leaves to protect its delicate stomata, openings that allow carbon dioxide and light to pass through for photosynthesis, and the leaf is narrow to reduce loss of water.

The best defence against sheep and rabbits is to grow low to the ground and form a mat. So rosette leaves are common like those on the **cowslip** (*Primula veris*) anchoring the plant to the ground. Only the yellow flowers are held upright so the bees can pollinate. Tea made from the drooping flowers is said to cure insomnia. **Horseshoe vetch** (*Hippocrepis comosa*), an important butterfly food plant (see p61), bears its small pea-flower-shaped yellow flowers on a dense close-fitting mat. Other strategies are to put out roots wherever a stem touches the soil or to interweave a network of stems just below the surface as **birdsfoot trefoil** (*Lotus corniculatus*) does.

The tiny yellow flower of **tormentil** (*Potentilla tormentilla*) can be seen hugging the ground in short grassland. It gets its name from an age when it was used as a medicinal remedy for diarrhoea and haemorrhoids: the taste is so foul that it tormented whoever took it.

Another tiny flower that can also be found close to the ground is the **scarlet pimpernel** (*Anagallis arvensis*), a member of the primrose family. The flowers are tiny at just 5mm in diameter but stand out from their grassy background thanks to their light red colour.

There are many **orchids** (see photos opposite) on the Downs and some are relatively common including the **early purple orchid** (*Orchis mascula*), as its name suggests, the first of the British orchids to flower from April onwards, and the widespread **bee orchid** (*Ophrys apifera*) which gets its name from the bee-shaped flowers produced in early summer. The National Nature Reserve at Wye is said to boast of no fewer than 21 different species of orchid.

The showiest plant is probably the **common poppy** (*Papaver rhoeas*), which splashes colour, with its deep-red petals, on the open fields of the Kent landscape in late summer.

Heath

Puttenham Heath, close to the path, is an isolated area of heath where acid-loving plants thrive on the greensand soil. The most common is **heather** (*Calluna vulgaris*), a versatile plant used for thatching, basket work, brooms and fuel for fires. You will also find a collection of acid-loving species about Hackhurst Downs (Map 10, p92).

Thorny **gorse** (*Ulex europaeus*) bushes brighten up the summer with their small yellow flowers that burst open from February until June.

Foxglove
Digitalis purpurea

Early Purple Orchid
Orchis mascula

Bee Orchid
Orchis apifera

Bell Heather
Erica cinerea

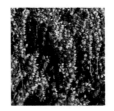

Heather (Ling)
Calluna vulgaris

Pyramidal Orchid
Anacamptis pyramidalis

Rosebay Willowherb
Epilobium angustifolium

Common Vetch
Vicia sativa

Forget-me-not
Myosotis arvensis

Rowan (tree)
Sorbus aucuparia

Old Man's Beard
Clematis vitalba

Red Campion
Silene dioica

Common Dog Violet
Viola riviniana

Common Centaury
Centaurium erythraea

Honeysuckle
Lonicera periclymemum

Wild marjoram
Origanum vulgare

Germander Speedwell
Veronica chamaedrys

Herb-Robert
Geranium robertianum

Lousewort
Pedicularis sylvatica

Self-heal
Prunella vulgaris

Scarlet Pimpernel
Anagallis arvensis

Viper's Bugloss
Echium vulgare

Ramsons (Wild Garlic)
Allium ursinum

Bluebell
Hyacinthoides non-scripta

Dog Rose
Rosa canina

Meadow Buttercup
Ranunculis acris

Gorse
Ulex europaeus

Tormentil
Potentilla erecta

Birdsfoot-trefoil
Lotus corniculatus

Ox-eye Daisy
Leucanthemum vulgare

St John's Wort
Hypericum perforatum

Primrose
Primula vulgaris

Cowslip
Primula veris

Common Ragwort
Senecio jacobaea

Red Admiral butterfly (*Vanessa atalanta*) on
Hemp Agrimony (*Eupatorium cannabinum*)

Using this guide

This trail guide has been described from west to east and divided into 12 stages. Each stage is approximately a days's walk in length though that doesn't mean you have to divide the trail up this way; with such good transport links and plenty of accommodation, you can of course divide the trail up however you wish.

There is excellent access by public transport if you're doing the walk in day stages, but it is not the only way to structure the walk. Much will depend on the speed you walk at, your interests and where you stay. See pp30-1 for some suggested itineraries.

To enable you to plan your own itinerary **practical information** is presented clearly on the trail maps. This includes walking times for both directions, places to stay, camp and eat, as well as shops where you can buy supplies. Further service **details** are given in the text under the entry for each place. For an overview of this information see the village and town facilities table on pp28-9.

For **map profiles** see the colour pages at the end of the book.

TRAIL MAPS

Scale and walking times

The trail maps are to a scale of 1:20,000 (1cm = 200m; $3^1/_8$ inches = one mile). Walking times are given along the side of each map and

---

❏ **Important note – walking times**
Unless otherwise specified, **all times in this book refer only to the time spent walking**. You will need to add 20-30% to allow for rests, photography, checking the map, drinking water etc. When planning the day's hike count on 5-7 hours' actual walking. To research this book I walked alone so kept a faster pace than if I were walking with companions. Most health and fitness professionals calculate average walking speed at 2mph/3kph. After a few days you will hopefully know how fast you walk compared to the time bars and can plan your day more accurately.

(Opposite) Top: The attractive hamlet of Seale, with St Laurence Church at its centre, lies only five minutes from the trail and is the first place where walkers can get refreshments. **Centre**: Puttenham is the first village lying right on the trail. **Bottom, left**: The stunning gesso murals in the terracotta-tiled Watts Cemetery Chapel (see p76) were completed in 1904. **Bottom, right**: Taking a breather on a commemorative bench, just a mile from the start of the trail.

the arrow shows the direction to which the time refers. Black triangles indicate the points between which the times have been taken. **See p65 for note on walking times.** The times on the maps are there as an aid to planning your walk not to judge your ability. There are many variables which will affect your speed including weather, ground conditions, whether you are walking alone or with company and how interesting you find parts of the landscape.

Up or down?

Other than when on a track or bridleway the trail is shown as a dotted line. An arrow across the trail indicates the slope; two arrows show that it is steep. Note that the arrow points towards the higher part of the trail. If, for example, you are walking from A (at 80m) to B (at 200m) and the trail between the two is short and steep, it would be shown thus: A- – – – >>- – – -B. Reversed arrow heads indicate a downward gradient.

Accommodation

The accommodation shown on the maps is either on the trail or within easy reach of it. Some owners are prepared to collect walkers from points on the trail where the accommodation is a mile or two off the path and it is worth asking if this is possible when booking. An offer to pay petrol money will generally be appreciated for this added service.

Details of each place are given in the accompanying text. The number and type of rooms is given for each place: **S** = single bed, **T** = twin beds, **D** = double bed or twin beds put together, **Tr/Qd** = triple/quad ie rooms that can sleep up to three/four people, but note that this often means two people sharing a double bed and the other(s) in bunk beds; these rooms can also be used as doubles or twins.

Rates given are **per person (pp)** based on two people sharing a room for a one-night stay – rates are almost always discounted for a longer stay. Where a single room (**sgl**) is available the rate for that is quoted if different from the per person rate. The rate for single occupancy (**sgl occ**) of a double/twin is generally higher, and the rate for three or more sharing a room may be lower. Unless specified, rates are for B&B. At some places the only option is a room rate; this will be the same whether one or two people share. Don't bank on negotiating a discount in the off-season; year-round demand from business travellers, holidaymakers and weekenders for accommodation along and near the North Downs Way keeps prices high. But some of the larger establishments catering to business travellers may offer a lower weekend rate; it's worth checking when you book. See pp18-21 for more details on prices.

The text also mentions whether the premises have **wi-fi** (WI-FI); if a **bath** is available (⬤) in, or for, at least one room; and whether **dogs** (🐾) are welcome. Most places will not take more than one dog in a room and also accept them subject to prior arrangement. Many make an additional charge (usually per night but occasionally per stay), while others may require a deposit which is refundable if the dog doesn't make a mess. See also pp201-3.

Other features

Features marked on the maps are pertinent to navigation but, to avoid clutter, not all features have been marked.

The route guide

FARNHAM [MAP 1a, p69]

The accident of the Surrey Hills made all men who wished to get to the south-western ports from the Thames Valley and the east pass through Farnham. Travellers going west and north from the Weald were equally compelled, if they would avoid the ridge, to pass through Farnham. The former had to come down north of the Hog's Back, the latter from the south of it, and it was ever at Farnham they met…and after Farnham the western tracks, now all in one, proceed to the Straits of Dover.

Hilaire Belloc, *The Old Road*

Situated roughly halfway between Winchester and London, Farnham made its money from trade in wool, then corn, and in the 19th century its wealth came from brewing. Now it services well-off commuters but it also has a vibrant arts scene, a wonderful museum housed in a Grade 1 listed building and a fine medieval street pattern with a well-preserved Georgian streetscape in Castle St, West St and The Borough.

This is the reputed birthplace of William Cobbett, the 18th-century politician and author of *Rural Rides*, in which he writes glowingly of the area covered in the first stage of the North Downs Way; his actual home and birthplace is now a pub named after him just outside the centre in Bridge Square.

What to see and do

If you have the time, follow the comprehensive **Farnham Heritage Trail**; a free leaflet may be downloaded from 🖳 farnham.gov.uk/discover/history-and-heritage/heritagetrail.

If you are time poor visit **Farnham Castle Keep** (☎ 01252-721194, 🖳 www .english-heritage.co.uk; Mon-Fri 9am-5pm, Sat & Sun 10am-4pm; free).

Overlooking the town, construction was commenced in 1138 under Henry de Blois and it provided accommodation for the bishops of Winchester until 1955. Mary Tudor stayed here on her way to marry Philip of Spain in Winchester and Elizabeth I visited several times.

Another worthwhile place to visit is the **Museum of Farnham** (☎ 01252-715094, 🖳 farnhammaltings.com/museum; Tue-Sat 10am-5pm; free); it's located in Wilmer House, West St, a graciously proportioned Grade 1 listed building, dating from 1718, with a pretty garden and the exhibits are well displayed.

There is a monthly market at **Farnham Maltings**, Bridge Square (☎ 01252-745444, 🖳 farnhammaltings.com; first Sat in the month 9am-4.30pm; £1), which is also the focus of a thriving music and arts scene, and a **Farmers' Market** (see box p22) on the fourth Sunday of every month (10am-1.30pm), in the Central Car Park, off Victoria Rd.

Services

Tourist information is only available online (🖳 farnham.gov.uk/discover).

There are branches of various banks and building societies with **ATMs** on The Borough as well as a main **post office** (Mon, Wed-Fri 9am-5.30pm, Tue 9am to 9.30am, Sat 9am-12.30pm); there is another post office on Station Hill.

Sainsbury's **supermarket** (Mon-Sat 7am-8pm, Sun 10am-4pm) is on South St and there is a Boots **pharmacy** (Mon-Sat 8.30am-6pm, Sun 10.30am-4pm) on The Borough.

Also on The Borough is Breaking Free **outdoor shop** (☎ 01252-724347, 🖳 breakingfree.co.uk; Mon-Sat 9.30am-5.30pm), for last-minute gear purchases.

ROUTE GUIDE AND MAPS

Transport
The **railway station**, on Station Hill, is about five minutes away. South Western Railway operate services (see box pp42-3) to Guildford (change at Aldershot) and direct to London Waterloo.

National Express **coach service** NX031 (see p44; London to Portsmouth) drops off at the bus stop on The Borough and picks up from the stop on South St.

Several Stagecoach **bus services** (pp45-8) call here: Nos 4 & 5 (to Aldershot); Nos 18 & 19 (Aldershot to Haslemere); No 46 (to Guildford); and No 65 (Alton to Guildford). The No 65 only stops on The Borough, but all the other services call also at Farnham railway station.

For a **taxi** try Farnham Station Taxis (☎ 01252-735735, 🖥 farnhamstationtaxis .co.uk) or Home James (☎ 01252-722296, 🖥 homejamestaxis.co.uk).

Where to stay
Farnham now has a hostel: *The Mulberry* (☎ 01252-726673, 🖥 mulberryfarnham.co .uk; 1 x 2- / 3 x 4- /1 x 5-bed dorms; WI-FI) sits near the station and has en suite dorms furnished with between three and six beds, with rates starting at £25pp – and you don't have to walk far from the pub in the evening!

For a great location and lodgings in an historic property at a fair price it's hard to beat *1 Park Row* (☎ 01252-710249, 🖥 1parkrow.co.uk; 1S/1D shared bathroom, 2D/1T all en suite; WI-FI). B&B costs £34-44pp (sgl from £45, sgl occ £58-78). It's just off Castle St and next door to the popular Nelson Arms.

At No 73 Lodge Hill Rd, about 1.75km south of the station off Tilford Rd, is the spacious *High Wray* (☎ 01252-715589, 🖥 c5555827.myzen.co.uk; 2T, shared bathroom; ➿; WI-FI; 🐾) charging from £30pp.

If location, not price, is your mantra try the 17th-century former coaching inn, *Bush Hotel* (☎ 01252-234800, 🖥 www.mercure.com; 94D or T, all en suite; ➿; WI-FI; 🐾) on The Borough (though the entrance is round the corner on South St). Rates vary depending on demand, though the rack rates are seldom less than £50pp

(sgl occ room rate) without breakfast; online, however, you should be able to secure a room for around £40pp (sgl occ room rate); breakfast costs £10pp.

Smaller but still central, *The Bishop's Table* (☎ 01252-710222, 🖥 www.bishops table.com; 2S/1T/21D, all en suite; ➿; WI-FI) sits at the other end of The Borough at 27 West St. Room rates also vary according to demand but are around £45pp (sgl £75-80, sgl occ room rate); breakfast is available.

Where to eat and drink
For a **coffee**, there are the usual nationwide chain outlets such as *Caffè Nero* (Mon-Fri 7am-6.30pm, Sat 7.30am-6.30pm, Sun 7.30am-6pm), at the bottom of Castle St, and *Costa* (Mon-Sat 7am-7pm, Sun 9am-6pm) on West St. For something more independent, *The Spire Café* (Mon-Fri 10am-2pm, to noon on Sat) offers decent, warm coffee (£1.50) served by decent, warm people, as well as some great-value light meals (soups £2.50) served Monday-Friday only. Back on Castle St, you can grab a quick **sandwich** from the smart kiosk, *Emma @ The Stirling* (☎ 01252-727253; Mon-Fri 8am-4pm, Sat & Sun 9.30am-4pm, gen closed on Sun in winter) at the southern end of Castle St.

Castle St is also the best place to head for **breakfasts**. Near Caffè Nero is a branch of that upmarket eatery *Bill's* (☎ 01252-716589, 🖥 bills-website.co.uk; Mon-Sat 8am-11pm, Sun to 10.30pm; WI-FI) charging £8.95 for their Full English; they also have some delicious lunchtime options (£10.50-15.95). Right by Caffè Nero, *Gail's* (☎ 01252-722955, 🖥 gailsbread.co .uk/bakeries/farnham; Mon-Fri 7am-6pm, Sat, Sun & Bank Hols 8am-6pm) is a branch of an 'artisan bakery' chain, though one that also does a fine line in breakfasts with porridge (£4) and granola (£5.50).

If this is all a bit fancy, on the corner of South St and the A325 (East St) is *The Gorge* (☎ 01252-726070; Mon-Sat 7am-5pm, Sun 8.30am-4pm), where an all-day breakfast costs just £3.75.

Brasserie Blanc (☎ 01252-899970, 🖥 brasserieblanc.com; Mon-Fri 9am-10pm,

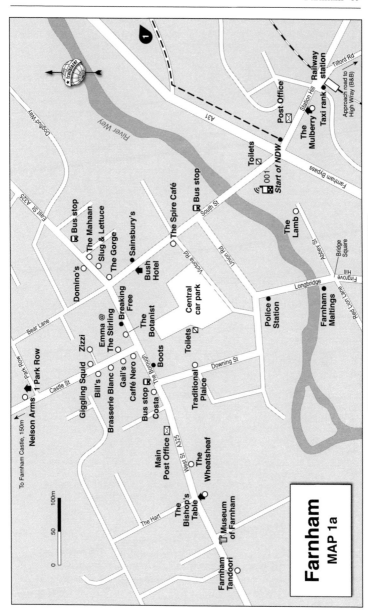

Farnham
MAP 1a

ROUTE GUIDE AND MAPS

River Wey

Dogflud Way

East St, A325

Bus stop
The Mahaan
Slug & Lettuce
The Gorge
Sainsbury's

Domino's

Bear Lane

Park Row
1 Park Row
Nelson Arms

To Farnham Castle, 150m

Castle St

Zizzi
Giggling Squid
Bill's
Brasserie Blanc
Gail's
Caffè Nero

Emma @
The Stirling

Breaking
Free

The
Botanist

Boots

Bus stop
Costa
The Borough

Traditional
Plaice

Downing St

Toilets

Central
car park

The Spire Café
Bus stop
South St

Start of NDW

Toilets

Victoria Rd

Bush Hotel

Main
Post Office

West St, A325

The
Wheatsheaf

The Hart

The
Bishop's
Table

Museum
of Farnham

Farnham
Tandoori

A31

Post Office

Railway
station

Tilford Rd

Station Hill

The
Mulberry
Taxi rank

Approach road to
High Wray (B&B)

Farnham Bypass

The Lamb

Union Rd

Longbridge

Police
Station

Farnham
Maltings

Bridge
Square

Firgrove Hill

Red Lion Lane

0   50   100m

Sat 8.30am-10.30pm, Sun 9am-9pm) is one of celebrity chef Raymond Blanc's babies. It's a cut above the quality – and cost – of your average trekker's repast with mains starting at around £14.90 for a chicken salad, though they do offer a couple of fixed price menus at lunchtime (£11.95 for two courses, £15.45 for three) that are better value. The food is lovely, of course, but maybe save this sort of fare for the end of your trek – otherwise you may never start!

Across the way, *Giggling Squid* (☎ 01252-727552, 🖳 gigglingsquid.com; Tue-Thur noon-10pm, Fri & Sat to 10.30pm, Sun & Mon to 9.30pm) is a Thai tapas restaurant at lunchtime, an unusual combination, though it reverts to a more typical Thai eatery at night, with that old favourite, green curry, for £9.95.

The Botanist (☎ 01252-718089, 🖳 the botanist.uk.com; food Mon-Thur 11am-4pm & 6-11pm, Fri 11am-11pm, Sat & Sun 10am-11pm), on The Borough, has mains from £10.95 up to £19.95 for a whole rotisserie chicken plus trimmings.

For takeaway fare, fish & chip fans – and many walkers are – should make for *Traditional Plaice* (☎ 01252-718009; Mon-Sat 11.30am-2.15pm & 5-10pm), at 50 Downing St.

Indian food is at its best in Farnham at *The Mahaan* (☎ 01252-718171, 🖳 thema haan.co.uk; daily noon-2pm & 5.30-11.30pm) on East St, or try *Farnham Tandoori* (☎ 01252-716853, 🖳 farnham-tandoori.com; daily noon-2pm & 6-11.30pm, to midnight Fri & Sat), 47 West St, with the ubiquitous chicken tikka masala at £11.50.

Back on Castle St, *Zizzi* (☎ 01252-719231, 🖳 zizzi.co.uk; Mon-Sat 11.30am-11pm, Sun to 10.30pm) is a lively Italian joint with pizzas from £7.95; on the subject of pizzas, there's a branch of *Domino's* (☎

01252-717000, 🖳 www.dominos.co.uk/farnham; Mon-Thur 11am-11.30pm, Fri & Sat 11am-12.30am, Sun to 11pm) on East St.

As a former brewery town, you'd expect to find a number of pubs, including several that serve food too. *The Mulberry* (see Where to stay; Mon-Thur noon-2.30pm & 6-10pm, Fri & Sat noon-10pm, Sun noon-8pm; WI-FI; 🐾 bar area only), opposite the station, does a nice line is tasty burgers including a Man versus Mulberry challenge for £25: four 8oz burgers, four house cheeses, tomatoes, red onion, dill pickles, spicy salsa, pickled jalepeños, hash browns, onion rings, ketchup, mayo and mustard – eat it all and you win a T-shirt!

The Wheatsheaf (☎ 01252-717135, 🖳 thewheatsheaffarnham.co.uk; food Mon-Thur noon-2.30pm & 5.30-9.30pm, Fri & Sat noon-9.30pm, Sun noon-8.30pm) uses local ingredients to concoct some lovely dishes including a delicious chargrilled red onion, cherry tomato and brie tart (£12.95).

Nelson Arms (☎ 01252-712554, 🖳 nelson-arms.co.uk; food served Mon-Sat noon-2.30pm & 6-9.30pm, Sun noon-8pm), on Castle St, is a low-beamed gastropub dating back to the 16th century (so pre-Nelson) with mains from £10 for the honey and mustard roast ham, two fried eggs & hand-cut chips.

The *Slug & Lettuce* (🖳 www.slugand lettuce.co.uk/farnham; 🐾), on the A325 (East St), is a huge place, part of a chain and not to everyone's taste. Nevertheless, they serve good-value food (mains from £7.79, with a beef & ale pie for £9.99) and they do allow **dogs**.

For drinking only, *The Lamb* (☎ 01252-714133, 🖳 lambfarnham.co.uk; Mon-Fri 11am-11pm, Sat noon-midnight, Sun noon-10.30pm), on Abbey St, serves lovely Spitfire ale from Shepherd Neame.

FARNHAM TO GUILDFORD [MAPS 1-6b]

Not too strenuous, very pretty and punctuated by plenty of points of interest – this first **12-mile/19.3km (3hrs 50mins to 4hrs 50mins** to a reunion with the River Wey and the turn-off to Guildford) stage of the NDW is, in many ways, a microcosm of the whole trail. *(cont'd on p74)*

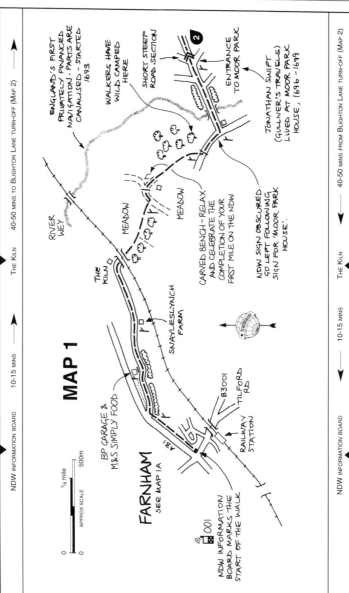

MAP 1

ENGLAND'S FIRST PRIVATELY FINANCED NAVIGATION - PARTS ARE CANALISED - STARTED 1693

WALKERS HAVE WILD CAMPED HERE

SHORT STEEP ROAD SECTION

ENTRANCE TO MOOR PARK

JONATHAN SWIFT (GULLIVER'S TRAVELS) LIVED AT MOOR PARK HOUSE, (1696 - 1699)

RIVER WEY

MEADOW

MEADOW

THE KILN

CARVED BENCH - RELAX AND CELEBRATE THE COMPLETION OF YOUR FIRST MILE ON THE NDW

NDW SIGN OBSCURED. GO LEFT FOLLOWING SIGN FOR 'MOOR PARK HOUSE'.

SNAYLESLYNCH FARM

BP GARAGE & M&S SIMPLY FOOD

¼ mile

500m

APPROX SCALE

0

0

FARNHAM
SEE MAP 1A

B3001 TILFORD RD

RAILWAY STATION

A31

NDW INFORMATION BOARD MARKS THE START OF THE WALK

NDW INFORMATION BOARD   10-15 MINS   THE KILN   40-50 MINS TO BLIGHTON LANE TURN-OFF (MAP 2)

NDW INFORMATION BOARD   10-15 MINS   THE KILN   40-50 MINS FROM BLIGHTON LANE TURN-OFF (MAP 2)

ROUTE GUIDE AND MAPS

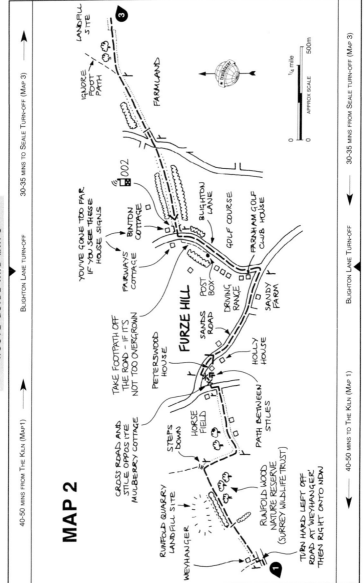

MAP 2

40-50 MINS FROM THE KILN (MAP1) ——▶   BLIGHTON LANE TURN-OFF ▶   30-35 MINS TO SEALE TURN-OFF (MAP 3)

40-50 MINS FROM THE KILN (MAP 1) ——▶   BLIGHTON LANE TURN-OFF ▶   30-35 MINS FROM SEALE TURN-OFF (MAP 3)

3

LANDFILL SITE

IGNORE FOOT PATH

FARMLAND

002

BLIGHTON LANE

GOLF COURSE

FARNHAM GOLF CLUB HOUSE

YOU'VE GONE TOO FAR IF IT'S YOU SEE THESE HOUSE SIGNS

BINTON COTTAGE

FAIRWAYS COTTAGE

POST BOX

DRIVING RANGE

SANDY FARM

TAKE FOOTPATH OFF THE ROAD – IF IT'S NOT TOO OVERGROWN

PETERSWOOD HOUSE

FURZE HILL

SANDS ROAD

HOLLY HOUSE

CROSS ROAD AND STILE OPPOSITE MULBERRY COTTAGE

STEPS DOWN

HORSE FIELD

PATH BETWEEN STILES

RUNFOLD QUARRY LANDFILL SITE

WEYHANGER

RUNFOLD WOOD NATURE RESERVE (SURREY WILDLIFE TRUST)

1

TURN HARD LEFT OFF ROAD AT 'WEYHANGER' THEN RIGHT ONTO NDW

1/4 mile

APPROX SCALE

500m

0   0

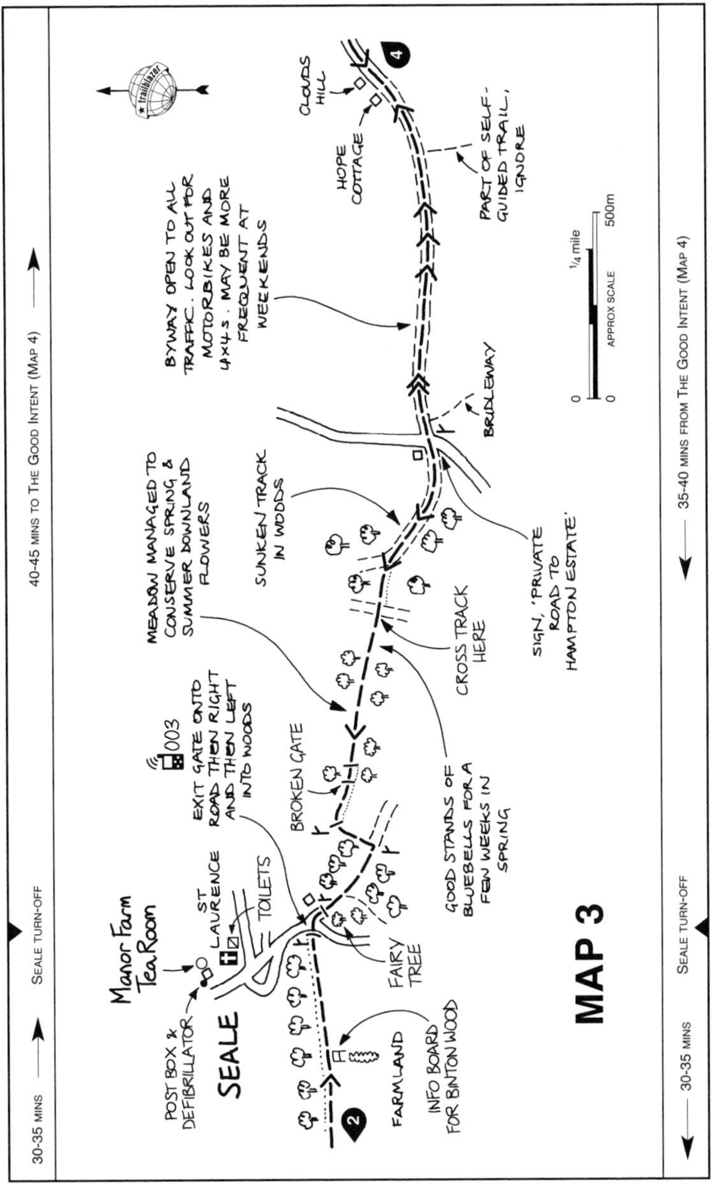

MAP 3

SEALE

POST BOX & DEFIBRILLATOR

Manor Farm TeaRoom

ST LAURENCE

TOILETS

INFO BOARD FOR BINTON WOOD

FARMLAND

FAIRY TREE

GOOD STANDS OF BLUEBELLS FOR A FEW WEEKS IN SPRING

BROKEN GATE

EXIT GATE ONTO ROAD THEN RIGHT AND THEN LEFT INTO WOODS

003

MEADOW MANAGED TO CONSERVE SPRING & SUMMER DOWNLAND FLOWERS

SUNKEN TRACK IN WOODS

CROSS TRACK HERE

SIGN, 'PRIVATE ROAD TO HAMPTON ESTATE'

BRIDLEWAY

BYWAY OPEN TO ALL TRAFFIC. LOOK OUT FOR MOTORBIKES AND 4X4'S. MAY BE MORE FREQUENT AT WEEKENDS

HOPE COTTAGE

CLOUDS HILL

PART OF SELF-GUIDED TRAIL, IGNORE

APPROX SCALE

0   ¼ mile

0   500m

30-35 MINS   SEALE TURN-OFF   40-45 MINS TO THE GOOD INTENT (MAP 4)

35-40 MINS FROM THE GOOD INTENT (MAP 4)

(cont'd from p70) True, for some people this opening walk may all be a bit tame – but fear not, for it does get wilder in subsequent stages. So do up those laces and thread your arms through the straps of your backpack – you've got a long way to go between here and Dover. We've talked the talk: now it's time to walk the chalk.

The start of the trail is fairly unspectacular. Having freed yourself from Farnham's civilised clutches (though if you've forgotten anything there's a small 24-hr M&S Simply Food at the petrol station by the side of the trail), the first place of note occurs just a couple of miles into the trek as the trail passes the drive of **Moor Park House**, one-time home of Jonathan Swift, author of *Gulliver's Travels*. It's your own travels – and travails – that are probably of more interest to you now however, and if the trail is already proving a little tough sustenance can be sought at **Seale**, just a few minutes from the trail and the first possible stopover on the North Downs Way.

SEALE   [MAP 3, p73]
A five-minute detour will bring you to this hamlet with its attractive church, **St Laurence**, and the great-value *Manor Farm Tea Room* (☎ 01252-783661; Tue-Sun 10am-5pm; WI-FI). Set in a converted milking parlour with a wood-burning stove to take the chill away in winter, a cup of tea or coffee and a cheese scone will cost about a fiver and will set you up nicely for the climb before Puttenham.

Stagecoach's **bus** No 65 (Alton to Guildford; see pp45-8) calls here.

Don't tarry too long over your teacake in Seale, however, for you've still got a fair way to go before you reach Guildford. In fact, you've got several 'fairways' to go as the trail traces a course through a couple of golf courses; this is, after all, wealthy Surrey, where for some people golf is a way of life. How appropriate, therefore, that the village which precedes the second golf course of the day should be called Puttenham…

PUTTENHAM   [MAP 4]
'*Puttenham was a modest little village nine stories high, with silos, a poultry farm, and a small vitamin-D factory.*'
Thus did **Aldous Huxley** imagine the future of Puttenham in his 1932 work, *Brave New World*. His vision may still come to pass, of course, though if it does, this long village, lined with pretty brick, stone, timber and tile-hung cottages, is going to have to undergo a complete transformation.

Unfortunately the village shop and post office have closed but Puttenham retains a pub and a restaurant and walkers will benefit from *Puttenham Eco Camping Barn* (☎ 01483-811001, 🖳 puttenhamcampingbarn .co.uk; open 5pm-10am, up to 11 spaces, booking essential; Easter to end Oct), which provides budget accommodation from £15pp). The barn is a listed building restored over a period of ten years using sustainable materials and solar energy.

Sleeping accommodation is on a three-section foam-lined wooden platform; sleeping bag essential but can be hired (£3). Kitchen, toilet and shower facilities are available. Note that dogs are not allowed.

The Good Intent (☎ 01483-810387, 🖳 thegoodintentpub.co.uk; food served Mon-Fri noon-2pm, Sat to 2.30pm, Sun to 3pm, Tue-Sat 7-9.30pm; WI-FI; 🐾) is a popular low-beamed pub with inglenook fireplace and it does a good line in food, with lunchtime sandwiches, ciabattas and jacket potatoes in the £6-7 range.

Leaving the village the trail passes opposite *The Jolly Farmer* (☎ 01483-810374; food served daily 11.30am-10pm, Sat & Sun from 9am; WI-FI; 🐾 bar area only), part of the Harvester chain.

Stagecoach's **bus** No 65 (Alton to Guildford; see pp45-8) stops by The Good Intent.

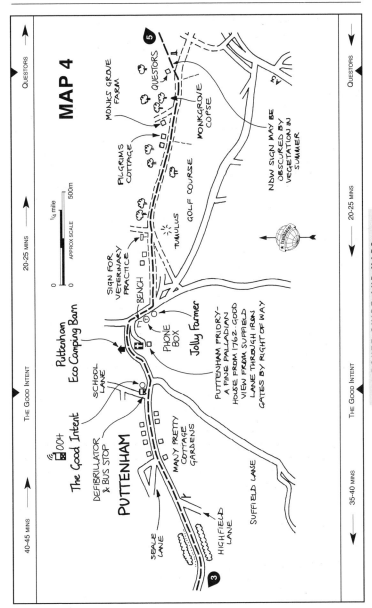

MAP 4

MONKS GROVE FARM

QUESTORS

MONKGROVE COPSE

PILGRIMS COTTAGE

GOLF COURSE

NDW SIGN MAY BE OBSCURED BY VEGETATION IN SUMMER

1/4 mile

500m

0

0   APPROX SCALE

SIGN FOR VETERINARY PRACTICE

TUMULUS

BENCH

PHONE BOX

Jolly Farmer

PUTTENHAM PRIORY – A FINE PALLADIAN HOUSE FROM 1762. GOOD VIEW FROM SUFFIELD LANE THROUGH IRON GATES BY RIGHT OF WAY

Puttenham Eco Camping Barn

SCHOOL LANE

The Good Intent

DEFIBRILLATOR & BUS STOP

PUTTENHAM

MANY PRETTY COTTAGE GARDENS

SUFFIELD LANE

SEALE LANE

HIGHFIELD LANE

trailblazer

In our experience, most walkers prefer the words 'cream' and 'tea' to 'green' and 'tee', so having departed Puttenham from opposite The Jolly Farmer, and after marching briskly past golf course and woodland bordering Puttenham Heath – geologically unusual in this area of chalk – it is with some relief to find yourself emerging onto the outskirts of Compton and its fine Tea Shop.

COMPTON [MAP 5]

The trail brings you out just a few metres below **Watts Gallery** (☎ 01483-810235, 🖳 wattsgallery.org.uk; Tue-Sun 11am-5pm; £9.50), an intimate space exhibiting works of the Victorian artist and sculptor George Frederic Watts, which is well worth a visit. Next door, in the former pottery workshop of Compton Potters Guild, is *Compton Tea Shop* (☎ 01483-813590; daily 10.30am-5pm; WI-FI), just the place for gooey Welsh rarebit (from £5.50).

Also on Down Lane is the red-brick **Watts Cemetery Chapel** (Mon-Fri 9am-5pm, Sat & Sun 10am-5pm; free), built by Watts's wife. His remains are interred in the cloister nearby. Irish yews line the path up to the chapel and the floral forms, tendrils and crosses on the exterior reveal the Art Nouveau, Celtic, Romanesque and Egyptian influences. Some may need to continue walking and recover their balance after seeing the incredible interior, every available surface decorated with red, silver and gold images and angels. Continue past

the chapel and take a left at the end of the lane and you come to the centre of the village, though unfortunately the constant moan of traffic does rather detract from one's appreciation of the fine collection of 19th- and 20th-century cottages. Still, the **parish church of St Nicholas**, dating from the 11th century, is worth a visit, particularly to see the two-storey sanctuary with a magnificent vault and nine-arch balustrade above it. Nearby is the old **Harrow Inn**, now a Thai restaurant called *Lemongrass* (☎ 01483-810594, 🖳 lgguildford.co.uk; daily noon-2.15pm & 5.30-10.45pm; mains from £6.50).

The upmarket eatery *The Withies Inn* (☎ 01483-421158, 🖳 www.thewithiesinn .com; bar food Mon-Sat noon-2.30pm & 6-9.30pm, Sun noon-2.30pm; WI-FI) lies outside the village; mains cost from £13.75 for a vegetable pancake rising to £25.50 for the fillet steak.

There's a **bus** stop outside the gallery, with Stagecoach's No 46 (Farnham to Guildford; see pp45-8) calling here.

From Compton the path meanders somewhat as it makes its way through yet more land belonging to the Loseley Estate.

Passing above **Littleton** (see Map 6, p79), you soon emerge at the dog-friendly *Ye Olde Ship Inn* (☎ 01483-575731, 🖳 yeoldeshipinn.pub; food served Mon-Thur noon-3pm & 6-9pm, Fri-Sun noon-9pm; WI-FI; 🐾) on the outskirts of Guildford. There are plenty of pizzas: £7 for a basic tomato and basil, or create your own from over 20 toppings at £1-1.50 a topping. Note that if they aren't busy they may close between 3pm and 5pm Monday to Thursday.

From here, steep Ferry Lane takes you down to the River Wey where you have a choice to make: right and south to Shalford, or left and north to Guildford along the towpath.

❏ Important note – walking times

All times in this book refer only to the time spent walking. You will need to add 20-30% to allow for rests, photography, checking the map, drinking water etc.

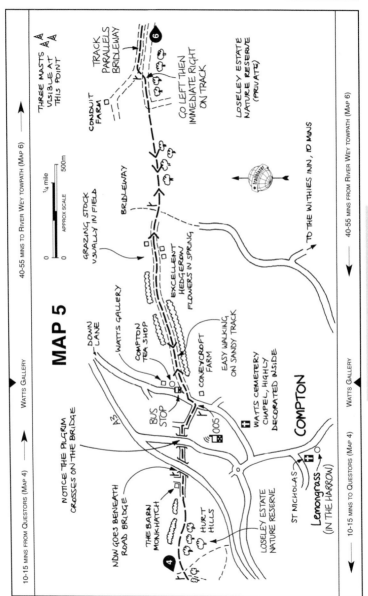

ROUTE GUIDE AND MAPS

SHALFORD [MAP 6a]

Shalford has an attractive village green complete with cricketers most of the summer, a church with a **John Bunyan** connection, a National Trust **restored mill** and the remnants of some **WWII defences**.

The timber-framed **Shalford Mill** (☎ 01483-561389, 🖳 nationaltrust.org.uk/shalford-mill; Mar-Oct Wed & Sun 11am-5pm; £2.50/1.25 adult/child, free for NT members) was given to the National Trust in 1932 by anonymous benefactors calling themselves Ferguson's Gang.

On the main road opposite the turn-off to the mill is The Seahorse (see p80), on the wall of which is a plaque marking the location of a **WWII road block** (Map 6), the last-ditch defence against an expected German invasion in 1940.

Further along the A281 is the parish **Church of St Mary the Virgin** where a large embroidery work by the Women's Institute depicting **John Bunyan's** *Pilgrim's Progress* hangs on the south wall. Bunyan's book is an allegory of Christian life where the main character, Christian, sets off on a journey from the city of Destruction to the Celestial City with countless temptations placed in his way on the road to Salvation. Bunyan allegedly came to the Surrey Hills when his preaching got him in trouble. Some claim that the boggy ground on Shalford Common inspired the description which has entered the English language: the Slough of Despond.

Services and transport

At the eastern end of the village is the **post office** (Mon-Fri 9am-5.30pm, Sat 9am-12.30pm). Before it, at 8 Kings Rd, is **Boots Pharmacy** (Mon-Fri 9am-6pm, Sat to 5pm) at 8 Kings Rd. Before either of these, if coming from the trail, just round the corner and near the station, **Snooty's Groceries** (see also The Snooty Fox, Where to stay; Mon-Sat 6.30am-8.30pm, Sun 8am-6pm) can help with essential provisions and is home to the **ATM**.

Shalford is a stop on GWR's **rail service** between Redhill and Reading; see box pp42-3.

Both Arriva's No 53 and Compass Travel's No 24 **bus services** run between Guildford and Cranleigh via Shalford. Compass and Buses Excetera share the No 32 (Guildford to Dorking) service, and Arriva's No 63 and X1 (Horsham to Guildford) also call here. They all depart from the railway station; see pp45-8 for details.

Where to stay and eat

If you need to stay, *Parrot Inn* (☎ 01483-561400, 🖳 parrotinn.co.uk; 3D/1T; all en suite; WI-FI bar area only; 🐾), with **B&B** (inc continental breakfast, £7.95 extra for a cooked breakfast) from £32.50pp (sgl occ room rate), is just off the River Wey towpath over the bridge on Broadford Rd and is very popular for its food (see p80).

The owners of *The Laurels* (☎ 01483-565753, 🖳 jeandeeks565@btinternet.com; 1T/1D shared bathroom; 🛌; WI-FI), 23 Dagden Rd, are refreshingly welcoming towards walkers. B&B costs from £35pp.

Snooty's Groceries (see Services) is the sister of *The Snooty Fox* (☎ 01483-303038, 🖳 thesnootyfox.uk; Mon-Fri 7am-4.30pm, Sat & Sun 8am-4.30pm; WI-FI) which comes with a very good reputation. It's nearly always busy and the food is good too – if you can catch the eye of the

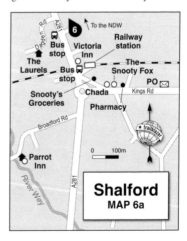

Shalford
MAP 6a

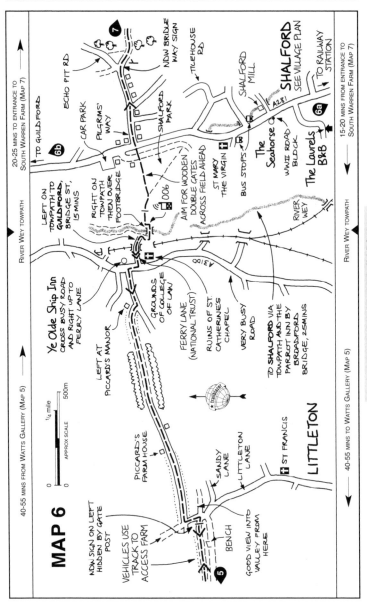

MAP 6

40-55 MINS FROM WATTS GALLERY (MAP 5)

RIVER WEY TOWPATH

20-25 MINS TO ENTRANCE TO SOUTH WARREN FARM (MAP 7)

¼ mile
500m
0   APPROX SCALE

NDW SIGN ON LEFT HIDDEN BY GATE POST

VEHICLES USE TRACK TO ACCESS FARM

PICCARD'S FARM HOUSE

GOOD VIEW INTO VALLEY FROM HERE

BENCH

SANDY LANE

LITTLETON LANE

✝ ST FRANCIS

LITTLETON

LEFT AT PICCARD'S MANOR

Ye Olde Ship Inn
CROSS BUSY ROAD AND RIGHT UP TO FERRY LANE

GROUNDS OF COLLEGE OF LAW

FERRY LANE (NATIONAL TRUST)

RUINS OF ST. CATHERINE'S CHAPEL

VERY BUSY ROAD

A3100

TO SHALFORD VIA TOWPATH AND THE PARROT INN BY BROADFORD BRIDGE, 25 MINS

RIVER WEY

RIVER WEY TOWPATH

40-55 MINS TO WATTS GALLERY (MAP 5)

ECHO PIT RD

TO GUILDFORD

CAR PARK

PILGRIMS' WAY

LEFT ON TOWPATH TO GUILDFORD, BRIDGE ST, 15 MINS

RIGHT ON TOWPATH THEN OVER FOOTBRIDGE

AIM FOR WOODEN DOUBLE GATES ACROSS FIELD AHEAD

ST MARY THE VIRGIN ✝

BUS STOPS

NDW BRIDGE WAY SIGN

TILEHOUSE RD

SHALFORD PARK

SHALFORD MILL

A281

SHALFORD
SEE VILLAGE PLAN

The Seahorse

WWII ROAD BLOCK

The Laurels B&B

TO RAILWAY STATION

20-25 MINS TO ENTRANCE TO SOUTH WARREN FARM (MAP 7)

15-20 MINS FROM ENTRANCE TO SOUTH WARREN FARM (MAP 7)

ROUTE GUIDE AND MAPS

half-dozen staff who bustle around looking busy doing anything except, it would seem, actually serving customers. Sandwiches start at £3.10.

Next door is a Thai restaurant and takeaway, *Chada* (☎ 01483-452550; daily 6-10.30pm) with mains from £7.50.

The three **pubs** also serve food. If you stay at The Laurels (see p78), *The Seahorse* (☎ 01483-514351, 🖥 theseahorse guildford.co.uk; food served Mon-Thur noon-9.30pm, Fri & Sat to 10pm, Sun to 9pm; WI-FI; 🐾 bar area only) is conveniently around the corner off the busy Shalford Rd and boasts one of the most

extensive menus on the whole trail, with mains from £9.95 for the chargrilled gammon steak & fried eggs with chunky chips and honey-roasted pineapple.

Parrot Inn (see p78; food Mon-Sat noon-2.30pm & 6.30-9.30pm, Sun noon-2.45pm) offers simpler fare with sandwiches from £5.60. Note they are closed on Sunday evenings.

Near the station, *Victoria Inn* (food Mon-Sat noon-2.30pm & 6-9pm, Sun noon-2.30pm) serves standard pub meals (eg ham, egg & chips £8.95) in a relaxed, unfussy setting.

GUILDFORD [MAP 6b]

'*To the east of Guildford is Leith Hill which, at 960ft above sea level, is the highest point in Surrey. From the summit on a good day you can see Hampstead Heath. On a bad day you can see Croydon.*'

Jack Dee, from the Radio 4 show *I'm Sorry I haven't a Clue.*

Guildford is the lively county town of Surrey and an ideal access point to the North Downs Way with good public transport links, plenty of accommodation, a wide range of restaurants and lots to see and do. The River Wey that runs through it cuts through the North Downs, and as such down the centuries Guildford emerged in importance as a 'gap town' for those heading north to London or south towards the coast.

Charles Dickens described Guildford High St as 'the most beautiful in the kingdom' and there is still much to recommend it, including many significant historic buildings including the Guildhall with its projecting town clock, the one surviving coaching inn, The Angel Posting House (now Angel Hotel, see Where to stay), and the almshouses of Abbot's Hospital. Indeed the whole car-free cobbled High St, crisscrossed by alleys and lanes, is one of the more attractive on the trail. Much of the town is given over to shopping and nightlife these days, but whether wandering

through The Shambles, a maze of narrow alleys, around the castle, or along Tunsgate take time to look up and admire the façades and get a sense of the town's medieval, Jacobean and Regency market town past.

What to see and do
It's easy to go from medieval to modern so rich is Guildford's architectural history despite the best efforts of 1960s' planners and busy roads scything close to the High St.

The **Guildhall** (🖥 guildford.gov.uk/guildhall; May-Sep Sun 11am-5pm, also Aug daily 10am-5pm; tours Sun 2.30pm & 3.30pm; £2) was built in 1683 and its bracket clock jutting over the High St is the town's symbol.

Further east is **Abbot's Hospital** (🖥 abbotshospital.org; main gates open Mon-Sat 9am-4pm; guided tours May-Sep Thur & Fri at 11am for £5), an almshouse that is still providing accommodation for the elderly poor. Access is limited but you can peer into the courtyard and admire the fine Jacobean brickwork.

Guildford Castle (☎ 01483-444751, 🖥 guildford.gov.uk/castle; Apr-Sep daily 10am-5pm, Oct half-term daily 11am-4pm, Mar & Oct Sat & Sun 11am-4pm; 🐾 on lead; £3.20) dates from the 13th century. There are spectacular displays of bedding plants in the grounds (free, dogs on leads please) in summer.

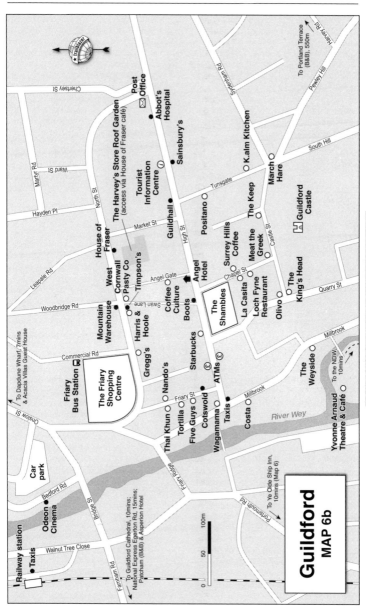

Guildford
MAP 6b

Guildford Cathedral (☎ 01483-547860, 🖳 www.guildford-cathedral.org; Mon-Fri 8.10am-6.15pm, Sat 8.40am-5pm, Sun 8am-7.30pm; donations appreciated) overlooks the town from its commanding position (to the west of town) on Stag Hill. Movie buffs will recognise it from the 1976 classic *The Omen*. Italian marble floors and Somerset sandstone grace the pale interior of the first post-Reformation cathedral to be built on a new site.

Accessible from the town centre via a towpath or Woodbridge Rd, the National Trust's **Dapdune Wharf** (☎ 01483-561389, 🖳 www.nationaltrust.org.uk; Easter/Apr-end Oct Mon & Thur-Sun 11am-5pm; £4.20, boat trip £3.95 free for NT members) tells the story of England's first privately financed navigation – the River Wey.

Harvey's Store Roof Garden at the House of Fraser was refurbished in 2000-1 and access is via the café, which is on the 5th floor. Designed in 1958 by landscape architect Sir Geoffrey Jellicoe, the circular planters were inspired by the launch of the Russian satellite Sputnik. It's a remarkable example of 1950s' elements which do not appear dated. Have lunch there if you scrub up well, or ask nicely at the café to see it.

If you want to rest your legs you might like to go to a show at the Yvonne Arnaud **theatre** (☎ 01483-440000, 🖳 yvonne-arnaud.co.uk) – a lot of the productions are pre West End – or see a **film** at the Odeon cinema.

Services
The **tourist information centre** (TIC; ☎ 01483-444333, 🖳 guildford.gov.uk/visit-guildford/16175; May-Sep Mon-Sat 9.30am-5pm, Sun & Bank Hols 11am-4pm, Oct-Apr Mon-Sat only) is at 155 High St.

If you've forgotten any essential kit – or the stuff you've brought with you needs replacing already – there are several **trekking stores** who'll be glad of your custom, including Cotswold (Mon-Wed & Fri-Sat 8.30am-6pm, Thur to 7pm, Sun 11am-5pm), on Friary Passage, and Mountain Warehouse (Mon-Sat 9am-6pm, Sun 11am-5pm) on North St.

If it's your footwear that's fallen apart you can always try to get it fixed at Timpson's (Mon-Fri 8.30am-5.30pm, Sat to 5pm, Sun 10am-4pm), the **shoe repairers** on North St.

There is a **post office** (Mon & Wed-Fri 9am-5.30pm, Tue 9.30am-5.30pm, Sat 9am-1pm) at the junction of North and High streets and plenty of banks with **ATMs** on those streets. **Sainsbury's** supermarket (Mon-Sat 7am-9pm, Sun 11am-5pm) is just a little way down the High St; there is also a Boots **chemist** (Mon-Sat 8.30am-6pm, Thur to 7pm, Sun 11am-5pm). There is also a **farmers' market** (see box p22) on the High St on the first Tuesday of every month.

Transport
The **bus station** for local services is Friary Bus Station by the eponymous shopping centre. Compass Travel's Nos 24, 25 & 32 services call here; Buses Excetera shares the No 32 route with Compass. Stagecoach's KITE, No 46 & No 65 and Arriva's Nos 53, 63 & X1 also call at the bus station; see pp45-8 for details.

National Express **coaches** No 030 service (see p44) between London and Southsea drop off and collect by the large Tesco superstore on Egerton Rd, way out from the town centre to the west; to get there walkers will have to turn off Farnham Rd at Guildford Park Rd.

The **railway station** is a stop on South Western Railway's London Waterloo and Portsmouth service; SWR also operates services to Ascot via Aldershot; for Farnham change at Aldershot. GWR's services between Gatwick Airport/Redhill and Reading also call here. See box pp42-3.

For a **taxi** call Surrey Cars (☎ 01483-577677) or A3 Cars (☎ 01483-606060).

Where to stay
Patcham (☎ 01483-570789, 🖳 simplicity websites.co.uk/patchambb; 1S/1T shared facilities, 1T en suite; WI-FI), at 44 Farnham Rd – look for the white squirrel on the gatepost – is a comfortable place less than ten minutes to the west of the railway station; rates, including a continental breakfast,

are £25-27.50pp (sgl £35, sgl occ £40-45).

Across the road at No 73 is *Asperion Hotel* (☎ 01483-579299, 🖳 asperionhotels .com/asperion; 3S/11D all en suite, 1S private bathroom; WI-FI) with singles starting at £65 and doubles for £44.50-60pp (sgl occ room rate) depending on the room size.

Close to the cricket ground (north of town) at 29 Woodbridge Rd is *Acacia Villas Guest House* (☎ 01483-458884, 🖳 sucord@gmail.com; 2T en suite, 2T/1D shared facilities; WI-FI; 🐾) where room only costs £25-30pp (sgl occ £50-60); breakfast (from £5pp) is available in the café over the road.

If you feel you are carrying too much weight *Angel Hotel* (see p80; ☎ 01483-564555, 🖳 angelpostinghouse.com; 24D, all en suite; 🍺; WI-FI; 🐾), at 91 High St, will lighten your wallet with rates from 'as little as' £42.50pp (sgl occ room rate), though rack rates in the £75-100pp (sgl occ room rate) bracket are more common. Parts of the vaulted undercroft or basement, where banquets are sometimes held, date back to the 1300s including the remains of a spiral staircase. Note that rates generally don't include breakfast, but a continental breakfast is available.

Portland Terrace (☎ 01483-575231, 🖳 portlandterrace.co.uk; 1S/1T/1Tr, all en suite; WI-FI), named after the road on which it stands (it's No 2), charges from £35pp (sgl from £50, sgl occ rates on request); the rate includes an extensive buffet breakfast. Guests can use the kitchen in the evening to cook a meal.

Where to eat and drink

Guildford has a wealth of good independent **coffee shops** in addition to the usual *Starbucks* (Mon-Sat 6am-6.30pm, Sun from 8am), on the High St opposite Quarry St, and *Costa* (Mon-Wed & Fri-Sat 9am-5.30pm, Thur to 7.30pm, Sun 11am-4.30pm) in Debenhams by the river. All do lunches and snacks as well as excellent coffee. They include *Coffee Culture* (☎ 01483-564200; Mon-Fri 8am-5pm, Sat to 6pm, Sun 9am-5pm) down an alleyway called Angel Gate; *K.alm Kitchen* (☎ 01483-813360, 🖳 kalmkitchen.co.uk/k-

cafe-new; Mon-Fri 8am-5pm, Sat to 5.30pm, Sun 9.30am-5pm; WI-FI) near the top of Tunsgate; *Surrey Hills Coffee* (🖳 surreyhillscoffee.co.uk; Mon-Sat 9.30am-5pm, Sun 11am-5pm; WI-FI; 🐾) on Chapel St; and *Harris & Hoole* (☎ 01483-561035, 🖳 www.harrisandhoole.co.uk; Mon-Sat 7.30am-6.30pm, Sun 8am-6pm; WI-FI; 🐾) on North St – which is actually something of a chain itself now, with 36 branches in London and the South-East.

For a bite on the go try *West Cornwall Pasty Co* (Mon-Sat 9am-5pm, Sun 11am-4pm) on North St, or the Guildford branch of *Gregg's* (Mon-Fri 7am-6.30pm, Sat from 7.30am, Sun 8.30am-5pm); for a healthy, traditional Greek kebab head to *Meat the Greek* (☎ 01483-458644, 🖳 meatthegreek .co.uk; daily noon-11pm) on Chapel St.

For food in the evening there are two main centres for **restaurants**, each different in character. The first is Friary St, where the restaurants are vast, shiny, glass-fronted affairs, with many of the eateries branches of international chains including: the Japanese-style restaurant *Wagamama* (☎ 01483-457779, 🖳 wagamama.com; Mon-Sat noon-11pm, Sun 12.30-10pm); the chicken specialists *Nando's* (☎ 01483-568083, 🖳 nandos.co.uk; Sun-Thur 11am-10pm, Fri & Sat to 11pm); the Thai street-food outlet *Thai Khun* (☎ 01483-678800, 🖳 thaikhun.co.uk; daily 11.30am-10pm); the fun and lively burger-joint *Five Guys* (☎ 01483-570580, 🖳 fiveguys.co.uk; Sun-Thur 11am-10pm, Fri & Sat 11am-11pm); and *Tortilla* (☎ 01483-573974, 🖳 tortilla.co.uk; daily 11.30am-9.30pm).

The other hotbed of restaurants is Chapel St, where you'll find more independent and more discreet options than those on Friary St. They include *La Casita* (☎ 01483-455155, 🖳 lacasitarestaurant .org; Mon-Thur noon-3pm & 5.30-10pm, Fri to 10.30pm, Sat noon-10.30pm, Sun noon-9pm), a Mediterranean restaurant serving tapas (bowls from £2.80) as well as mains (from £8.50, rising to £16.50 for the baked fish casserole with cod, mussels, prawns, squid rings & potatoes, served in a rich tomato, garlic & chilli sauce) and the upmarket fish restaurant and oyster bar

ROUTE GUIDE AND MAPS

84 Guildford

Loch Fyne Restaurant (☎ 01483-230550, 🖥 lochfyneseafoodandgrill.co.uk; Mon-Thur noon-10pm, Fri noon-11pm, Sat 9am-11pm, Sun 9am-10pm) where you can dine on a whole baked lobster for £33.95.

For **pub food**, the first place you come to from the path is *The Weyside* (☎ 01483-568024, 🖥 theweyside.co.uk; WI-FI; 🐕; food Mon-Sat noon-9.45pm, Sun noon-8.45pm) – and a lovely place it is to stop too, particularly if you have a dog, with dog towels, blankets and biscuits available. The menu is good but short, though, with mains from £12.25 for the Cumberland sausage ring & mash. The terrace overlooking the river is a lovely place to sit in the sun and air those blisters.

There are also some great choices down Castle St, which separates the High St from the castle. These include *March Hare* (☎ 01483-401530, 🖥 marchhareguild ford.com; food Mon-Thur noon-10pm, Fri & Sat to 10.30pm, Sun noon-9pm; WI-FI; 🐕 bar area only), a pub and brasserie opposite the top of Tunsgate. They have a range of menus, though it's their à la carte that is the most imaginative (mains from £12) and they do a classic slow-cooked bœuf bourguignon with mash (£16.95).

A little further down Castle St is *The Keep* (☎ 01483-450600, 🖥 thekeepguild ford.pub; food Mon-Fri noon-3pm, Sat

noon-6pm; WI-FI; 🐕) a more traditional place with a more traditional menu, too, with no meal above a tenner and including home-made cottage pie with seasonal vegetables & gravy (£8.95). They also serve Silent Pool gin.

At the bottom of Castle St and the junction with Quarry St is *The King's Head* (☎ 01483-575004, 🖥 thekingsheadpub .co.uk; food served Mon-Fri noon-3pm & 5-9pm, Sat noon-9pm, Sun noon-4pm; WI-FI; 🐕), reputedly haunted, with a pretty standard pub menu (mains around a tenner including ham, egg & chips, £9.50).

Opposite is *Olivo* (☎ 01483-303535, 🖥 olivo.co.uk; Mon-Thur noon-4.30pm & 5.30-10.30pm, Fri & Sat noon-10.30pm, Sun noon-9.30pm). Housed in an old Tudor beamed house this cosy Italian restaurant serves classic and classy Italian dishes; if you can stretch to it, try the *pesce spada* (char-grilled swordfish steak with prawns, cherry tomato, black olives, capers & garlic, served with mixed vegetables, £15.95).

There's another fine Italian, *Positano* (☎ 01483-563277, 🖥 positano-restaurant .co.uk; Mon-Fri noon-3pm & 5.30-10.30pm, Sat noon-10.30pm, Sun noon-9.30pm), just off the High St on Tunsgate, with a large menu and a good line in risotto (from £10.50).

GUILDFORD TO DORKING   [MAPS 6-12a]

'It has been very fine to-day. Yesterday morning there was snow on Reigate Hill, enough to look white from where we were in the valley. We set off about half-past one o'clock, and came all down the valley, through Buckland, Betchworth, Dorking, Sheer and Aldbury, to this place. Very few prettier rides in England, and the weather beautifully fine.'
William Cobbett, *Rural Rides*

Whilst the names 'Guildford' and 'Dorking' may not in themselves be enough to arouse excitement in those walkers seeking isolation and an escape from the modern world, nor conjure up images of untainted wilderness and nature at its most untrammelled, there is actually much to enjoy on this **12.9-mile/20.7km** stage. The trail certainly does its utmost to show off the best that Surrey has to offer, including two very fine churches, the county's prettiest village and the country's largest vineyard. There are also large tracts of walking in mature and beautiful woodland on this stage – a feature of the North Downs Way that is as surprising as it is welcome. But it's the views that walkers are afforded throughout the day that are this stage's real highlight. Those good folk whose job it is

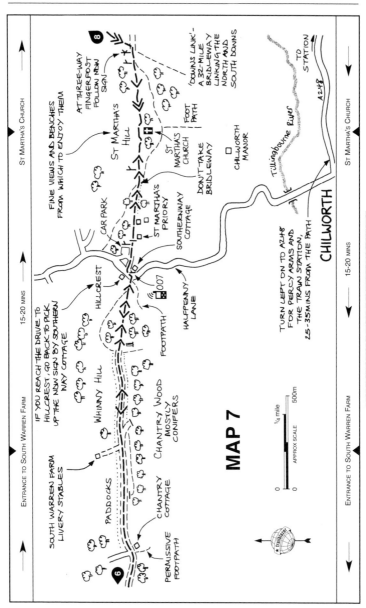

ENTRANCE TO SOUTH WARREN FARM ◀ ── 15-20 MINS ── ▶ ST MARTHA'S CHURCH

MAP 7

¼ mile
0 ─────── APPROX SCALE ─────── 500m

SOUTH WARREN FARM
LIVERY STABLES

HILLCREST

IF YOU REACH THE DRIVE TO
HILLCREST, GO BACK TO PICK
UP THE NEW SIGN BY SOUTHERN
WAY COTTAGE

FINE VIEWS AND BENCHES
FROM WHICH TO ENJOY THEM

ST MARTHA'S HILL

CAR PARK

AT THREE-WAY
FINGERPOST
FOLLOW NEW
SIGN

8

ST
MARTHA'S
CHURCH

FOOT
PATH

'DOWNS LINK' -
A 32-MILE
BRIDLEWAY
LINKING THE
NORTH AND
SOUTH DOWNS

ST MARTHA'S PRIORY

SOUTHERNWAY
COTTAGE

DON'T TAKE
BRIDLEWAY

CHILWORTH
MANOR

WHINNY HILL

CHANTRY WOOD
MOSTLY
CONIFERS

007

HALFPENNY
LANE

FOOTPATH

Tillingbourne River

TO
STATION

A248

CHILWORTH

PADDOCKS

CHANTRY
COTTAGE

PERMISSIVE
FOOTPATH

6

TURN LEFT ON TO A248
FOR PERCY ARMS AND
THE TRAIN STATION,
25-35 MINS FROM THE PATH

ENTRANCE TO SOUTH WARREN FARM ◀ ── 15-20 MINS ── ▶ ST MARTHA'S CHURCH

to maintain and enhance the North Downs Way clearly recognise this fact, for throughout the day there are benches aplenty to entice you to slow down, put your feet up and just drink in the scenery; thus ensuring that this stage, which should take only **4hrs 20mins-5¼hrs** if no breaks are taken, usually takes a whole day to complete.

The first of these stretches of woodland walking – and the first breathtaking views – occur early on this stage with a climb through **Chantry Wood** and up the slopes of **St Martha's Hill** to the **church** that shares its name. It is believed that pilgrims visited the church on the way to Canterbury, so it is often referred to as the Pilgrims' Church, though it's debatable whether there was ever only one route pilgrims followed. Nevertheless, it's likely that they found the church a convenient place to stop and rest. And few are those who don't find their spirits soaring when they visit, for even if the sermons within the church fail to rouse, the panorama over the Surrey Hills outside the church surely will; it's a lovely spot to rest for a few minutes and enjoy the view over nearby Chilworth and, further east, Albury.

CHILWORTH   [off MAP 7, p85]

Reached by turning right off the trail (down Halfpenny Lane) before St Martha's Hill, Chilworth straggles along the A248 but has a good pub, *The Percy Arms* (☎ 01483-561765, 🖥 thepercyarms.net; 1T or D/4D, all en suite; 🛏; WI-FI; 🐾 bar area only), with a curious South African theme, rather incongruous given its rural Surrey setting. Nevertheless the rooms are pretty opulent and the **food** (Mon-Fri noon-3pm & 6-10pm, Sat noon-10pm & Sun noon-8.30pm), particularly the steaks (£19.95 for the 10oz rump), are renowned. **B&B** costs £62.50-72.50pp (sgl occ room rate); additional beds can be put in some rooms for children. Note that booking well in advance is essential particularly for a room but also for meals on Sunday.

GWR's Reading to Redhill service (see box pp42-3) calls at the **railway station**. Buses Excetera and Compass Travel operate the No 32 **bus service** (Guildford to Dorking/Redhill) which also stops at the station; see pp45-8 for details.

ALBURY   [off MAP 8]

Albury is an estate village belonging to the Duke of Northumberland and buildings owned by the estate are painted in green trim. The village was mentioned in the Domesday Book under its original name, Eldeberie, when it was said to consist of one church, one mill and woodland worth 30 hogs; little has changed in the intervening nine and half centuries.

Well known locally for its highly decorative **Pugin** chimneys, the estate yard also has a restored **dovecote**. Ten minutes east on the A248 is the **Catholic Apostolic Church** (not open) and the **Saxon Old Church, Albury Park** (daily 10am-5pm or dusk), which is worth a visit for its Pugin mortuary chapel. The building is now managed by the Churches Conservation Trust.

You can get **supplies** at Pratt's Stores and **post office** (☎ 01483-202123; Mon-Fri 7.30am-5.30pm, Sat to 1pm) and at the smart and sumptuous *Drummond at Albury* (☎ 01483-202039, 🖥 thedrummond arms.co.uk; 4D/6T/1Qd, all en suite; 🛏; WI-FI; 🐾 bar area only), **B&B** costs £42.50-47.50pp (sgl occ £66-75). **Food** is served (Mon-Sat noon-3pm & 6-9.30pm, Sun noon-8pm, also a snack menu on Sat 3-6pm), with mains for £9.95-14.95 (steaks from £22.75) and there is a delightful beer garden bordering the Tillingbourne River.

Buses Excetera and Compass Travel operate the No 32 **bus service** (Guildford to Dorking/Redhill) which stops by The Drummond; see pp45-8 for details.

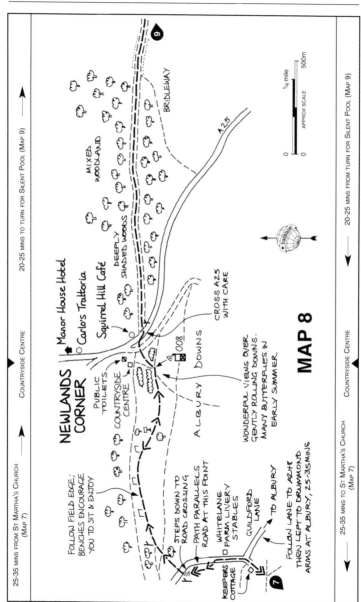

25-35 MINS FROM ST MARTHA'S CHURCH (MAP 7)

COUNTRYSIDE CENTRE

20-25 MINS TO TURN FOR SILENT POOL (MAP 9)

25-35 MINS TO ST MARTHA'S CHURCH (MAP 7)

COUNTRYSIDE CENTRE

20-25 MINS FROM TURN FOR SILENT POOL (MAP 9)

NEWLANDS CORNER

Manor House Hotel
Carlo's Trattoria
Squirrel Hill Café

PUBLIC TOILETS

COUNTRYSIDE CENTRE

008

CROSS A25 WITH CARE

ALBURY DOWNS

MIXED WOODLAND

DEEPLY SHADED WOODS

BRIDLEWAY

A25

WONDERFUL VIEWS OVER GENTLY ROLLING DOWNS. MANY BUTTERFLIES IN EARLY SUMMER

MAP 8

FOLLOW FIELD EDGE; BENCHES ENCOURAGE YOU TO SIT & ENJOY

STEPS DOWN TO ROAD CROSSING

PATH PARALLELS ROAD AT THIS POINT

WHITELANE FARM LIVERY STABLES

GUILDFORD LANE

TO ALBURY

FOLLOW LANE TO A248 THEN LEFT TO DRUMMOND ARMS AT ALBURY, 25-35MINS

KEEPERS COTTAGE

APPROX SCALE
0   ¼ mile
0   500m

Tearing yourself away from the views, as you eventually must, you'll find more benches along **Albury Downs** before you gain the North Downs Way ridgeline at busy **Newlands Corner**.

NEWLANDS CORNER   [MAP 8, p87]

The views from here are spectacular on a clear day and this beauty spot was the scene of the 10-day disappearance of Agatha Christie, the mystery writer, (see box below) in December 1926.

There are plans in the pipeline to update the facilities at Newlands Corner, to improve accessibility and modernise the existing toilets and Countryside Centre, so the description in this book may be dated by the time you visit.

The trail passes to the front of **Surrey Wildlife Trust Countryside Centre** (daily 9am to around 4.30pm, depending on the weather, only staffed on Sun), which has an informative display on the flora and fauna of this part of the Downs (see pp58-64).

Squirrel Hill Café (☎ 01483-222659, ☐ squirrel-hill.co.uk; summer daily 9.30am-5pm, winter Tue-Sun 9.30am-4.30pm; 🐾) is often crowded, especially at

the weekend, with people feasting on the view and Welsh rarebit (£6.95).

A short walk down the busy A25 (there is no footpath so use the overgrown grass verge) is *Carlo's Trattoria* (☎ 01483-224180, ☐ carlostrattoria.com; Mon-Fri noon-2.30pm & 6.30-10pm, Sat 6.30-10.30pm, Sun noon-2.30pm); Italian food at its best is the veal escalope in a creamy white wine sauce with field & porcini mushrooms (£12.80).

If you can go no further after that *Manor House Hotel* (☎ 01483-222624, ☐ manorhouse-hotel.com; 50D or T, all en suite; 🛏; WI-FI) charges from £35pp (sgl occ from £50) including breakfast; rates without breakfast are also available.

The only **bus** service, and a limited one at that, is Compass Travel's No 25 (Cranleigh to Guildford); see pp45-8 for details.

Those extensive views disappear as suddenly as Agatha Christie did in 1926 (see box below) as you strike east along a drove road to undertake perhaps the most extensive stretch of woodland walking of any national trail, a stretch that continues, on and off, all the way to Ranmore Common. That said, few and

❏ Agatha Christie and the Mysterious Affair at Newlands Corner

When Agatha Christie disappeared from here in December 1926 she was on the best-seller lists so was well known; thus her disappearance had thousands out searching for her.

She abandoned her car here on a Friday evening. Since it was close to Silent Pool (off Map 9) it prompted fears that she had committed suicide. The pool was dredged but no body was found. It turned out that she had travelled to Harrogate, the Yorkshire spa town.

Did she get there by train and was it from Chilworth, Gomshall or nearby Guildford? We shall never know as she refused to talk about her 'lost days'. She booked into a hotel under the name Neele, her husband's mistress's name, and was eventually found when guests recognised her from newspaper photographs.

On her return the story was put about that she suffered amnesia following her mother's death. But why did she do what she did? Were they the actions of someone unhinged by jealousy, or were they pre-planned to embarrass her husband and get away from a bad marriage? Perhaps someone else was in on it and helped her travel from deepest Surrey to Yorkshire? Maybe it's time to call Poirot.

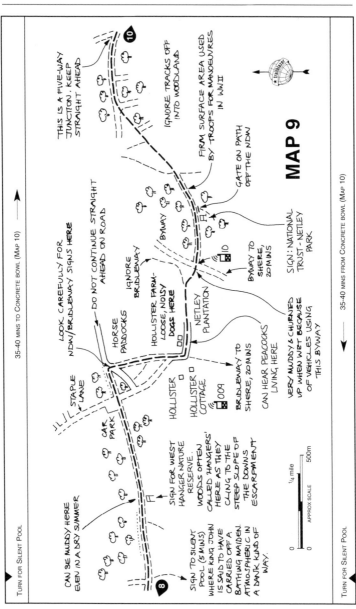

35-40 MINS TO CONCRETE BOWL (MAP 10)

TURN FOR SILENT POOL

THIS IS A FIVE-WAY JUNCTION. KEEP STRAIGHT AHEAD

IGNORE TRACKS OFF INTO WOODLAND

FIRM SURFACE AREA USED BY TROOPS FOR MANOEUVRES IN WWII

GATE ON PATH OFF THE NDW

MAP 9

BYWAY

SIGN: NATIONAL TRUST - NETLEY PARK

BYWAY TO SHERE, 20 MINS

LOOK CAREFULLY FOR NDW/BRIDLEWAY SIGNS HERE

DO NOT CONTINUE STRAIGHT AHEAD ON ROAD

IGNORE BRIDLEWAY

HOLLISTER FARM-LOOSE, NOISY DOGS HERE

NETLEY PLANTATION

HORSE PADDOCKS

STAPLE LANE

CAR PARK

HOLLISTER COTTAGE

HOLLISTER

BRIDLEWAY TO SHERE, 20 MINS

CAN HEAR PEACOCKS LIVING HERE

VERY MUDDY & CHURNED UP WHEN WET BECAUSE OF VEHICLES USING THIS BYWAY

SIGN FOR WEST HANGER NATURE RESERVE. WOODS OFTEN CALLED 'HANGERS' HERE AS THEY CLING TO THE STEEP SLOPE OF THE DOWNS ESCARPMENT

CAN BE MUDDY HERE EVEN IN A DRY SUMMER

¼ mile

500m

APPROX SCALE

SIGN TO SILENT POOL (5 MINS) WHERE KING JOHN IS SAID TO HAVE CARRIED OFF A BATHING MAIDEN. ATMOSPHERIC IN A DANK KIND OF WAY.

TURN FOR SILENT POOL

35-40 MINS FROM CONCRETE BOWL (MAP 10)

foolish are those who don't take a break from all this sylvan strolling by turning off the trail at Hollister Farm to visit Surrey's prettiest village, **Shere**. This joins a by-way, crosses the A25 and enters Shere by the car park (see Map 9).

SHERE [MAP 9a]

Described as the prettiest village in Surrey, Shere suffers as a result and may claim the title as one of the busiest. But it's packed with pretty 15th- and 16th-century **timbered buildings** and attractive cottages, and has a stream with ducks.

The 12th-century parish **church of St James** is open daily and the lychgate was designed by Sir Edwin Lutyens (see box below). Film buffs may also recognise it from 2004's *Bridget Jones: The Edge of Reason*, where it features in the final wedding season at the end.

Shere Museum (☎ 01483-202769, 🖳 www.exploringsurreyspast.org.uk), focusing on local history, is open all year (Sat & Sun 2-5pm as well as Apr-Oct Tue & Thur 10am-3pm) and is free but donations are welcome. Shere also has useful **services**, a choice of **accommodation** and several **eateries**.

Services

There is a **post office** where you can take money out at the **Welcome** store (store hours Mon-Fri 7am-10pm, Sat/Sun 8am-10pm, post office open Mon-Tue & Thur-Fri 8am-10pm, Wed 8am-6pm, Sat & Sun 9am-6pm), part of the Co-op group.

You'll find the village rather expensive but **Crumbs Bakery** (Mon-Fri 7.30am-2.30pm, Sat 7am-12.30pm) does the best-value food (a decently sized and stuffed pasty costs £2.50).

A little surprisingly, Shere also has its own **trekking outfitter**, Trek Hire UK (☎ 01483-209559, 🖳 trekhireuk.com; Mon, Tue & Thur-Sat 10.30am-5pm, Sun 11am-3pm, closed Wed), beyond William Bray Inn on Shere Lane.

Transport

[See pp45-8] Compass Travel's No 25 **bus service** and their No 32 (shared with Buses Excetera) stop near the Village Hall. Metrobus's No 22 calls here on schooldays only (1/day).

Where to stay

Cherry Trees (☎ 01483-202288, 🖳 www.cherrytreesshere.com; 1D en suite, 1T shared facilities; ☛; WI-FI), a large brick and hung-tile home, does B&B for £40-50pp (sgl occ from £80). They also have a Garden Cottage sleeping up to three people (from £115) that they usually rent out by the week but will offer on a B&B basis if it's not occupied.

To the west of the main hubbub at Coombe End, Upper St, *Shere B&B* (☎ 01483-203313, 🖳 sherebnb.co.uk; 1D en suite, 2D shared bathroom; ☛; WI-FI; early Jan to mid Dec) is a super-stylish option charging £50-70pp (sgl occ £95-135). The bathroom for the two doubles upstairs is private if only one room is booked. Note that there is a minimum two-night stay policy here.

❏ Sir Edwin Lutyens (1869-1944) and the Surrey Style

Surrey saw a revival in vernacular architecture – the architecture of ordinary buildings – in the late 19th and early 20th century. Lutyens favoured the distinctive Surrey style using materials that would blend in with existing buildings and the surrounding countryside. This was typically oak framing, white plaster infilling, or brick and hanging clay tiles decorating the walls of the first floor. Dormer windows were used and chimneys tended to be large and separately built. His first commission was for the lychgate of **St James's Church** in Shere. His career took off when he met and collaborated with the well-connected doyenne of English garden design, Gertrude Jekyll.

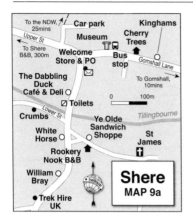

Back near the centre on The Square, **Rookery Nook** (☎ 01483-209382, 🖳 rookerynook.info; 2D, shared bathroom; ✆; WI-FI) is a bit of tourist attraction in its own right, a 15th-century Grade II listed cottage with original wattle-and-daub walls as well as views of the North Downs Way from one of its rooms. B&B costs from £55pp (sgl occ from £80).

Where to eat and drink

The **White Horse** (☎ 01483-202518, 🖳 chefandbrewer.com; food served Mon-Sat noon-9pm, Sun noon-8pm; WI-FI; 🐾) is perhaps the most reasonably priced option in Shere, and as a result is very popular – it's a good idea to book in advance. It's a lovely beamed pub, with an open fire and an extensive menu (mains from £11); on the latter are burgers, pies, steaks and pub clas-

sics as well as more imaginative fare such as a seafood grill (including cod loin, salmon, sea bass fillets, wild Patagonian king prawns & fries) for £15.79.

Just up the road, **William Bray** (☎ 01483-202044, 🖳 thewilliambray.co.uk; food Mon-Thur noon-3pm & 6-9pm, Fri & Sat to 10pm, Sun noon-4pm; WI-FI; 🐾 bar area) has some lovely outside seating and an interesting menu (mains from £13, with the Thai pork burger and fries just a pound more), though they're most famous for their takeaway fish-and-chips (£9.95).

Their attempt to be the finest dining option in Shere, however, is thwarted by **Kinghams** (☎ 01483-202168, 🖳 kinghams-restaurant.co.uk; Tue-Sat noon-2pm & 7-9pm, Sun noon-2pm), a more formal experience packed with the good burghers of Surrey and booking is essential. Mains start at £16.95 for the corn-fed spring chicken stuffed with leek, chive & cream cheese mousse on a shallot & carrot velouté. Even if not eating there do walk past the terraced garden dining room in summer – it's glorious.

The Dabbling Duck Café and Deli (☎ 01483-205791, 🖳 thedabblingduck.uk .com; late Mar to late Oct Mon-Fri 9am-5pm, Sat & Sun to 5.30pm, late Oct to late Mar Mon-Fri 9am-4.30pm, Sat & Sun to 5pm; WI-FI; 🐾) certainly isn't cheap but is very likeable nevertheless, with mains from £9 (for the pulled pork bap) up to £13 for the burger, though sandwiches are £7-8.50.

Ye Olde Sandwich Shoppe (daily 7.30am-3.30pm) will do you a sandwich and a cold drink for about a fiver.

HOLMBURY ST MARY
[off MAP 10, p92]

Called 'Little Switzerland' by the Victorians because of the surrounding hills and valleys, dedicated hostellers and campers face an hour's walk off the path to stay at YHA Holmbury St Mary, or you could take Metrobus No 22 (see pp45-8) from near The Royal Oak pub. **YHA Holmbury St Mary** (☎ 0345-371 9323, 🖳 yha.org.uk/hostel/holmbury-st-mary; 10 x

4-bed dorms, 2T/1Tr rooms; WI-FI communal areas; Mar/Apr-end Oct) charges from £15pp for a dorm bed though at weekends in summer it can rise to £25pp; the private twins are £29-59.99.

There are also two **bell tents** (sleeping up to four people; Easter to end Aug; 🐾) and 15 **tent pitches** (🐾) from £12.99pp. There is a self-catering kitchen but meals are also available.

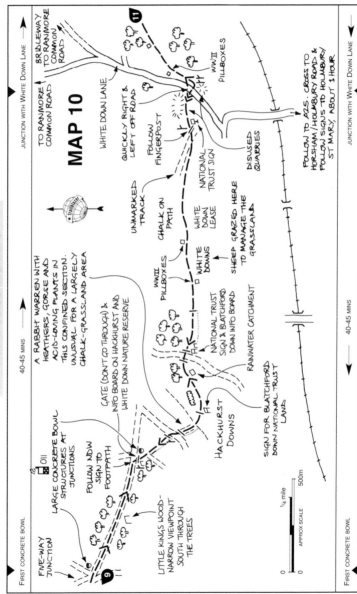

ROUTE GUIDE AND MAPS

MAP 10

FIRST CONCRETE BOWL

JUNCTION WITH WHITE DOWN LANE

40-45 MINS

FIVE-WAY JUNCTION

LARGE CONCRETE BOWL STRUCTURES AT JUNCTIONS

OII

FOLLOW NDW SIGN TO FOOTPATH

LITTLE KING'S WOOD - NARROW VIEWPOINT SOUTH THROUGH THE TREES

A RABBIT WARREN WITH HEATHERS, GORSE AND ACID-LOVING PLANTS IN THIS CONFINED SECTION. UNUSUAL FOR A LARGELY CHALK-GRASSLAND AREA

GATE (DON'T GO THROUGH) & INFO BOARD ON HACKHURST AND WHITE DOWN NATURE RESERVE

HACKHURST DOWNS

SIGN FOR BLATCHFORD DOWN NATIONAL TRUST

NATIONAL TRUST SIGN & BLATCHFORD DOWN INFO BOARD

RAINWATER CATCHMENT

WWII PILLBOXES

UNMARKED TRACK

CHALK ON PATH

WHITE DOWNS

WHITE DOWN LEASE

SHEEP GRAZED HERE TO MANAGE THE GRASSLAND

NATIONAL TRUST SIGN

DISUSED QUARRIES

FOLLOW FINGERPOST

QUICKLY RIGHT & LEFT OFF ROAD

WHITE DOWN LANE

TO RANMORE COMMON ROAD

BRIDLEWAY TO RANMORE COMMON ROAD

11

WWII PILLBOXES

JUNCTION WITH WHITE DOWN LANE

FOLLOW TO A25. CROSS TO HORSHAM/HOLMBURY ROAD & FOLLOW SIGNS TO HOLMBURY ST MARY. ABOUT 1 HOUR

40-45 MINS

1/4 mile

500m

0

0

APPROX SCALE

9

FIRST CONCRETE BOWL

The Royal Oak (☎ 01306-898010, 🖥 royaloak.timewellspent.co.uk; WI-FI; 🐾) serves pub grub (Mon-Sat noon-9pm, Sun to 6pm).

Metrobus's No 22 (Crawley to Abinger Common; see pp45-8) **bus service** calls here on weekdays only.

Back on the trail, you emerge from beneath the forest canopy at Ranmore Common to pass the Gothic-style **church of St Barnabas**. This is known as the 'Church on the North Downs Way', though it is not, of course, the only one on the Way – you passed lovely St Martha's (see p86), which bagged the title

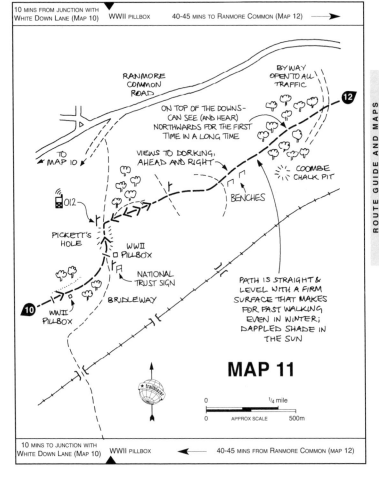

10 MINS FROM JUNCTION WITH WHITE DOWN LANE (MAP 10)   WWII PILLBOX   40-45 MINS TO RANMORE COMMON (MAP 12)

RANMORE COMMON ROAD

BY WAY OPEN TO ALL TRAFFIC

12

ON TOP OF THE DOWNS – CAN SEE (AND HEAR) NORTHWARDS FOR THE FIRST TIME IN A LONG TIME

TO MAP 10

VIEWS TO DORKING, AHEAD AND RIGHT

COOMBE CHALK PIT

012

BENCHES

PICKETT'S HOLE

WWII PILLBOX

NATIONAL TRUST SIGN

PATH IS STRAIGHT & LEVEL WITH A FIRM SURFACE THAT MAKES FOR FAST WALKING EVEN IN WINTER; DAPPLED SHADE IN THE SUN

10

WWII PILLBOX

BRIDLEWAY

MAP 11

★ trailblazer

0   ¼ mile
0   APPROX SCALE   500m

ROUTE GUIDE AND MAPS

10 MINS TO JUNCTION WITH WHITE DOWN LANE (MAP 10)   WWII PILLBOX   ◀   40-45 MINS FROM RANMORE COMMON (MAP 12)

'Pilgrims' Church', earlier on this stage. St Barnabas was built by Sir George Gilbert Scott in 1859 for the Cubit family, then owners of the nearby Denbies Estate. Scott also designed the Albert Memorial and the enormous Grand Midland Hotel at St Pancras Station in London, while his grandson, Sir Giles, designed the original Battersea Power Station – which is currently undergoing a redevelopment and being converted largely into flats, Bankside (now the Tate Modern) and the iconic red phone boxes that were once so common all over Britain.

RANMORE COMMON   [MAP 12]

YHA Tanners Hatch (off Map 12; ☎ 0345-371 9542, 🖳 yha.org.uk/hostel/tanners-hatch-surrey-hills; 1 x 6-/1 x 7-bed dorm, 1D; Mar-Dec), off Ranmore Common Rd and about 20 minutes from the North Downs Way, is a much better option for hostellers (dorm bed £15-19pp, double room at £49-79) and **campers** (seven tent pitches; from £12pp; 🐾) than Holmbury St Mary. Once described as 'famously basic',

this charming beamed cottage is deep in the woods and has a rambling garden, a small, comfortable lounge with open wood fire, outside toilet and showers. Note that it's self-catering only, and you'll probably need a torch too.

Ranmore Common Road is the last stop on Carlone Buses No 533 service from Ewhurst via Dorking but it only runs on a Tuesday.

From Ranmore Common it is a mere hop and a skip to the Denbies Estate, England's largest vineyard, situated on the outskirts of Dorking. A short diversion to the visitor centre (see below) and the winery tour are recommended.

DENBIES WINE ESTATE
                    [MAP 13, p97]

With your thirst sharpened along the 13-mile stage, a detour to England's largest vineyard, Denbies (☎ 01306-876616, 🖳 denbies.co.uk), could be in order. An outdoor train tour of the vines costs £7 and can be booked at the **visitor centre** (daily 9.30am-5.30pm).

The stylish *Gallery Restaurant* (Mon-Sat noon-2.30pm, Sun to 3.30pm, also Thur-Sat 6-8.30pm) on the third floor has panoramic views of the vineyard, and a 2-course fixed-price menu for £16.95. The *Conservatory Restaurant* is the cheaper, more informal restaurant (daily 9.30am-5.30pm; WI-FI) with a wide range of salads and sandwiches as well as a decent breakfast.

Surrey Hills Brewery (🖳 surreyhills .co.uk) is also based on the estate and you can visit their operation on a pre-arranged tour (£12pp); call ☎ 01306-883603 for details.

B&B is offered at *Denbies' Farmhouse* (☎ 01306-876777, 🖳 denbies .co.uk/accommodation; 5D/1Tr/1Qd, all en suite; ♥; WI-FI) for £55-60pp (sgl occ £80-102), a whitewashed farmhouse.

Another option nearby is the luxurious *Burford Bridge Hotel* (☎ 01306-884561, 🖳 mercure.com; 57D, all en suite; ♥; WI-FI; 🐾). Nelson is said to have stayed here before departing for Trafalgar and reputedly Keats completed his poem *Endymion* during a stay; room rates start at about £50pp (sgl occ room rate); breakfast costs £16.50, though B&B rates are available.

Stepping Stones (☎ 01306-889932; food Mon-Sat noon-9pm, Sun noon-7pm; WI-FI; 🐾 bar area), at Westhumble, is both walker and dog friendly, with a range of pizzas and burgers and other familiar pub fare (mains £10.95-16.95).

And if you want fast food before tackling Box Hill there is *Ryka's Café* (🖳 rykas .co.uk; daily 7.30am-6pm, summer Wed to

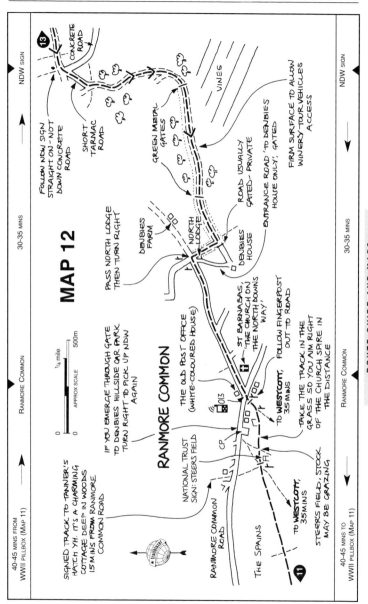

MAP 12

40-45 MINS FROM
WWII PILLBOX (MAP 11)

RANMORE COMMON

30-35 MINS

NDW SIGN

FOLLOW NDW SIGN STRAIGHT ON - NOT DOWN CONCRETE ROAD

CONCRETE ROAD

13

SHORT TARMAC ROAD

VINES

GREEN METAL GATES

PASS NORTH LODGE THEN TURN RIGHT

ROAD USUALLY GATED - PRIVATE

ENTRANCE ROAD 'TO DENBIES HOUSE ONLY; GATED

FIRM SURFACE TO ALLOW WINERY TOUR VEHICLES ACCESS

DENBIES FARM

NORTH LODGE

DENBIES HOUSE

0   ¼ mile
0   APPROX SCALE   500m

RANMORE COMMON

THE OLD POST OFFICE (WHITE-COLOURED HOUSE)

013

NATIONAL TRUST SIGN: STEERS FIELD

CP

ST BARNABAS, 'THE CHURCH ON THE NORTH DOWNS WAY'

TO **WESTCOTT**, 35 MINS

FOLLOW FINGERPOST OUT TO ROAD

TAKE THE TRACK IN THE GRASS SO YOU AIM RIGHT OF THE CHURCH SPIRE IN THE DISTANCE

IF YOU EMERGE THROUGH GATE TO DENBIES HILLSIDE CAR PARK TURN RIGHT TO PICK UP NDW AGAIN

SIGNED TRACK TO TANNER'S HATCH YH. IT'S A CHARMING COTTAGE DEEP IN WOODS 15 MINS FROM RANMORE COMMON ROAD

RANMORE COMMON ROAD

THE SPAINS

TO **WESTCOTT**, 35MINS

STEERS FIELD, STOCK MAY BE GRAZING

11

40-45 MINS TO
WWII PILLBOX (MAP 11)

RANMORE COMMON

30-35 MINS

NDW SIGN

9pm), popular with the burger and biker crowd since the 1920s!

Box Hill & Westhumble railway station is a couple of minutes' walk away from Stepping Stones B&B and has services to both London Waterloo (South Western Railway) and Victoria (Southern Railway); see box pp42-3.

Quality Line's No 465 **bus service** (Kingston-upon-Thames to Dorking) stops on the A24; see pp45-8 for details.

The end of the estate is marked by the horribly busy A24. Tempting as it may be to try to run straight across the road, we urge you not to; instead, turn north for 500m to take the underpass – or, even better, head south to Dorking, which has plenty of accommodation options and good transport links. You can either walk along the A24 – though that's not a pleasant option; instead, we urge you to take the turn-off from the trail marked on Map 13.

DORKING   [MAP 13a, p99]

Dorking is a thriving town at the foot of the North Downs' chalk ridge and Box Hill. It is reputed to have more antique shops per head of population than any other town in England, but even if you don't fancy wandering around the shops – and remember: a full-size Victorian mahogany wardrobe is not the easiest thing to carry on the North Downs Way – there's still enough good eateries and accommodation to warrant a visit.

What to see and do

Dorking Museum (🖳 dorkingmuseum.org .uk; Thur-Sat 10am-4pm; £2) has exhibits of the town's history and there is memorabilia of composer **Ralph Vaughan Williams** who lived locally; there is now a statue of him outside **Dorking Halls**, at the eastern end of the High St. At 26 Wathen Rd, a blue plaque commemorates **Sir Lawrence Olivier** who was born there.

West Street is the centre of the antique trade; by the sign to the museum notice the plaque above the former home of **William Mullins** (at No 58), a shoemaker who joined the Pilgrim Fathers and sailed on the *Mayflower* to America in 1620.

You need to book visits to **Dorking Caves**, the maze of passages under South St which were used as warehouses, smugglers' dens and for illegal cock-fighting in the past. There are guided tours (end Mar to end Oct last Sat of month 10am, 11am, 1pm & 2pm); to check the dates and make a booking visit the Dorking Museum website.

Dorking Traditional **Market** (including clothes, mobile phones for sale too, but with local produce available too; see box p22) is held every Friday at St Martin's Walk, off High St.

Services

The tourist information centre in Dorking has closed down but there's still **online information** available at 🖳 visitdorking .com.

There are **three supermarkets** within the town centre, Marks & Spencer (Mon-Sat 8.30am-6pm, Sun 10am-4pm), Sainsbury's (Mon-Sat 7am-8pm, Sun 10am-4pm) and Waitrose (Mon-Sat 8am-9pm, Sun 10am-4pm). There is also a Boots **chemist** (Mon-Sat 8.30am-5.30pm, Sun 10am-4pm) on the High St and a couple of outdoor shops: **SC Fuller** (☎ 01306-882177, 🖳 scfuller.co.uk; Mon-Sat 8am-5.30pm, Sun 10am-3.30pm), 28-32 South St, which claims to be the oldest in Dorking; and a branch of **Millets** (Mon-Sat 9am-6pm, Sun 10am-4pm) on St Martin's Walk.

There are several **ATMs** on West St and High St. The main **post office** (Mon-Fri 9am-5.30pm, Sat 9am-12.30pm) is on High St. If you'd rather try to repair your existing boots than get a new pair there is a branch of the **shoe repairer** Timpson (Mon-Fri 9.30am-5.30pm, Sat to 5pm).

Transport

There are three **railway stations**: Dorking (sometimes referred to as Dorking North) is

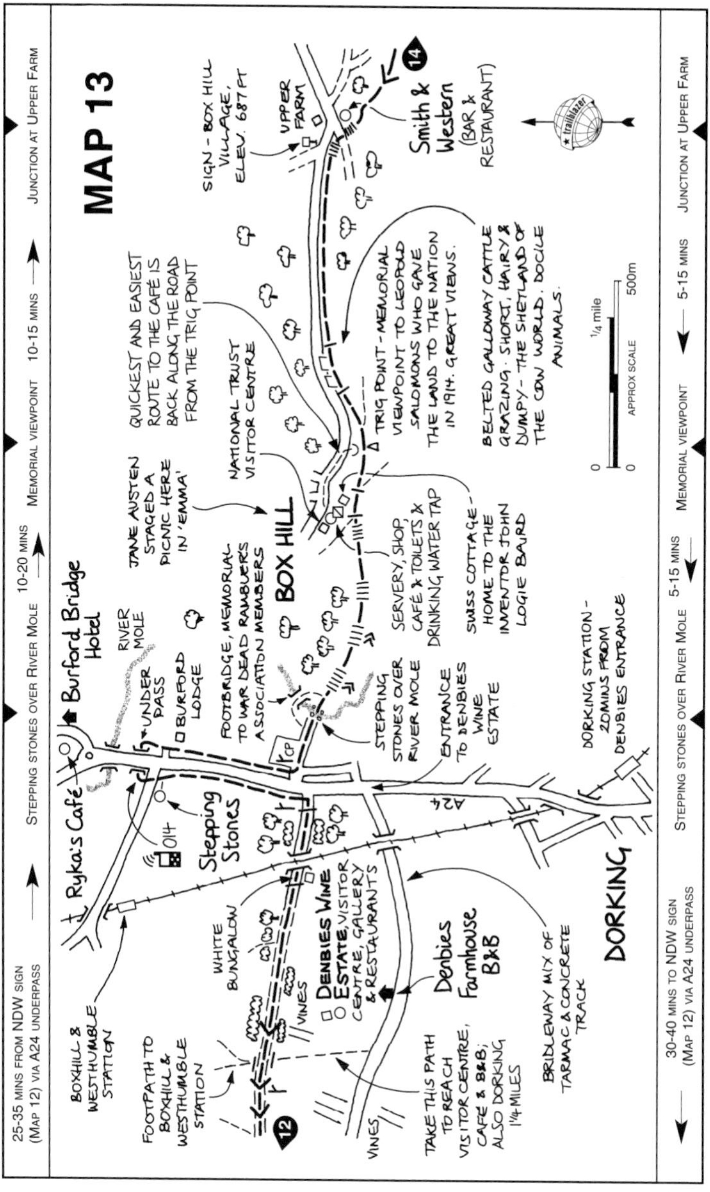

25-35 MINS FROM NDW SIGN (MAP 12) VIA A24 UNDERPASS
STEPPING STONES OVER RIVER MOLE
10-20 MINS
MEMORIAL VIEWPOINT
10-15 MINS
JUNCTION AT UPPER FARM
MAP 13
BOXHILL & WESTHUMBLE STATION
FOOTPATH TO BOXHILL & WESTHUMBLE STATION
Ryka's Café
Burford Bridge Hotel
RIVER MOLE
UNDER PASS
BURFORD LODGE
014
Stepping Stones
WHITE BUNGALOW
VINES
DENBIES WINE ESTATE, VISITOR CENTRE, GALLERY & RESTAURANTS
FOOTBRIDGE, MEMORIAL TO WAR DEAD RAMBLERS ASSOCIATION MEMBERS
JANE AUSTEN STAGED A PICNIC HERE IN 'EMMA'
BOX HILL
NATIONAL TRUST VISITOR CENTRE
QUICKEST AND EASIEST ROUTE TO THE CAFÉ IS BACK ALONG THE ROAD FROM THE TRIG POINT
SIGN - BOX HILL VILLAGE, ELEV. 687 FT
UPPER FARM
Smith & Western (BAR & RESTAURANT)
14
12
VINES
TAKE THIS PATH TO REACH VISITOR CENTRE, CAFÉ & B&B; ALSO DORKING 1¼ MILES
Denbies Farmhouse B&B
BRIDLEWAY MIX OF TARMAC & CONCRETE TRACK
DORKING
A24
STEPPING STONES OVER RIVER MOLE
ENTRANCE TO DENBIES WINE ESTATE
DORKING STATION - 20MINS FROM DENBIES ENTRANCE
SERVERY, SHOP, CAFÉ & TOILETS & DRINKING WATER TAP
SWISS COTTAGE - HOME TO THE INVENTOR JOHN LOGIE BAIRD
TRIG POINT - MEMORIAL VIEWPOINT TO LEOPOLD SALOMONS WHO GAVE THE LAND TO THE NATION IN 1914. GREAT VIEWS.
BELTED GALLOWAY CATTLE GRAZING. SHORT, HAIRY & DUMPY - THE SHETLAND OF THE COW WORLD. DOCILE ANIMALS.
0 ¼ mile
0 APPROX SCALE 500m
trailblazer
30-40 MINS TO NDW SIGN (MAP 12) VIA A24 UNDERPASS
STEPPING STONES OVER RIVER MOLE
5-15 MINS
MEMORIAL VIEWPOINT
5-15 MINS
JUNCTION AT UPPER FARM

ROUTE GUIDE AND MAPS

used by South Western Railway for services to London Waterloo and by Southern Railway (London Victoria to Horsham); GWR's services (Gatwick Airport/Redhill to Reading) call at Dorking West and Dorking Deepdene. See box pp42-3 for details.

Metrobus's **bus services** No 21 (Crawley to Epsom) & 22 (Crawley to Holmbury St Mary), Compass Travel's and Buses Excetera's No 32 (Guildford to Dorking/Redhill), Buses Excetera's No 489 (Leatherhead to Merstham) and Quality Line's No 465 (to Kingston-upon-Thames via Denbies) all stop by White Horse Hotel (see Where to stay/eat). See pp45-8.

For a **taxi** call Dorking Taxis (☎ 01306-885533).

Where to stay

Coming into town off the A24, about 300m to the east along the A25, is a *Travelodge* (☎ 0871-984 6026, 🖳 travelodge.co.uk; 45D/10Tr, all en suite; ☛; WI-FI 30 mins free; 🐾). Each room has an extra sofa bed so it can sleep up to three walkers. Non-refundable Saver room rates can be as low as £29.99 but expect to pay around £56, or £71.50 with wi-fi and a breakfast box; for a Flexi rate you may have to pay about £82/95.50. What it lacks in character is more than made up for by its consistent quality and good value.

Just off the High St on Moores Rd is *Fairdene* (☎ 01306-888337, 🖳 fairdene-guesthouse.co.uk; 2D/2T/1Tr shared facilities, 1Tr/1Qd en suite; ☛; WI-FI; small, clean 🐾) charging £30-37.50pp (sgl occ rates on request); the rate includes a simple breakfast.

Centrally located on the High St is White Horse Hotel (☎ 01306-881138, 🖳 bespokehotels.com/dorking-white-horse; 9S/25D/19D or T, three luxury rooms, all en suite; WI-FI; 🐾) with prices varying according to demand but in the range of £65-100pp (sgl £100-140, sgl occ rates on request) for B&B. Some rooms can have an additional bed put in.

Further up on Rose Hill is the 19th-century *Waltons* (☎ 01306-883127, 🖳 the waltonsbedbreakfastdorking.epageuk.com; 1D/1T/1Qd, all en suite; ☛; WI-FI; 🐾),

charging from £45pp (sgl occ £75-85), including a continental breakfast (£10 for the full English, but this must be requested in advance).

If your legs just won't carry you any further coming into town along the A24 from the trail there is always *The Lincoln Arms Hotel* (☎ 01306-882820, 🖳 lincoln arms.co.uk; 4S/3D/10T/3Tr, all en suite; ☛; WI-FI) next to Dorking Station. It's seen a few incarnations but has always been a station hotel. Rates are £35-45pp (sgl £35-45, sgl occ from £55) including a continental breakfast, but for an additional charge a cooked breakfast can be provided. Note, however, that they usually require a two-night minimum stay during the summer months – though it can't hurt to ask.

Where to eat and drink

In addition to that ubiquitous coffee provider, *Costa* (Mon-Fri 7.30am-6pm, Sat 8am-6pm, Sun 9am-4.30pm) there are several quirky cafés too. Newest amongst them is the bicycle-themed *Musette Café* (☎ 01306-898040, 🖳 bakerstreetbikes.co.uk/ musette; Mon-Sat 8.30am-5pm, Sun 8.30am-4pm; WI-FI), at the start of the High St, which does a small range of tasty sandwiches including salt beef (£4.95).

Further along the High St is *Courtyard Café* (☎ 01306-888849; Mon-Sat 9am-4pm, but later if busy; 🐾) a simple, home-ly place with indoor and outdoor seating off the main drag and a large menu including hot meals such as a lightly seasoned chicken breast known as Dorking Cockrell (£6.95).

Two Many Cooks (☎ 01306-882200, 🖳 twomanycooks.com; Mon-Fri 8am-5pm, Sat 8.30am-5pm, Sun 9am-4pm; WI-FI; 🐾), on South St just before Waitrose, does some of the best food anywhere in Dorking including breakfasts, sandwiches and salads. Note, however, that there are no toilet facilities here.

For evening dining there are plenty of options down the eastern end of the High St where food from all over the globe can be found including: a Mexican, *Dos Bandidos* (☎ 01306-898083, 🖳 dosbandidos.co.uk; daily noon-11pm), on the corner of High St

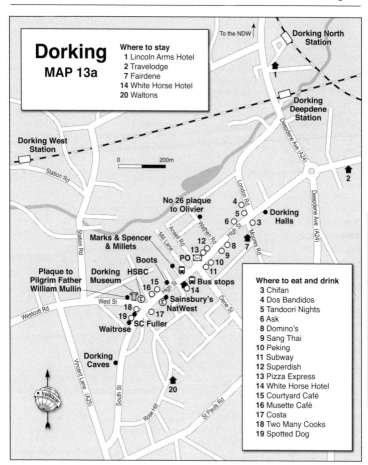

Dorking
MAP 13a

Where to stay
1 Lincoln Arms Hotel
2 Travelodge
7 Fairdene
14 White Horse Hotel
20 Waltons

To the NDW

Dorking North Station

Dorking Deepdene Station

Dorking West Station

Station Rd

0   200m

No 26 plaque to Olivier

Dorking Halls

Marks & Spencer & Millets

Boots

PO

Plaque to Pilgrim Father William Mullin

Dorking Museum

HSBC

West St

Waterhouse Rd

Westcott Rd

Vincent Lane (A25)

Bus stops

Sainsbury's
NatWest

Waitrose

SC Fuller

Dorking Caves

South St

Rose Hill

St Pauls Rd

Deepdene Ave (A24)

London Rd

High St

Moores Rd

Dene St

Where to eat and drink
3 Chifan
4 Dos Bandidos
5 Tandoori Nights
6 Ask
8 Domino's
9 Sang Thai
10 Peking
11 Subway
12 Superdish
13 Pizza Express
14 White Horse Hotel
15 Courtyard Café
16 Musette Café
17 Costa
18 Two Many Cooks
19 Spotted Dog

ROUTE GUIDE AND MAPS

and London Rd, with all your favourites
including empanadas (from £5.45), que-
sadillas (from £6.45), fajitas (from 11.95)
and tacos (from £5.95); a fine and lively
Indian next door, *Tandoori Nights* (☎
01306-887860, 🖳 www.tandoorinightsdor
king.com; daily noon-2pm & 5.30-11.30pm)
with tandoori dishes from £7.95; two
Chinese restaurants, *Chifan* (🖳 chinesedor
king.co.uk; Mon-Sat noon-2.30pm & 5.30-
11pm, Sun noon-10pm), down near the cinema, and the busier *Peking* (☎ 01306-

881222; Mon-Sat noon-2.30pm & 6-11pm,
Sun noon-10pm), at 272 High St, with an all-
you-can-eat buffet for £12.95. Next door
there's the ever-popular *Sang Thai* (☎
01306-888237, 🖳 sangthai restaurant.com;
daily noon-2pm & 6-10.30pm), a Thai
restaurant with vegetarian mains from £6.30
and carnivorous mains from £7.80.
    Nearby are branches of the Italian chain
Ask (☎ 01306-888669, 🖳 askitalian.co.uk;
Sun-Thur 11am-10pm, Fri & Sat to 11pm)
and also *Pizza Express* (☎ 01306-888236,

pizzaexpress.com/dorking; Mon-Tue noon-10pm, Wed & Thur to 10.30pm, Fri & Sat 11.30am-11.30pm, Sun 11.30am-10pm). Most of these run a takeaway service, too, though if you'd like more local fare there's a decent chippy, **Superdish** (Mon & Tue 10am-2.30pm, Wed-Fri 10am-10pm, Sat 1-9pm).

Pub food is available at **Spotted Dog** (☎ 01306-885218, 🖳 spotteddogdorking .co.uk; food Mon-Fri noon-4pm & 5-7pm, Sat noon-8pm, Sun to 4pm; WI-FI; 🐾), a few yards down from Waitrose, with nearly every dish under a tenner and sandwiches around the £5-6 mark. **White Horse Hotel** (see Where to stay; food daily noon-9.30pm) has an à la carte menu featuring standard British-style food and daily specials; it also offers a three-course set meal (£27.95) on Sunday lunch.

For takeaway-only fare you have **Subway** (Mon-Thur 7am-9pm, Fri & Sat to 10pm, Sun 8am-8pm) and **Domino's** (Sun-Thur 11am-midnight, Fri & Sat to 1am).

DORKING TO OXTED   [MAPS 13-21]

In the introduction to this book we talked about how the North Downs Way fights a not infrequent battle against the relentless incursions of the modern world and it is something of a wonder that the trail manages to plot such a beautiful course through a region so dissected, despoiled, choked and corrupted by the trepidations of *homo sapiens* and, in particular, the cacophony of the combustion engine. Well, it is on this lengthy **18.2-mile/29.4km stage (4¾hrs to 6hrs 40mins)** that this conflict is most keenly fought, and in truth the path, in some places, struggles to maintain the upper-hand against the incessant tumult of traffic. The A24, M25 and its diminutive but equally noisy sibling the A25, the A217, A23, M23, M25 (again) and A22 all scream for your attention at various points throughout this lengthy stage. Thankfully, the national trail has a clever way of distracting you from all the hubbub by cramming this stage with as many sights, panoramas, and points of interest as possible – and by being as pretty as it possibly can be in the circumstances too.

Indeed, no sooner do you trip off the A24 at the start of this stage than you encounter one of the stage's highlights, the National Trust-owned **Stepping Stones** that convey you across the River Mole. Having successfully negotiated them, you then find yourself confronted by the biggest climb on the North Downs Way, a sweaty, sweltering slog up a steep,

> 'Mole, that like a nousling mole doth make
> His way still underground, til Thames he
>   overtake'
>   **Edmund Spenser**, *The Faerie Queene*

slippery slope. Encourage yourself by thinking of the rewards that await you at the top including yet more lovely views and, even more welcome, a National Trust café (see p102) with plenty of outdoor seating.

Appropriately for a hill called Box, the man who invented the most significant 'box' of them all, the television, lived up here for four years (1929-32). That man was John Logie Baird who lived at Swiss Cottage (closed to the public) and carried out some of his most important experiments here. Rather than being named after the goggle box, however, the name **Box Hill** is believed to have been derived from the box trees that flourish up here. Now in the care of the National Trust, having been gifted to the nation by Leopold Salomons

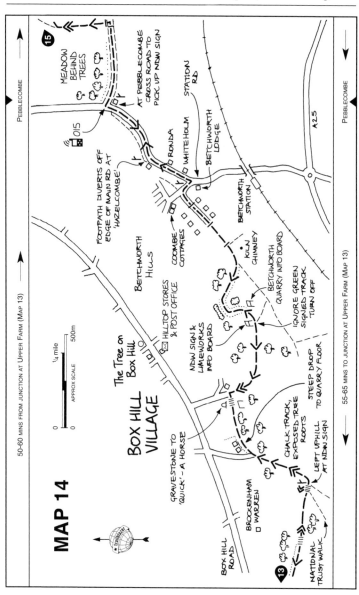

MAP 14

50-60 MINS FROM JUNCTION AT UPPER FARM (MAP 13)

PEBBLECOMBE

¼ mile
APPROX SCALE
0   500m

BOX HILL VILLAGE

The Tree on Box Hill

GRAVESTONE TO 'QUICK' - A HORSE

BROCKENHAM WARREN

BOX HILL ROAD

NATIONAL TRUST WALK

13

LEFT UPHILL AT NEW SIGN

CHALK TRACK, EXPOSED TREE ROOTS

STEEP DROP TO QUARRY FLOOR

NEW SIGN & LIMEWORKS INFO BOARD

HILLTOP STORES & POST OFFICE

BETCHWORTH HILLS

FOOTPATH DIVERTS OFF EDGE OF MAIN RD AT 'HAZELCOMBE'

COOMBE COTTAGES

KILN CHIMNEY

BETCHWORTH QUARRY INFO BOARD

IGNORE GREEN SIGNED TRACK TURN OFF

BETCHWORTH STATION

RONDA

WHITEHOLM

BETCHWORTH LODGE

STATION RD

A25

AT PEBBLECOMBE CROSS ROAD TO PICK UP NEW SIGN

MEADOW BEHIND TREES

015

15

PEBBLECOMBE

55-65 MINS TO JUNCTION AT UPPER FARM (MAP 13)

ROUTE GUIDE AND MAPS

(whose memorial you'll pass on the trail after the café), much of the hill is an SSSI (see p57), with two-thirds of Britain's butterfly species having been recorded here; it's also home to important chalk grassland plants, see pp63-4.

The hill is an important burial site, too, with two Bronze Age barrows close to Salomons' Memorial. There is a further grave of note on the hill, that of Peter Labilliere (mis-spelt Labelliere on the grave) an 18th-century political agitator, peace campaigner and eccentric who would come here to meditate, but whose rather low standards of personal hygiene led to his nickname of 'The Walking Dung Hill'.

BOX HILL & BOX HILL VILLAGE
[MAP 13, p97 & MAP 14, p101]
'They had a very fine day for Box Hill … Nothing was wanting but to be happy when they got there. Seven miles were travelled in expectation of enjoyment, and every body had a burst of admiration on first arriving…' **Jane Austen,** *Emma*

The *servery* (daily 9am-5pm in summer; 11am-4pm in good weather the rest of the year) has a big menu of snacks including cakes (£2-3.50), pasties (£3.95) and a daily homemade soup with crusty bread (£4). There is also a popular **café-cum-gift shop** (daily 9 or 10am-5pm) with a similar menu.

Further on, and opposite Upper Farm – though it's all but hidden by trees in full leaf in summer – is *Smith & Western* (☎ 01737-841666, ☐ smith-western.co.uk/restaurant-boxhill; Mon-Sat noon-11pm, Sun to 10pm; WI-FI) an American-themed

diner where the portions are huge though it's rather expensive, with burgers amongst the cheaper options (from £13.45).

Further on and more reasonable is *The Tree on Box Hill* (Map 14; ☎ 01737-845996, ☐ thetreeboxhill.co.uk; food Tue-Sat noon-9pm, Sun to 7pm; WI-FI; 🐾) offering a carvery for £11.95 as well as a full à la carte menu (mains from £5.75 for a caesar salad).

Before you get there, a mile down Box Hill Rd in the **village** there is **Hilltop Stores** (Mon-Fri 7am-7pm, Sat to 6.30pm, Sun 8am-3pm), incorporating the **post office** (same hours).

Metrobus's No 21 **bus** service (Crawley to Epsom; see pp45-8) stops at the National Trust Visitor Centre and at Upper Farm. Note that the Boxhill & Westhumble Station is actually a couple of miles from the village.

Plunging back into woodland soon after Salomons' Memorial, the trail now runs past a couple of former lime quarries, climbing short but steep hills to **Juniper Hill** (Map 15).

With the noise of the M25 now encroaching from the north, the Ridgeline is gained at Colley Hill. The path is now punctuated by masts, a water tower, a **monument to Lt Col Inglis**, who gave this land to public use, a **memorial to a plane** that crashed on the hill during WWII, a couple of **pillboxes** and **Napoleonic Reigate Fort** (see box p104) – enough distractions, I think you'll agree, to draw your attention away from both the M25's rumble and any weariness you may be feeling after all that climbing today.

REIGATE HILL　　　[MAP 16, p105]
The path passes above and behind *The Bridge House Hotel* (☎ 01737-246801, ☐ bridgehousereigate.com; 8S/23D/6T/2Tr, all en suite; ✆; WI-FI). Room rates vary

depending on demand but are around £28-55pp (sgl/sgl occ from £50); with breakfast an extra £7.50pp if booked in advance. The attached *restaurant* (daily noon-3pm &

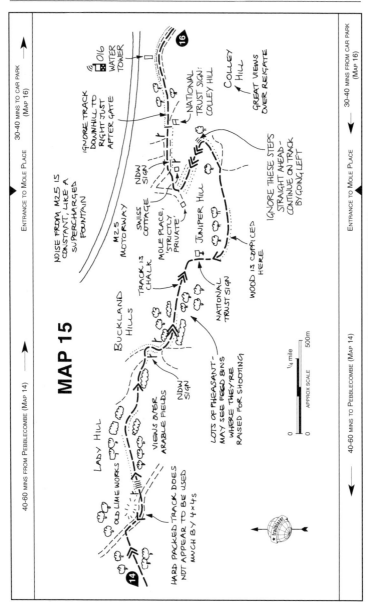

MAP 15

LADY HILL

OLD LIME WORKS

VIEWS OVER ARABLE FIELDS

NDW SIGN

BUCKLAND HILLS

HARD PACKED TRACK DOES NOT APPEAR TO BE USED MUCH BY 4×4s

LOTS OF PHEASANT - MAY SEE FEED BINS WHERE THEY'RE RAISED FOR SHOOTING

NATIONAL TRUST SIGN

WOOD IS COPPICED HERE

TRACK IS CHALK

NOISE FROM M25 IS CONSTANT, LIKE A SUPERCHARGED FOUNTAIN

M25 MOTORWAY

SWISS COTTAGE

MOLE PLACE, STRICTLY PRIVATE

NDW SIGN

JUNIPER HILL

IGNORE THESE STEPS STRAIGHT AHEAD - CONTINUE ON TRACK BY GOING LEFT

IGNORE TRACK DOWNHILL TO RIGHT JUST AFTER GATE

WATER TOWER

016

16

NATIONAL TRUST SIGN: COLLEY HILL

COLLEY HILL

GREAT VIEWS OVER REIGATE

14

¼ mile

APPROX SCALE

0   500m

6.30-9.30pm) with mains from £10.95 and up to £14.95 for the rump of lamb with minted gravy and celeriac mash. To reach the hotel you need to cross the footbridge over the A217 to the snack bar and car park, and then cross the A217 itself.

The **Junction 8 snack bar** (daily 9am-4pm) is conveniently situated at the top of Reigate Hill with a nice line in smoothies and a decent selection of wraps (£4) and ciabattas (£5 inc a drink). Below the car park is Wray Lane leading to Redhill, though be careful on this pavement-less winding road; you may find it easier to walk onto Merstham and get a bus back from there if Redhill is your destination.

❏ Wartime defences – Surrey's Maginot Line

Reigate Fort (see Map 16) was built in 1890 as one of 13 installations forming a defence chain over 70 miles of the Downs escarpment to protect London from invasion from the south and east. At the time the victory over Napoleon was recent and France was considered the greatest potential threat.

The structures were not forts in the ordinary sense but large gun encampments. At the time they were cutting-edge military tactics – a static defence line facing the enemy along the ridge of the North Downs. The same methods were adopted in WWII with pillboxes creating a Surrey Maginot Line – Maginot was the French General who devised the tactic.

The tank traps and pillboxes seen along the trail (see Map 6 p79, Map 10 p92, and Map 11 p93) are remnants of defence thinking in the inter-war years. The concrete boxes, complete with machine-gun slits and 17-inch thick walls, dotting the route in Surrey were part of a three-tier system of national defence – coastal defences on beaches, stop lines inland and finally a fixed line of tank traps and pillboxes 50 miles behind the south and east coasts.

REDHILL   [MAP 16a, p106]

Not exactly the most charismatic of places you'll visit on your walk, this commuter town would not normally warrant a mention in a guidebook such as this if it wasn't for the fact that it does at least have some useful services and good transport links; so for these reasons alone walkers may want to come here. The central area around High St, Station Rd and the Harlequin Centre is pedestrianised.

Services

There is an **outdoor shop**, Millets (Mon-Sat 9am-6pm, Sun 10am-4pm), on the High St. Footsore walkers will find relief at the **chemist**, Boots (Mon-Sat 9am-6pm, Sun 10am-4pm). The Sainsbury's **supermarket**, north of the Harlequin Centre, is open daily (Mon-Sat 7am-10pm, Sun 10am-4pm) and there's a branch of (cheaper) Iceland (Mon-Sat 8am-8pm, Sun 10am-4pm). The town centre is host to an open-air **market** (every Thur, Fri & Sat), and a farmers' market on the second Friday of every month (see box p22).

There are several banks with **ATMs** on Station Rd and a **post office** (Mon-Sat 9am-5.30pm, Sun 10.30am-2.30pm) in the branch of WH Smith in the Belfry Centre.

Transport

The most useful **bus** services are: Metrobus's No 400 (East Grinstead to Caterham), No 420 (to Sutton), Nos 430/435 (to Merstham) and No 460 (Epsom to Crawley); Compass's No 32 (to Guildford); Buses Excetera's No 489 (Leatherhead to Merstham); Southdown PSV's No 357 (Selsdon to Reigate), No 410 (to Hurst Green) and 424 (to Crawley); and London General's No 405 (to West Croydon). See pp45-8 for details.

The main bus station is opposite the **railway station**; Southern Railway, GWR

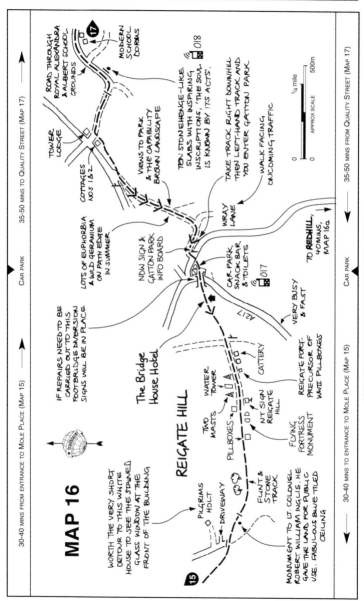

MAP 16

ROAD THROUGH ROYAL ALEXANDRA & ALBERT SCHOOL GROUNDS

MODERN SCHOOL DORMS

TOWER LODGE

COTTAGES NOS 1 & 2

VIEWS TO PARK & THE CAPABILITY BROWN LANDSCAPE

TEN STONEHENGE-LIKE SLABS WITH INSPIRING INSCRIPTIONS; 'THE SOUL IS KNOWN BY ITS ACTS'.

TAKE TRACK RIGHT DOWNHILL THEN LEFT-HAND TRACK AND YOU ENTER GATTON PARK

LOTS OF EUPHORBIA & WILD GERANIUM ON PATH EDGE IN SUMMER

IF REPAIRS NEED TO BE CARRIED OUT TO THIS FOOTBRIDGE DIVERSION SIGNS WILL BE IN PLACE

WRAY LANE

NDW SIGN & GATTON PARK INFO BOARD

CAR PARK, SNACK BAR & TOILETS

018

017

TO REDHILL, 40MINS, MAP 16a

VERY BUSY & FAST

A217

The Bridge House Hotel

REIGATE HILL

TWO MASTS

WATER TOWER

PILLBOXES

NT SIGN REIGATE HILL

CATTERY

REIGATE FORT, PRECURSOR OF WWII PILLBOXES

FLYING FORTRESS MONUMENT

FLINT & STONE TRACK

PILGRIMS HOLT

DRIVEWAY

WORTH THE VERY SHORT DETOUR TO THIS WHITE HOUSE TO SEE THE STAINED GLASS WINDOW AT THE FRONT OF THE BUILDING

MONUMENT TO LT. COLONEL ROBERT WILLIAM INGLIS. HE GAVE THE LAND FOR PUBLIC USE. FABULOUS BLUE-TILED CEILING

15

17

APPROX SCALE

0   ¼ mile

0   500m

and Thameslink operate train services to a number of destinations in the south of England; see box pp42-3. Road Runners **taxis** (☎ 01737-760076) can always drop you back on the trail.

Where to stay
At 2 Redstone Hill there's a *Travelodge* (☎ 08715-591843, 🖳 travelodge.co.uk; 5S/13T/16D/3Qd, all en suite; 🍸; WI-FI free for 30 mins; 🐕) offering the usual rather impersonal but, if you book far enough in advance, good-value accommodation can cost from £29.99 for a room). However, for a non-refundable Saver room rate expect to pay around £83 (£96.50 with wi-fi and breakfast box); Flexi rates may be around £97/110.50. If you would like a cooked breakfast there is a Toby Carvery (see Where to eat) next door. Close by is

Brompton Guesthouse (☎ 01737-765613, 🖳 www.bromptonguesthouse.com; 1S private bathroom, 3D or T/2Qd all en suite; 🍸; WI-FI; 🐕), at 6 Crossland Rd, a comfortable Edwardian house about five minutes from the station and charging from £42.50pp (sgl/sgl occ from £65/85).

Also a quarter of a mile (500 metres) away, though this time to the north of the town centre, is *Lynwood Guest House* (☎ 01737-766894, 🖳 lynwoodguesthouse.co.uk; 1D/2Qd all en suite, 2S/2T/2Qd shared facilities; 🍸; WI-FI; 🐕), on the corner of Lynwood Rd and London Rd. B&B costs £26.50-31.50pp (sgl £40, sgl occ room rate).

Where to eat and drink
The best of the culinary bunch in the heart of the town is *The Junction* (☎ 01737-762357; WI-FI; 🐕), a pub which welcomes

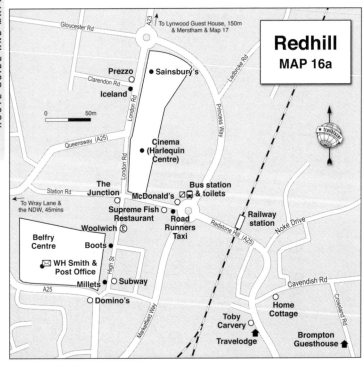

dogs and has a fine menu with food (*Sai Kitchen @ The Junction* 🖳 saikitchen .co.uk; Mon-Fri 11.30am-3pm & 5.30-9.30pm, Sat 11.30am-4pm & 5.30-9.30pm) from the Far East including Singapore noodles and Pad Thai (both £11.45).

For fast food you're spoilt for choice with, most conveniently of all, a 24-hour *McDonald's* by the bus station and a *Domino's* (☎ 01737-773737, 🖳 dominos .co.uk; Sun-Thur 11am-midnight, Fri & Sat to 1am) at the western end of the High St. There's also a branch of the upmarket Italian chain *Prezzo* (☎ 01737-779927, 🖳 prezzorestaurants.co.uk; Mon-Sat noon-11pm, Sun noon-10pm), opposite Sainsbury's, in a converted post office; pizza starts at £7.90 and the lasagne is £10.70. *Toby Carvery* (☎ 01737-768434;

food daily 8am-10pm; WI-FI), next to the Travelodge (see Where to stay), dishes up breakfasts (£4.49 for the full English) in addition to its better-known roast dinners.

Good pub grub can be had at *Home Cottage* (☎ 01737-762771, 🖳 homecottage redhill.com; food Mon-Sat noon-10pm, Sun to 9pm; WI-FI; 🐾 bar area only), a Victorian pub serving Young's and which is just around the corner from Brompton Guest House (see Where to stay); it's probably the most charming place in town to eat and the food is reasonable (pie of the day £13).

The spotless chippy *Supreme Fish Restaurant* (Mon-Fri 11am-2.30pm & 4.30-9.30pm, Sat 11am-9.30pm), on Station Rd, is licensed.

There are several **coffee shops** in the Belfry Centre.

Separating you from the first settlement of any note actually on the trail since Puttenham is a saunter down the Capability Brown designed landscape of **Gatton Park**, a chicane through school grounds and a saunter across Reigate Hill Golf Club, where you're likely to find skylarks pouring out their song as they spiral skyward from the rough. The North Downs Way enters Merstham by the quaintly named Quality St and its diverse collection of 18th-century houses.

MERSTHAM [MAP 17, p108]

There is no accommodation in Merstham – you'll have to catch a bus or train down to Redhill for that – but there are several other facilities. There's an **ATM** about 500m from the southern end of Quality St on Nutfield Rd.

The Esso petrol station **shop** is open 24 hours a day and below this the *Railway Arms* is home to *Tong Thai* (☎ 01737-213293; Tue-Sat noon-3pm & 5-9.30pm, Sun & Mon 6-9.30pm), with red and green curries from £6.50.

Across the busy road is *The Feathers* (☎ 01737-645643, 🖳 www.classicinns.co .uk/thefeathersmerstham; food daily noon-9.45pm; WI-FI; 🐾), with a diverse and good-value menu including sandwiches (£6.49), and with no main costing more than the £13.49 for the 10oz rib-eye steak.

By Station Rd North is *Hungers End* (☎ 01737-642291; Mon-Fri 8am-3pm, Sat 9am-2pm) which does filling warm baguettes and sandwiches from £2.60.

Quality Café (☎ 01737-644263; Mon-Fri 6.30am-3.30pm, Sat/Sun from 7/8am), Station Rd South, is a cabbies' hang out serving all your greasy favourites.

There is also a **newsagent** (Mon-Sat 5.30am-8.30pm, Sun to 6pm), and Station Cars **taxi** (☎ 01737-767676), who are based at the station.

Southern Railway operates **train** services (see box pp42-3) to a number of destinations including London Victoria and London Bridge; Thameslink services also stop here.

London General's **bus service** No 405 (West Croydon to Redhill), Southdown PSV's No 357 (Selsdon to Reigate) run along the main street (the A23). You'll need to walk to the south of town to catch either Metrobus's Nos 430 & 435 (circular route to Redhill station) or Buses Excetera's No 489 (to Leatherhead). See pp45-8 for details.

ROUTE GUIDE AND MAPS

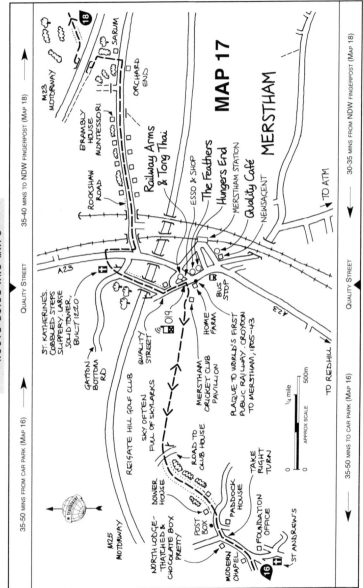

35-50 MINS FROM CAR PARK (MAP 16)   QUALITY STREET   35-40 MINS TO NDW FINGERPOST (MAP 18)

30-35 MINS FROM NDW FINGERPOST (MAP 18)

QUALITY STREET

35-50 MINS TO CAR PARK (MAP 16)

MAP 17

MERSTHAM

M23 MOTORWAY

SARUM

ORCHARD END

BRAMBLY HOUSE MONTESSORI

ROCKSHAW ROAD

Railway Arms & Tong Thai

ESSO & SHOP

The Feathers

Hungers End

MERSTHAM STATION

Quality Café

NEWSAGENT

TO ATM

A23

ST. KATHERINE'S. COBBLED STEPS SLIPPERY. LARGE SOLID TOWER, BUILT 1220

GATTON BOTTOM RD

QUALITY STREET

019

HOME FARM

BUS STOP

TO REDHILL

REIGATE HILL GOLF CLUB

SKY OFTEN FULL OF SKYLARKS

MERSTHAM CRICKET CLUB PAVILION

PLAQUE TO WORLD'S FIRST PUBLIC RAILWAY. CROYDON TO MERSTHAM, 1805-43

ROAD TO CLUB HOUSE

1/4 mile

500m

0

APPROX SCALE

0

M25 MOTORWAY

DOWER HOUSE

NORTH LODGE- THATCHED & CHOCOLATE BOX PRETTY

POST BOX

PADDOCK HOUSE

TAKE RIGHT TURN

MODERN CHAPEL

FOUNDATION OFFICE

ST ANDREW'S

16

18

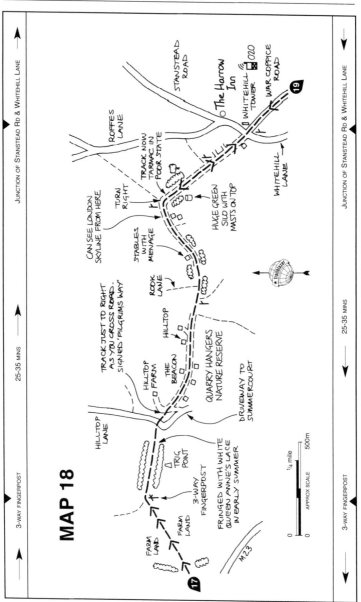

> ### ❏ Whitehill Tower
> Follies, bizarre and quirky buildings with no apparent practical use or purpose, were
> built by the grieving, the eccentric, and the out and out bonkers. Whitehill Tower (Map
> 18) is also known as Whitehill Folly Tower and the Sight Tower. Built in 1862 by
> Jeremiah Long, after his son was killed at sea, you are able, supposedly, to see the sea
> from the top. A fourth floor was reputedly added after the trees around the tower grew.
>   The bible on follies is *Follies, Grottoes and Garden Buildings*, Headley &
> Meulenkamp, Aurum Press, or visit 🖥 follies.org.uk.

Crossing the M25 and M23 in quick succession, the path climbs steadily to the
ridgeline where the traffic noise recedes. The level track continues past Quarry
Hangers Nature Reserve (see Map 18), a chalk grassland habitat managed by
Surrey Wildlife Trust (see box p57).

The track then leads to **Whitehill Tower** (see box above), a folly, from
where it is a short walk to ***The Harrow Inn*** (☎ 01883-343260, 🖥 harrowcater
ham.co.uk; food Mon-Sat noon-3pm & 6-9pm, Sun noon-5pm; WI-FI; 🐕 bar

ROUTE GUIDE AND MAPS

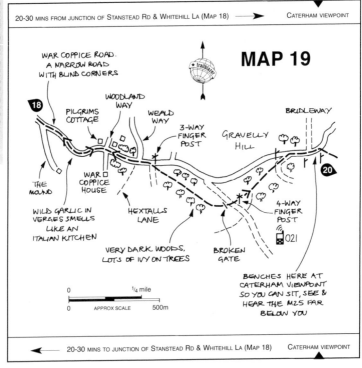

MAP 19

WAR COPPICE ROAD.
A NARROW ROAD
WITH BLIND CORNERS

WOODLAND WAY

PILGRIMS COTTAGE

WEALD WAY

BRIDLEWAY

3-WAY FINGER POST

GRAVELLY HILL

18

THE MOUND

WAR COPPICE HOUSE

20

WILD GARLIC IN VERGES SMELLS LIKE AN ITALIAN KITCHEN

HEXTALLS LANE

4-WAY FINGER POST

021

VERY DARK WOODS, LOTS OF IVY ON TREES

BROKEN GATE

BENCHES HERE AT CATERHAM VIEWPOINT SO YOU CAN SIT, SEE & HEAR THE M25 FAR BELOW YOU

0   ¼ mile
0   APPROX SCALE   500m

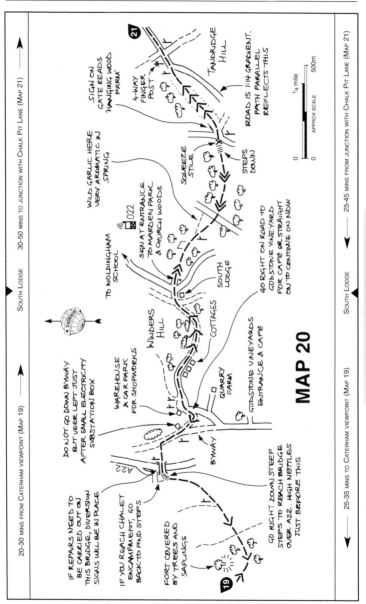

20-30 MINS FROM CATERHAM VIEWPOINT (MAP 19) — SOUTH LODGE — 30-50 MINS TO JUNCTION WITH CHALK PIT LANE (MAP 21)

25-35 MINS TO CATERHAM VIEWPOINT (MAP 19) — SOUTH LODGE — 25-45 MINS FROM JUNCTION WITH CHALK PIT LANE (MAP 21)

IF REPAIRS NEED TO BE CARRIED OUT ON THIS BRIDGE, DIVERSION SIGNS WILL BE IN PLACE

DO NOT GO DOWN BYWAY BUT VEER LEFT JUST AFTER SMALL ELECTRICITY SUBSTATION BOX

IF YOU REACH CHALET ENCAMPMENT, GO BACK TO FIND STEPS

FORT COVERED BY TREES AND SAPLINGS

GO RIGHT DOWN STEEP STEPS TO REACH BRIDGE OVER A22. HIGH NETTLES JUST BEFORE THIS

A22

BYWAY

WAREHOUSE & CAR PARK FOR SHOPWORKS

WINDERS HILL

QUARRY FARM

GODSTONE VINEYARDS ENTRANCE & CAFE

COTTAGES

SOUTH LODGE

GO RIGHT ON ROAD TO GODSTONE VINEYARD FOR CAFE OR STRAIGHT ON TO CONTINUE ON NDW

TO WOLDINGHAM SCHOOL

WILD GARLIC HERE VERY AROMATIC IN SPRING

SIGN AT ENTRANCE TO MARDEN PARK & CHURCH WOODS

022

SQUEEZE STILE

STEPS DOWN

SIGN ON GATE READS 'HANGING WOODS FARM'

4-WAY FINGER POST

TANDRIDGE HILL

ROAD IS 1:14 GRADIENT. PATH PARALLEL REFLECTS THIS

MAP 20

19

21

APPROX SCALE

0 — ¼ mile
0 — 500m

ROUTE GUIDE AND MAPS

area). The menu includes pie of the day (£10.50) as well as the usual pub standards, or you can settle for a sub (£4.95-6.50).

The only other refreshment possibility on this short section is just off the trail at Godstone Vineyards (see below), reached after a short section of road walking and a stretch in dense woodland leading, via **Caterham Viewpoint** (Map 19), to the A22. To get to *Godstone Vineyards* (see Map 20; ☎ 01883-744590, 🖥 godstonevineyards.com; Mar-Dec Thur-Fri 11am-4pm, Sat & Sun 10.30am-4.30pm, Jan & Feb Fri-Sun only) leave the Way opposite the warehouse and turn right onto the road following it downhill to the entrance. Their cream tea at £4.50 is a good energy booster which you'll appreciate on the 1:14 gradient that follows.

Once again a section of tree-lined trekking follows as you haul your wearying carcass up to the top of **Tandridge Hill**, only then to descend just as sharply via wooden steps to **Oxted Downs**, a chalk grassland habitat and SSSI (see p57) packed with wildflowers in spring and such a counterpoint to the M25 running below it. Cattle are grazed to conserve the downland habitat and prevent trees taking over. The trail then cuts across the grassland to **Chalk Pit Lane** from where it's a 25-minute or so walk to Oxted. Call Station **Taxis** (see below) if you prefer the thought of a lift.

OXTED   [MAP 21a, p115]

Oxted is separated from Old Oxted by the A25 and divided east and west by the railway line with a parade of shops either side of the station. Old Oxted and its high street is the most photogenic part, no doubt, though for something other than a pub you'll need to keep to the streets near the station where you'll find pretty much everything you'll need.

Services
There are several **ATMs** on both sides of the railway station and a **post office** (Mon-Fri 9am-5.30pm, Sat 2pm) on its western side.

Morrisons' **supermarket** (Mon-Sat 6am-10pm, Sun 10am-4pm) is the biggest of the supermarkets in town but there's also a Waitrose (Mon-Fri 7am-9pm, Sat 8am-8pm, Sun 10am-4pm), Sainsbury's (daily 7am-11pm) and Co-op (daily 6am-11pm) all on Station Rd East; and while we're on the subject of high street stalwarts there is also a Boots the **chemist** (Mon-Sat 8.30am-6pm, Sun 10am-4pm) on the same strip.

If your boots are falling apart already there's a branch of the **shoe repairer** Timpson (Mon-Sat 9am-5pm), and if they've disintegrated altogether you'll be

able to get some sort of replacement footwear at the **sports outfitter** Intersport (Mon-Fri 9am-6pm, Sat 8.30am-5.30pm).

Transport
The railway station is a stop on Southern Railway's frequent **services** (see box pp42-3) between London Victoria and East Grinstead and London Bridge to/from Uckfield. **Bus** services include: Southdown PSV's No 410 (Redhill to Hurst Green) and stops at the George (Old Oxted) and on Station Rd East (Oxted); their No 236 (to East Grinstead); and 594/595 (to Westerham) stop on Station Rd East. See pp45-8 for details.

For a **taxi** contact Station Taxis (☎ 01883-338027).

Where to stay
Meads (☎ 01883-730115, 🖥 bandbmeads .co.uk; 1T/1D, both en suite; ✆; WI-FI), 23 Granville Rd, is a substantial 1920s Tudor-style house where B&B costs £47.50-50pp (sgl occ from £75); note that they don't accept credit cards and at weekends and bank holidays in the high season they require a minimum of two nights.

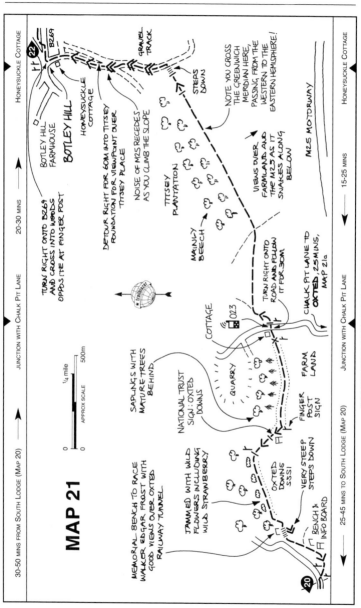

MAP 21

MEMORIAL BENCH TO RACE WALKER EDGAR FROST WITH GOOD VIEWS OVER OXTED RAILWAY TUNNEL

JAMMED WITH WILD FLOWERS INCLUDING WILD STRAWBERRY

OXTED DOWNS SSSI

VERY STEEP STEPS DOWN

BENCH & INFO BOARD

SAPLINGS WITH MATURE TREES BEHIND

NATIONAL TRUST SIGN: OXTED DOWNS

QUARRY

FINGER POST SIGN

FARM LAND

COTTAGE

023

TURN RIGHT ONTO ROAD AND FOLLOW IT FOR 30M

CHALK PIT LANE TO OXTED, 25 MINS, MAP 21a

TURN RIGHT ONTO B269 AND CROSS INTO WOODS OPPOS [SIC] AT FINGER POST

DETOUR RIGHT FOR 50M INTO TITSEY FOUNDATION FOR VIEWPOINT OVER TITSEY PLACE

NOISE OF M25 RECEDES AS YOU CLIMB THE SLOPE

TITSEY PLANTATION

MAINLY BEECH

BOTLEY HILL FARMHOUSE

BOTLEY HILL

HONEYSUCKLE COTTAGE

GRAVEL TRACK

B269

STEPS DOWN

NOTE YOU CROSS THE GREENWICH MERIDIAN HERE, PASSING FROM THE WESTERN TO THE EASTERN HEMISPHERE!

VIEWS OVER FARMLAND AND THE M25 AS IT SNAKES ALONG BELOW

M25 MOTORWAY

¼ mile

500m

APPROX SCALE

ROUTE GUIDE AND MAPS

Just along the way at No 58, *Arawa* (☎ 01883-714104, 🖳 arawa.co.uk; 2T private facilities, 1Qd en suite; 🐕; WI-FI; 🍴) is another good choice. Rates are from £37.50pp (sgl occ £40-50); add a fiver if it's a Saturday.

Where to eat and drink

There are cafés aplenty and you should find one that's to your taste.

Toast (☎ 01883-717617; Mon-Sat 8am-5pm, Sun 9am-2pm; WI-FI; 🍴), on Station Rd East, is all stripped floorboards and music played with the bass turned up to a thumping – though tolerable – level. Good coffee, perhaps the best in town, and a small but unusual menu (eg avocado, chilli and lime mash, feta and beet hummus on toast for £8.20) are just a couple of its attractions.

For something more traditional there's the bakery, *Coughlan's* (☎ 01883-716972; Mon-Sat 7.30am-5pm, Sun 10am-3pm), a regional chain that's been going since the thirties.

Café Papillon (☎ 01883-717031, 🖳 cafepapillon.co.uk; Mon-Sat 8am-5pm, Sun 9am-2pm) is a popular place to the west of the station with good breakfasts (eg egg Benedict £5.50), decent baguettes and sandwiches and hot meals for the rest of the day (all mains around a tenner).

Finally in this category, there are also outlets of the ubiquitous *Costa* (Mon-Fri 6am-6.30pm, Sat 7am-6.30pm, Sun 8am-5.30pm) and *Caffè Nero* (Mon-Fri 6.30am-6pm, Sat 7am-6pm, Sun 7.30am-5.30pm) chains as well as a branch of *Subway* (Mon-Thur 7am-7pm, Fri 7am-8pm, Sat 8am-7pm, Sun 10am-6pm) – all to the east of the station.

For lunches, all the above are good choices as is *Brisk Burgers* (☎ 01883-717071, 🖳 briskburgers.com; daily noon-9pm), a top-notch burger bar with friendly staff and three very good veggie-burger options (£7.25-8.25).

In the evening, for **pub grub** you can try the Wetherspoons-owned *Oxted Inn* (☎ 01883-723440, 🖳 jdwetherspoon.com; food daily 8am-11pm; WI-FI), by the station, but for a place with some character we

think you're better off heading to Old Oxted, to the far west of the station across the A25, where there are four pubs, three of which do food. The swishest of these is *Blue @ The George* (☎ 01883-713453, 🖳 thegeorgeoxted.co.uk; food Tue-Fri noon-2.30pm & 6-10pm, Sat noon-10pm, Sun noon-7pm; WI-FI; 🍴 bar area), the interior painted in muted but trendy tones; however, the food is refreshingly free of any pretension, with sandwiches for £6-7.50 and evening meals hearty and tasty, particularly their steaks (£19 for a 250g Argentinean rib-eye steak). Visit on Wednesday and the steaks are up to 40% off too – very good value.

A little further on, *The Old Bell* (☎ 01883-712181; food Mon-Sat noon-10pm, Sun noon-9.30pm; WI-FI; 🍴) serves food all day and packs them in for a roast on Sundays (£14.99 for slow-cooked lamb shoulder with all the trimmings).

Back towards the station, *The Crown* (☎ 01883-717853; food Mon-Sat noon-2.30pm & 7-9pm, Sun noon-6pm; WI-FI intermittent; 🍴) is a 17th-century dog-friendly place and the only independent pub left in Oxted, with a pleasant beer garden and big plates of pub grub; mains start at £11.95 for a duck & brie salad with plum sauce rising to £17.95 for a strip loin steak. Lunches are better value at £9.95 for a meal and a pint. Or, if you just want a pint, you could try *The Wheatsheaf*, the first place you come to when walking from the station.

For **international food** you're spoilt for choice with Oxted home to a couple of Chinese restaurants – the smart *Golden Palace* (☎ 01883-715323; Mon-Thur noon-2.30pm & 5-11pm, Fri & Sat to 11.30pm, Sun noon-3.30pm & 5-10.30pm; mains from £5), to the east of the station, and *China Garden* (☎ 01883-730754; Tue-Sat 5-11pm, Sun & Mon 5-10.30pm) to the west; a couple of subcontinental eateries, *Golden Bengal* (☎ 01883-717373, 🖳 bengaloxted.co.uk; daily noon-2pm & 6-11pm; mains from £5.75) and *Gurkha Kitchen* (☎ 01883-722621, 🖳 gurkhakitchen.co.uk; Mon 6-11pm, Tue-Thur noon-2.30pm & 6-11pm, Fri & Sat to 11.30pm, Sun 1-10pm; mains from £7.50 for the *pork bangoor*

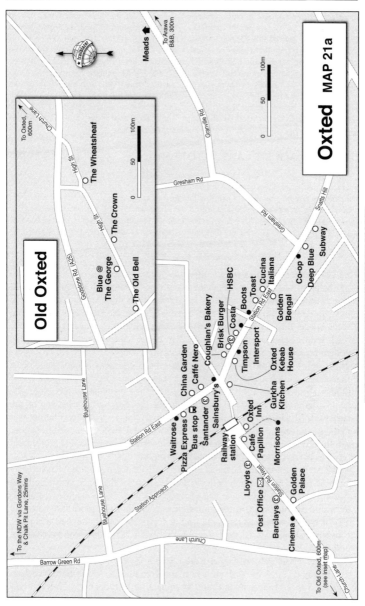

Oxted MAP 21a

Old Oxted

To Arawa B&B, 300m

Meads

Granville Rd

Gresham Rd

Snatts Hill

Gresham Rd

Subway

Co-op

Deep Blue

Cucina Italiana

Golden Bengal

HSBC

Toast

Boots

Station Rd East

Costa

Brisk Burger

Intersport

Coughlan's Bakery

Timpson

Oxted Kebab House

China Garden

Caffé Nero

Sainsbury's

Gurkha Kitchen

Waitrose

Pizza Express

Bus stop

Santander

Oxted Inn

Station Rd East

Railway station

Café Papillon

Morrisons

Station Rd West

Lloyds

Post Office

Golden Palace

Station Approach

Barclays

Bluehouse Lane

Church Lane

Barrow Green Rd

Cinema

To Old Oxted, 600m (see inset map)

To the NDW via Gordons Way & Chalk Pit Lane, 25mins

Church Lane

To Oxted, 600m

High St

High St

Godstone Rd (A25)

The Wheatsheaf

The Crown

Blue @ The George

The Old Bell

Church Lane

(pork cooked with onions, ginger, turmeric & coriander); and a couple of Italians, *Pizza Express* (☎ 01883-723142; Mon-Thur 11.30am-10pm, Fri & Sat to 11pm, Sun noon-10pm; pizzas from £8.95 for the cheapest version, a margherita) and *Cucina Italiana* (☎ 01883-713988, ☐ cucinaoxted .co.uk; Mon-Fri noon-2.30pm & 5.30-10.30pm, Sat noon-11pm, Sun noon-10pm), which does a great risotto starting at £11.25 for the vegetable option.

All of these also offer some sort of **takeaway** service, as does *Oxted Kebab House* (Mon-Thur 11.30am-11pm, Fri & Sat 11.30am-midnight, Sun 1-11pm), and the upmarket chippy, *Deep Blue* (☎ 01883-722666, ☐ deepbluerestaurants.com; Mon-Sat 11.30am-10pm, Sun noon-9pm), at the bottom of the hill on Station Rd East, which has its own restaurant (Mon-Sat 11.30am-9pm, Sun noon-8pm; cod fillet £8.50-10.60) attached.

OXTED (CHALK PIT LANE) TO OTFORD   [MAPS 21-26]

'*Sunrays, leaning on our wild southern hills and lighting*
wild cloud-mountains that drag the hill along,
Oft ends the day of your shifting brilliant laughter
Chill as a dull face frowning on a song.'
George Meredith (1828-1909), *Love in the Valley*. Meredith lived in Mickleham and was one of the founders of The Society of Sunday Tramps, a group of friends who would meet up to walk along the North Downs together. Their number included such literary luminaries as Robert Louis Stevenson, Rudyard Kipling, Henry James and JM Barrie.

This **11.6-mile/18.6km** (3¾hrs-5¼hrs) hike encompasses several milestones of importance to walkers. For this is the stage where you reach the **highest point of the North Downs Way** at Botley Hill (269.6m/885ft). On this stage you also **cross the county border** separating Surrey from its North Downs neighbour, Kent, a border that actually occurs, as far as we can tell, very near the milestone (which seems appropriate) on Map 23. No sooner have you achieved that than you then pass near the summit of Betsom's Hill – which, at 251m (823ft), is the **highest point in Kent**. And while such parochial concerns may perhaps be of little interest to you – and 251m is, in all honesty, not the most impressive of altitudes – maybe you'll be more impressed by the fact that on this stage you also pass from the Western Hemisphere to the Eastern, with a **crossing of the Greenwich Meridian** occurring very early on in today's walk (just before you join the track leading north through the Titsey Plantation; see Map 21, to be precise). Indeed, Greater London is only a few miles away at times and you should be able to catch glimpses of the skyline during the day.

Milestones aside, this is another stage that's haunted – but not ruined – by the whine of the M25, which greets you at the start of the stage and is on hand to wave you off just before the end of it too. The walking is also, to be honest, a little dull at times as you pass through a patchwork of arable farmland and fields of horses. After rejoining the trail at Chalk Pit Lane, you start this stage by walking alongside and then through the extensive beech woods of Titsey Plantation.

A short detour off the Way at Botley Hill is *Botley Hill Farmhouse* (Map 21; ☎ 01959-577154, ☐ botleyhill-farmhouse.co.uk; food Mon-Sat noon-3pm & 6-9pm, Sun 9-11am & noon-7pm; 🐾 on lead) a 16th-century pub-restaurant

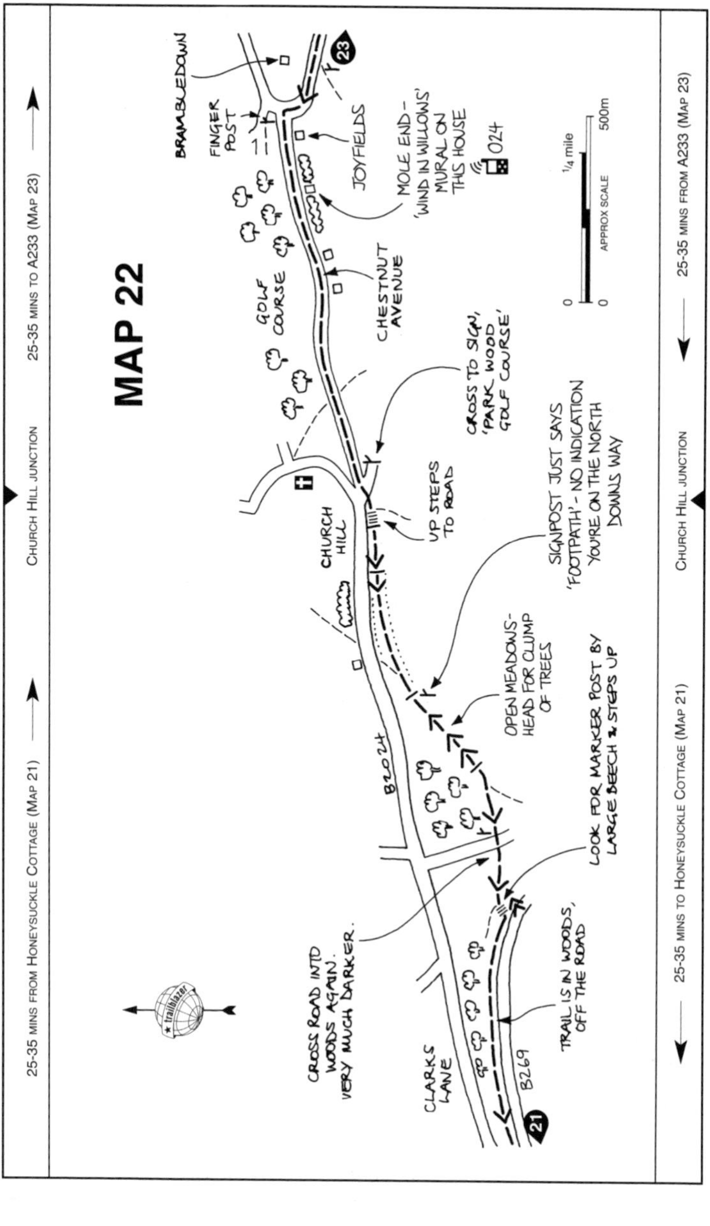
MAP 22
25-35 MINS TO A233 (MAP 23)
CHURCH HILL JUNCTION
25-35 MINS FROM HONEYSUCKLE COTTAGE (MAP 21)
25-35 MINS FROM A233 (MAP 23)
CHURCH HILL JUNCTION
25-35 MINS TO HONEYSUCKLE COTTAGE (MAP 21)
23
BRAMBLEDOWN
FINGER POST
JOYFIELDS
MOLE END – 'WIND IN WILLOWS' MURAL ON THIS HOUSE
024
GOLF COURSE
CHESTNUT AVENUE
CROSS TO SIGN, 'PARK WOOD GOLF COURSE'
CHURCH HILL
UP STEPS TO ROAD
SIGNPOST JUST SAYS 'FOOTPATH' - NO INDICATION YOU'RE ON THE NORTH DOWNS WAY
OPEN MEADOWS - HEAD FOR CLUMP OF TREES
B2024
LOOK FOR MARKER POST BY LARGE BEECH & STEPS UP
CROSS ROAD INTO WOODS AGAIN. VERY MUCH DARKER.
TRAIL IS IN WOODS, OFF THE ROAD
CLARKS LANE
B269
21
0
1/4 mile
0
APPROX SCALE
500m
trailblazer

which is said to sit at the highest point on the Downs. It's very popular especially on Sundays when there is a choice of roasts for £10.95 (nut roast) to £13.95 (beef) so booking is recommended. They also run *Sheep Shed Tea Shop* (Sun-Tue 10.30am-4pm, Wed-Sat 9.30am-4pm).

After crossing the B269 the trail continues through woods to emerge at Church Hill below **St Mary's Church** (see Map 22), a short way off the trail, a small 11th-century building with original Norman windows that may originally have been built by William the Conqueror's half brother.

From here you can saunter past the massive houses of Chestnut Avenue to the busy A233 and, should you wish it, a diversion to Westerham.

WESTERHAM   [MAP 23a, p120]
Westerham lies on the A25 but it remains an attractive town with historic connections (see box below).

There are banks with **ATMs** on Market Square. Services include a **Co-op** (daily 7am-10pm) and a **Nisa** convenience store (Mon-Fri 6am-9pm, Sat 7am-9pm, Sun 7am-8pm), a newsagent with a **post office** (Mon-Fri 9am-1pm & 1.30-5.30pm, Sat 9am-12.30pm) and a **pharmacy** (Mon-Fri 9am-6pm, Sat 9am-1pm).

Westerham Cyclery (Tue-Sat 9am-5pm, Sun 8.30am-1pm) advertises itself as a **tourist information point** which, in reality, is just a rack of brochures.

Southdown's 594/595 **bus services** (to Oxted) and their No 236 (Oxted to East Grinstead) call here by the King's Arms. London General's No 246 and Go Bus's No 401 (to Sevenoaks) stop at The Green. See pp45-8 for details.

Where to stay
For **accommodation**, *Kings Arms Hotel* (☎ 01959-562990, or ☎ 0845-608 6040, 🖳 old englishinns.co.uk; 3S/2T/8D/1Tr/3Qd, all en suite; ✆; WI-FI; 🐾), on Market Sq, could do with a lick of paint in some of the rooms but if you're lucky it can be good value with rates depending on demand:

❏ **Westerham's historic connections**
The childhood home of General James Wolfe, who captured Quebec in the French Indian war in 1759 only to die a few days later of gunshot wounds, **Quebec House** (for further information call Chartwell) is open to visitors (late Feb-end Oct Wed-Sun & Bank Holiday Mondays noon-5pm, Nov-Dec weekends only 1-4pm; £5.60, £6.20 inc Gift Aid, NT members free). The house contains Georgian memorabilia as well as a Battle of Quebec exhibition and is run by the National Trust.

Chartwell (☎ 01732-868381; late Feb-end Oct house daily 11am-5pm; garden daily 10am-5pm, winter to 4pm; house & garden/garden & studio £14.40/7.20, £16/8 inc Gift Aid, NT members free), Sir Winston Churchill's former home, is also run by the National Trust and is one of its most popular properties. Winston Churchill lived here from 1924 till the end of his life and the house is still much as he left it. Parts of the garden were created by him and his wife. Timed tickets for the house are issued on arrival (though afternoon tickets can be pre-booked on the website) so it could be a while before you get in. A third NT property, **Emmetts Garden** (for further information call Chartwell; late Feb-end Oct daily 10am-5pm, winter to 4pm; spring £10.30, £11.50 inc Gift Aid, rest of year £8.50, £9.50 inc Gift Aid, NT members free), an old Edwardian estate with panoramic views over the Weald, can be reached via a path from Chartwell.

Chartwell is about three miles south of the trail; London General's **bus** No 246 (Bromley to Westerham) calls here; see also pp45-8.

For more information on both properties visit 🖳 nationaltrust.org.

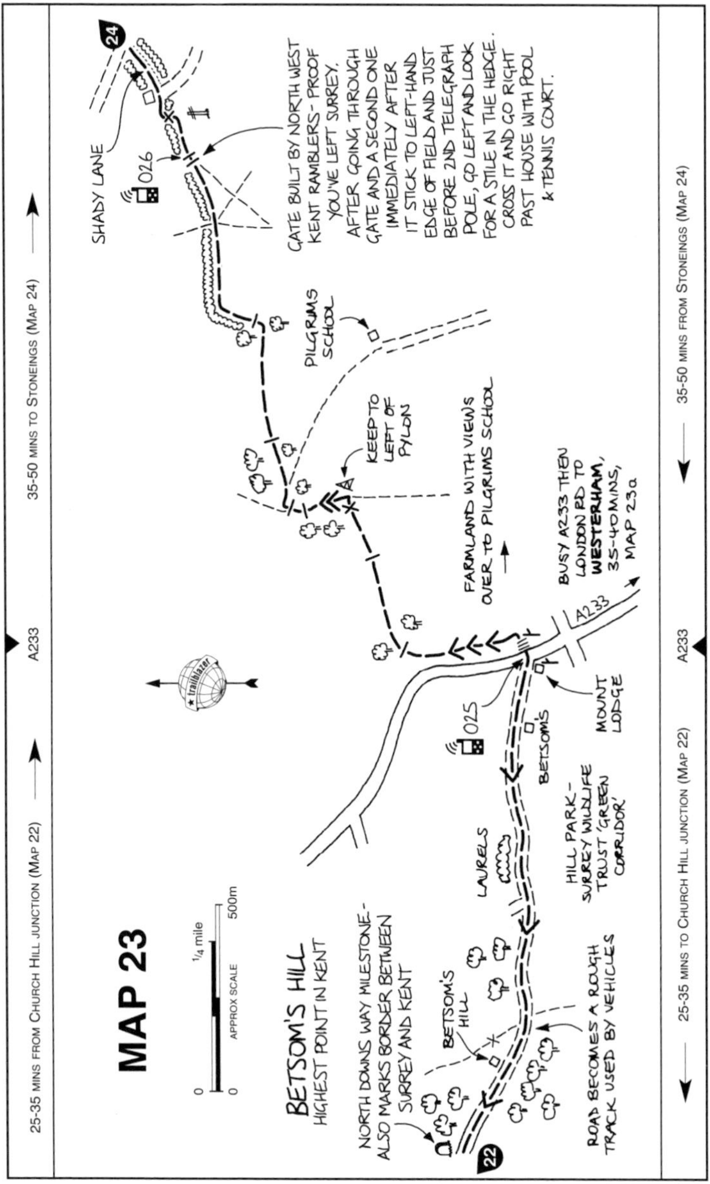

MAP 23

1/4 mile

0   500m
APPROX SCALE

BETSOM'S HILL
HIGHEST POINT IN KENT

NORTH DOWNS WAY MILESTONE –
ALSO MARKS BORDER BETWEEN
SURREY AND KENT

ROAD BECOMES A ROUGH
TRACK USED BY VEHICLES

BETSOM'S
HILL

LAURELS

HILL PARK –
SURREY WILDLIFE
TRUST ('GREEN'
CORRIDOR)

MOUNT
LODGE

BETSOM'S

025

BUSY A233 THEN
LONDON RD TO
WESTERHAM,
35-40 MINS,
MAP 23a

FARMLANDS WITH VIEWS
OVER TO PILGRIMS SCHOOL

KEEP TO
LEFT OF
PYLON

PILGRIMS
SCHOOL

SHABY LANE

026

GATE BUILT BY NORTH WEST
KENT RAMBLERS – PROOF
YOU'VE LEFT SURREY.
AFTER GOING THROUGH
GATE AND A SECOND ONE
IMMEDIATELY AFTER
IT STICK TO LEFT-HAND
EDGE OF FIELD AND JUST
BEFORE 2ND TELEGRAPH
POLE, GO LEFT AND LOOK
FOR A STILE IN THE HEDGE.
CROSS IT AND GO RIGHT
PAST HOUSE WITH POOL
& TENNIS COURT.

24

22

A233

25-35 MINS FROM CHURCH HILL JUNCTION (MAP 22) — A233 — 35-50 MINS TO STONEINGS (MAP 24)

25-35 MINS TO CHURCH HILL JUNCTION (MAP 22) — A233 — 35-50 MINS FROM STONEINGS (MAP 24)

ROUTE GUIDE AND MAPS

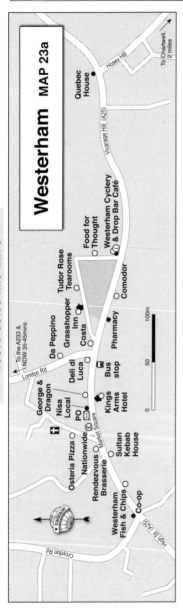

Westerham MAP 23a

from £33.50pp, though this can rise to £75pp (sgl £40-67.50, sgl occ room rate).

The friendly **Grasshopper Inn** (☎ 01959-563136, ☐ faucetinn.com/grasshopperinn; 9D, all en suite; ✆; WI-FI most rooms) charges from £40pp for a standard room and up to £87.50pp for the Bridal Suite, though there is no discount for single occupancy for any room.

Where to eat and drink
You won't go hungry or thirsty in Westerham. Nor will you suffer from coffee withdrawal, with several places dedicated to the bean with the caffeine. In addition to a branch of the **Costa** chain (Mon-Fri 7am-6pm, Sat 8am-6pm, Sun 9am-6pm) there are several local and more 'individual' places including: the popular **Deli Di Luca** (Mon-Fri 8am-5pm, Sat & Sun from 8.30am), which also serves a very good line in breakfasts including toasted bagel with salmon & cream cheese (£3.95); **Tudor Rose Tearooms** (Mon 9am-4pm, Tue-Fri 8am-4.30pm, Sat to 5pm, Sun 9am-5pm), with some great specials including a fishfinger sandwich (£6.10); the jolly **Food for Thought** (daily 9am-5pm), under new ownership but still great for coffee and cakes (from £3.25 for a Victoria sponge); and Westerham Cyclery which has its own café, the **Drop Bar** (Tue-Sat 9am-5pm, Sun 8.30am-1pm), boasting a decent range of ciabattas (from £2.90 for the basic cheese and tomato).

Moving onto evening dining there are a few Italian places, our favourite being **Osteria Pizzeria** (Tue-Sun noon-3pm & 6-11pm), on the western side of The Square; it is certainly the best choice for pizzas (from £8.50).

Rivals include **Da Peppino** (☎ 01959-564924, ☐ dapeppinorestaurant.com; Mon-Sat noon-10pm, Sun noon-9pm), 6 London Rd, with mains from £11.95 for the homemade lasagne.

For pub food we make straight for **The Grasshopper Inn** (see Where to stay; food Mon-Thur 7-11am, noon-3pm & 6-9pm, Fri 7-11am, noon-4pm & 6-10pm, Sat 7-11am & noon-10pm, Sun 8-11am & noon-8pm; WI-FI; 🐾 bar area) is an old coaching inn with a restaurant serving some lovely twists on pub favourites including hay-smoked lamb rump (£15.50); they also claim to offer the best breakfasts in town too including a classic eggs Benedict (£8).

Just up a little way, *The George & Dragon* (☎ 01959-563071; food daily noon-8pm; WI-FI; 🐾) serves up mains from £11.95 including a fish stew (£12.75); while directly opposite the *Kings Arms Hotel* (see Where to stay; food daily noon-10pm) has a similarly tempting menu with a sea bass & scallop risotto (£12.79).

Other options include *Comodor* (☎ 01959-565600; daily noon-11pm), also on The Square, with a Spanish-inspired menu designed, we think, to appeal to pretty much everybody, including steaks from £7.95 and tapas items for about £3.50.

Perhaps the smartest place to eat in town, however, is *Rendezvous Brasserie* (☎ 01959-561408, 🖳 rendezvous-brasserie.co.uk; May-Sep Mon-Thur 9am-9.30pm, Fri & Sat 8.30am-9.30pm, Sun 8.30am-5pm, rest of year Mon-Fri from 10am, Sat from 9am & Sun 9am-4pm), serving imaginative fare from southern France including a fish parmentier (cod, haddock, prawns & salmon in a creamy leek, chive & mushroom sauce; £14).

For simpler meals, *Westerham Fish & Chips and Chinese Food To Take Away* (☎ 01959-562462; Tue-Sat 11.45am-2pm, daily 5-10pm) leaves you in no doubt what it does and *Sultan Kebab House* (☎ 01959-565589; daily 11.30am-11.30pm) is next door.

If Westerham's too far out of your way then a few fields later you come to **Stoneings Lane** (see Map 24), at the end of which is *Tally Ho* (☎ 01959-533602; bar Tue-Sun noon-11pm, food Tue-Sun noon-2.30pm; WI-FI; 🐾), a walker-friendly pub attracting locals for a lunchtime pint; note that the pub is closed on Mondays. Tasty baguettes range from £4.95 to £6.95, the latter for a Lincoln sausage and fried onion number.

Thirty minutes further along is **Chevening Lane** (see Map 25) and the turn-off to Knockholt Pound.

KNOCKHOLT POUND
[off MAP 25, p123]
The Three Horseshoes (☎ 01959-532102; food Mon-Sat noon-9pm, Sun to 6pm; WI-FI; 🐾 bar area) is about 15 minutes down Chevening Lane; it's a fine old place though with a surprisingly modern restaurant area. For food, the best place we found was up the road at *The Harrow Inn* (☎ 01959-928734, 🖳 harrowinn.net; food Wed-Sat noon-2.30pm & 6-8/9pm, Sun noon-2.30pm only; WI-FI; 🐾 on lead) serving a range of burgers from £9.95 or for something truly warming try the lamb shank for £15.95. Note food is not served here on Monday or Tuesday.

Go Bus's No 431 **bus service** (see pp45-8 for details) calls here en route between Sevenoaks and Orpington; it also calls at Knockholt station which is a stop on South Eastern Railway's Charing Cross/Cannon Street to Sevenoaks **rail** service (see box pp42-3).

The North Downs Way skirts the mixed woodland of the grounds of Chevening House, the Foreign Secretary's country house, and descends quickly with views over to the M25/M26 interchange. **Chevening** is not on the trail, the house isn't open to the public and the church is often locked so there's not much reason to go there. But there is accommodation about 25 minutes away at the 18th-century *Crossways House* (☎ 01732-456334, 🖳 lelaweavers@gmail.com; 3D one private bathroom, two en suite; 🛏; WI-FI) with room rates from £30pp (sgl occ from £60).

Crossing over the M25 after Morants Court Farm, you now head towards Dunton Green.

DUNTON GREEN   **[MAP 26, p125]**
Well it probably won't be the most memorable detour of your trip but Dunton Green has a few facilities (off Map 26) including a railway station about half a mile from the path on the London Rd.

However, on the Way is *The Rose & Crown* (Map 26; ☎ 01732-462343, 🖥 vintageinn.co.uk; food Mon-Sat noon-10pm, Sun to 9.30pm; WI-FI; 🐾), where a two-course fixed price lunch is £11.95, or it's £14.95 for three courses.

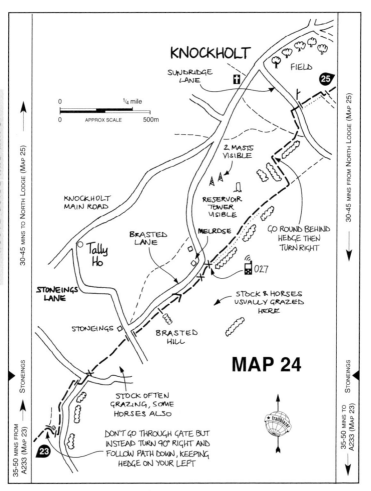

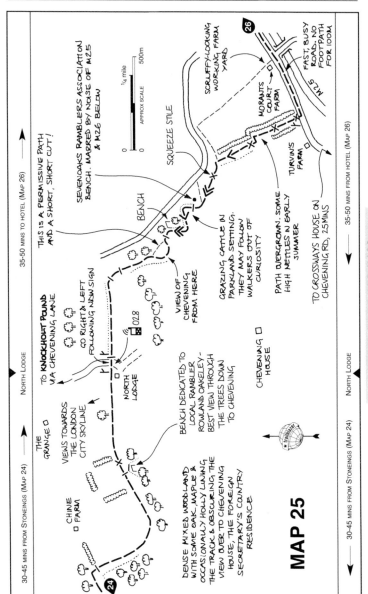

30-45 MINS FROM STONEINGS (Map 24) →

← NORTH LODGE

35-50 MINS TO HOTEL (MAP 26) →

THIS IS A PERMISSIVE PATH AND A SHORT, SHORT CUT!

SEVENOAKS RAMBLERS ASSOCIATION BENCH. MARRED BY NOISE OF M25 & M26 BELOW

¼ mile

500m

APPROX SCALE

SQUEEZE STILE

26

SCRUFFY-LOOKING WORKING FARM YARD

FAST, BUSY ROAD. NO FOOTPATH FOR 100M

M25

MORANTS COURT FARM

TURVINS FARM

BENCH

GRAZING CATTLE IN PARKLAND SETTING. THEY MAY FOLLOW WALKERS OUT OF CURIOSITY

PATH OVERGROWN. SOME HIGH NETTLES IN EARLY SUMMER

THE GRANGE

VIEWS TOWARDS THE LONDON CITY SKYLINE

TO KNOCKHOLT POUND VIA CHEVENING LANE

GO RIGHT & LEFT FOLLOWING NEW SIGN

VIEW OF CHEVENING FROM HERE

TO CROSSWAYS HOUSE ON CHEVENING RD, 25 MINS

← NORTH LODGE

35-50 MINS FROM HOTEL (MAP 26) →

NORTH LODGE

02.8

CHEVENING HOUSE

BENCH DEDICATED TO LOCAL RAMBLER ROWLAND OAKELEY - BEST VIEW THROUGH THE TREES DOWN TO CHEVENING

CHINE FARM

DENSE MIXED WOODLAND WITH SOME OAK, MAPLE & OCCASIONALLY HOLLY LINING THE TRACK & OBSCURING THE VIEW OVER TO CHEVENING HOUSE, THE FOREIGN SECRETARY'S COUNTRY RESIDENCE

MAP 25

24

← 30-45 MINS FROM STONEINGS (Map 24)

trailblazer

(**Dunton Green** *cont'd*) For accommodation consider Best Western's ***Donnington Manor Hotel*** (Map 26; ☎ 01732-462681, 💻 donningtonmanorhotel .co.uk; 63D or T, all en suite; WI-FI), also right on the path, charging at least £50pp (sgl occ rates on request) inc breakfast.

Near the railway station there's a clutch of shops including a **newsagent** (Mon-Fri 6.30am-8pm, Sat 7am-8pm, Sun 8am-8pm); a café, ***Bojangles*** (Mon-Fri 8am-5pm, Sat from 8.30am, Sun 10am-4pm); a Chinese, ***Hei's*** (☎ 01732-462335; Tue-Sat noon-2pm, Mon-Thur 5-10pm, Fri & Sat to 10.30pm); ***Taj Tandoori*** (☎ 01732-462277; daily noon-2.30pm & 6-11pm) optimistically rises above the ordinariness of the area with curries starting at £5.75;

and a pub, ***The Dukes Head*** (☎ 01732-456123, 💻 dukesheadduntongreen.co.uk; food Mon-Thur noon-3pm, Fri & Sat noon-4pm; WI-FI; 🐾), serving an all-day full English breakfasts for £6.50 or their 'mega breakfast' (with two eggs and rashers) for £8.50; all mains are good value with nothing over £8.95.

There's also a 24-hour Tesco **supermarket**, a quarter of a mile due south at the roundabout.

Train-wise (see box pp42-3) Dunton Green is a stop on South Eastern Railway's Charing Cross/Cannon Street to Sevenoaks service.

Both Arriva's **bus** service No 402 and Go Bus's No 431 stop by The Dukes Head on their way to Sevenoaks; see pp45-8.

Back on the route, you say a temporary ta-ta to the tarmac for the time being by **Donnington Manor Hotel** (see above). From here it is a pleasant walk through fields, then along a hard track through a **lavender nursery** before rejoining the pavement to cross over the **River Darent** and arrive at Otford's picturesque duck pond.

OTFORD   [MAP 26a, p126]
Called Otta's Ford by the Anglo-Saxons, Otford is a lovely village with the **ruins of** an archbishop's palace, which went into decay following its surrender to Henry VIII, and the world's largest scale **model of the solar system** (see box below).

Services
The **pharmacy** (☎ 01959-522072; Mon-Fri 8.35am-6.30pm, Sat 9am-1pm & 2.15-5pm) is by the roundabout.

There is an **ATM** outside the **One Stop** (daily 6am-11pm) convenience store and the **post office** (Mon-Fri 9am-5.30pm,

Sat 9am-2.30pm) is down the road from that. The **Heritage Centre** (☎ 01959-524808; Mon-Fri 9am-noon, Sat & Sun 2.30-4.30pm) has local history displays.

Transport
Otford is a stop on South Eastern Railway's services to London Victoria and also Thameslink Railway's line to West Hampstead; see box pp42-3.

Go bus No 421 (Sevenoaks to Swanley) calls here; there's also Centaur Coaches' No 789/790 commuter service to/from London. See pp45-8 for details.

❏ **Otford's Solar System Model**
As part of Otford Parish Council's Millennium celebrations the world's largest scale model of the solar system was built in Otford – 💻 solarsystem.otford.info. Starting at the recreation ground, pillars mark the position of the planets at midnight on 1 January 2000. Pick up a leaflet map from the Heritage Centre (see above) and 'walk' the solar system if you have time, bearing in mind that every millimetre you walk represents 4595.7km in space!

The Sun Marker Pillar is the closest to the path – see Otford town plan on p126.

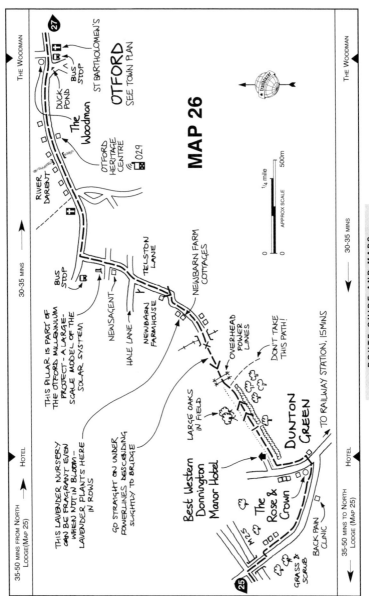

THE WOODMAN

35-50 MINS FROM NORTH
LODGE(MAP 25)

HOTEL

THE WOODMAN

30-35 MINS

30-35 MINS

35-50 MINS TO NORTH
LODGE (MAP 25)

HOTEL

MAP 26

1/4 mile

500m

0

0

APPROX SCALE

27

OTFORD
SEE TOWN PLAN

ST BARTHOLOMEW'S

BUS
STOP

DUCK
POND

The
Woodman

OTFORD HERITAGE
CENTRE

029

RIVER
DARENT

BUS
STOP

NEWSAGENT

HALE LANE

NEWBARN
FARMHOUSE

TELSTON
LANE

NEWBARN FARM
COTTAGES

THIS PILLAR IS PART OF
THE OTFORD MILLENNIUM
PROJECT – A LARGE-
SCALE MODEL OF THE
SOLAR SYSTEM

OVERHEAD
POWER
LINES

DON'T TAKE
THIS PATH!

TO RAILWAY STATION, 15MINS

THIS LAVENDER NURSERY
CAN BE FRAGRANT EVEN
WHEN NOT IN BLOOM –
LAVENDER PLANTS HERE
IN ROWS

GO STRAIGHT ON UNDER
POWERLINES DESCENDING
SLIGHTLY TO BRIDGE

LARGE OAKS
IN FIELD

DUNTON
GREEN

Best Western
Donnington
Manor Hotel

The
Rose &
Crown

BACK PAIN
CLINIC

GRASS &
SCRUB

M25

25

ROUTE GUIDE AND MAPS

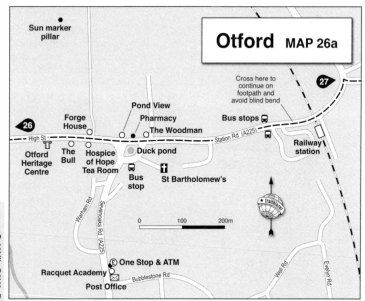

Where to stay and eat

The nearest place to stay is actually in Kemsing, see Up the Downs B&B opposite, though it's only a 10-minute walk from Otford railway station.

The Bull (☎ 01959-523198; food Mon-Sat noon-10pm, Sun to 9pm; WI-FI; 🐾 bar area) serves food all day with lunch options from £4.99 and evening mains from £8.49 (for a Caesar salad) and including slow-cooked pork belly (£12.59). The pub's fireplace is reputedly 16th century and said to have come from the ruined archbishop's palace.

The Woodman (☎ 01959-522195; food Tue-Sun noon-3pm; WI-FI; 🐾) does bar food including a good line in baguettes (eg beef baguette with roast potatoes, £7.50). At

the upmarket end there is *Forge House* (☎ 01959-522463, 🖥 the forgehouse restaurant.co.uk; Tue-Sat noon-2.30pm & 6-10pm, Sun noon-4pm) with mains from £13.95 including sea bass fillets with garlic, chilli & mash potato (£16.95).

Pond View Café (Mon-Sat 9am-4.30pm, from 10am on Sun) has an enviable location by the roundabout, but we prefer the more peaceful *Hospice of Hope Tea Room* (Mon-Sat 10am-5pm) at the rear of the charity shop. A pot of tea and a toasted tea cake, slathered with butter, is £3.10 while sandwiches start at £2.95. Dogs are allowed in the outdoor seating area.

For a takeaway sandwich *Racquet Academy* (Mon-Fri 8.30am-5pm, Sat 9.30am-4.30pm) is near the post office.

❏ Where to stay: the details

In the descriptions of accommodation in this book: 🛏 means at least one room has a bath; Ⓛ means a packed lunch can be prepared if arranged in advance; 🐾 signifies that dogs are welcome in at least one room but also subject to prior arrangement, an additional charge may also be payable; WI-FI means wi-fi is available. See also p66.

OTFORD TO ROCHESTER   [MAPS 27-36a]

This **17.8-mile/28.6km stage (5hrs 10mins to 6¾hrs)** takes you deeper into the heart of Kent and, as it does so, the very nature of the North Downs Way changes. While this section of the trail still offers far-reaching views aplenty and large stretches of woodland, the highways are noticeably fewer now (though on this stage you do have to cross over the M20 as well as overcome the worst part of the entire trail, a crossing of the River Medway on a path adjacent to the roaring M2). You also start to encounter ancient burial sites and other Neolithic constructions that are very much a feature of both this and the next stage. But perhaps most importantly of all, the path also starts to feel like a proper pilgrimage trail – which was, after all, if not the reason for its foundation (the Neolithic sites prove that ancient man walked these trails way before Christians did) it was at least this trail's main role for many centuries. I'm not quite sure what it is about the path that gives it this new character, but we felt it initially after passing Kemsing, on the lovely cow-parsley-lined chalk path that traces the course of the foot of the Downs as it makes its arrow-straight way to Wrotham.

But first of all you have to get to Kemsing, or at least the turn-off to it; this is reached by climbing out of Otford to meadow and woodland, which is an important chalk grassland habitat, and across pleasant farmland, much of it now given over to horse paddocks.

KEMSING   [MAP 27, p128]

There is only one **accommodation** option in pretty, historical Kemsing.

Up The Downs B&B (☎ 07759 268115, ☎ 01959-526869, 🖳 upthedowns .com; 1D en suite, 1T private bathroom; ☛; WI-FI; Mar-end Oct) sits at the end of a quiet cul-de-sac about halfway between the centre of Kemsing and Otford Station (so many guests prefer to head to Otford for their dinner as there's more choice there). Rates are £34.50-39.50pp (sgl occ from £55).

In Kemsing itself there is food at *The Bell* (☎ 01732-761550, 🖳 thebellkemsing .com; food Mon-Sat noon-3pm & 6-9pm,

Sun noon-5pm; WI-FI; 🐾) where a decent roast costs £11.95. Round the corner, *Kemsing Italian Deli* (☎ 01732-761581; Tue-Sat 8.30am-5pm, Sun 9am-3pm) is a new **deli** and coffee shop with panini from £5.50 and superior coffee.

The **railway station** is about 20 minutes to the south of the village; South Eastern Railway has services (see box pp42-3) between London Victoria and Ashford International with onward connections from there to Folkestone and Dover. Arriva's **bus** No 452 serves Sevenoaks and stops by St Mary's Church; see pp45-8.

Back on the trail, and having survived any equine encounters, you then find yourself dropping steeply to land on the chalk path leading to Wrotham.

(cont'd on p130)

❑ **Important note – walking times**
Unless otherwise specified, **all times in this book refer only to the time spent walking**. You will need to add 20-30% to allow for rests, photography, checking the map, drinking water etc. When planning the day's hike count on 5-7 hours' actual walking.

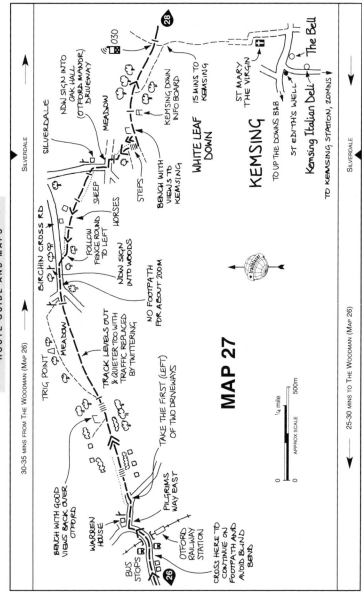

30-35 MINS FROM THE WOODMAN (MAP 26)

SILVERDALE

25-30 MINS TO THE WOODMAN (MAP 26)

SILVERDALE

MAP 27

¼ mile

500m

APPROX SCALE

0

0

Map labels:

28

030

NEW SIGN INTO OAK HALL (OTFORD MANOR DRIVEWAY)

SILVERDALE

MEADOW

KEMSING DOWN INFO BOARD

15 MINS TO KEMSING

ST MARY THE VIRGIN

KEMSING

TO UP THE DOWNS B&B

ST EDITH'S WELL

Kemsing Italian Deli   The Bell

TO KEMSING STATION, 20 MINS

WHITE LEAF DOWN

STEPS

BENCH WITH VIEWS TO KEMSING

SHEEP

HORSES

FOLLOW FENCE ROUND TO LEFT

NEW SIGN INTO WOODS

NO FOOTPATH FOR ABOUT 200M

BIRCHIN CROSS RD

TRIG POINT

MEADOW

TRACK LEVELS OUT & QUIETER TOO WITH TRAFFIC REPLACED BY TWITTERING

BENCH WITH GOOD VIEWS BACK OVER OTFORD

WARREN HOUSE

BUS STOPS

26

OTFORD RAILWAY STATION

PILGRIMS WAY EAST

TAKE THE FIRST (LEFT) OF TWO DRIVEWAYS

CROSS HERE TO CONTINUE ON FOOTPATH AND AVOID BLIND BENDS

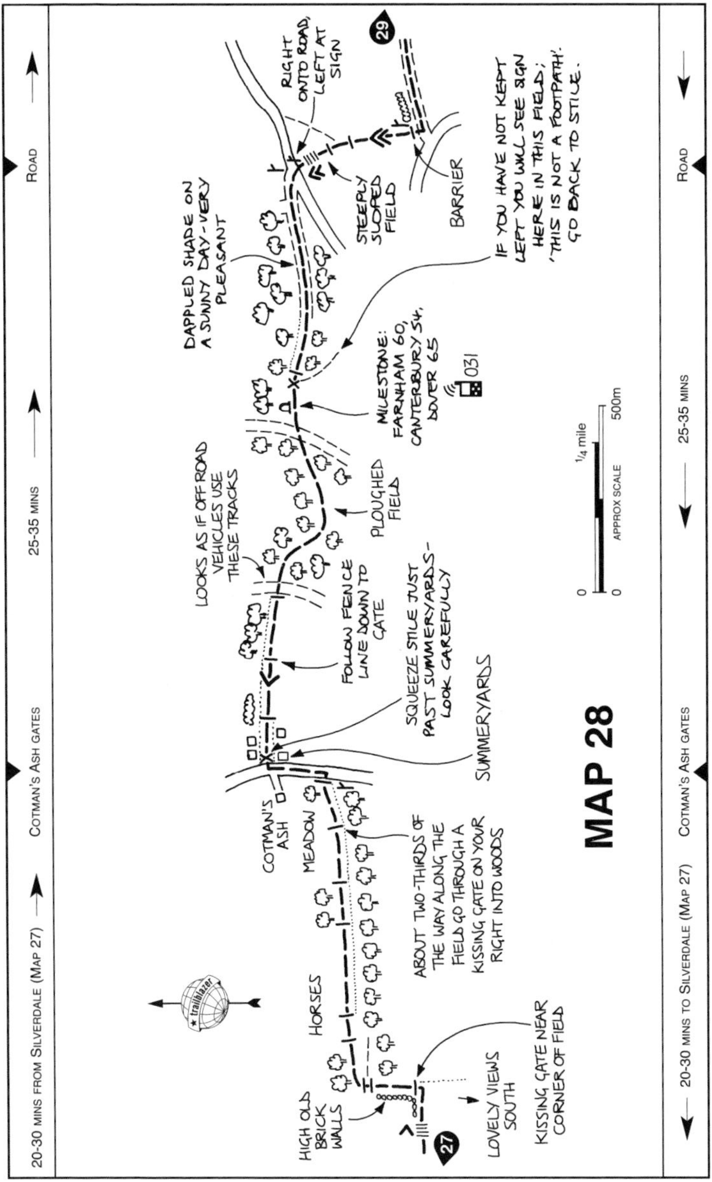

MAP 28

RIGHT ONTO ROAD, LEFT AT SIGN

DAPPLED SHADE ON A SUNNY DAY - VERY PLEASANT

STEEPLY SLOPED FIELD

BARRIER

IF YOU HAVE NOT KEPT LEFT YOU WILL SEE SIGN HERE IN THIS FIELD: 'THIS IS NOT A FOOTPATH'. GO BACK TO STILE.

MILESTONE: FARNHAM 60, CANTERBURY 54, DOVER 65

📷 031

LOOKS AS IF OFF ROAD VEHICLES USE THESE TRACKS

PLOUGHED FIELD

FOLLOW FENCE LINE DOWN TO GATE

SQUEEZE STILE JUST PAST SUMMER/YARDS - LOOK CAREFULLY

SUMMER/YARDS

COTMAN'S ASH

MEADOW

ABOUT TWO-THIRDS OF THE WAY ALONG THE FIELD GO THROUGH A KISSING GATE ON YOUR RIGHT INTO WOODS

HIGH OLD BRICK WALLS

HORSES

LOVELY VIEWS SOUTH

KISSING GATE NEAR CORNER OF FIELD

27

29

APPROX SCALE

0 — ¼ mile

0 — 500m

| 20-30 MINS FROM SILVERDALE (MAP 27) → | COTMAN'S ASH GATES | 25-35 MINS | ROAD ► |

← 20-30 MINS TO SILVERDALE (MAP 27) | COTMAN'S ASH GATES | 25-35 MINS | ROAD ►

WROTHAM [MAP 29]

Pronounced 'Root ham' the village lies relatively unspoilt below the M20/A20 interchange and above the M26. The remains of an archbishop's palace lies east of the squat old church. There is accommodation here and a few services. **Harden's Mini Market** (Mon-Sat 7am-8pm, Sun 8am-8pm) has an **ATM** (£1.85 fee) and sells all the lunch supplies you'd need. If you need more choice a bus ride away is Borough Green (see below), home of the nearest railway station.

Arriva's No 308 **bus service** (Gravesend to Sevenoaks) and the evening No 306 (to Bluewater, in case you have a need for some retail therapy) call opposite the Bull Hotel as does Autocar Bus No 222 (to Tonbridge); see pp45-8.

The nearest **railway station** to Wrotham is at Borough Green (the station is called Borough Green & Wrotham); see below.

Accommodation is thin on the ground in Wrotham but dedicated **campers** (with their own tents) will find pitches at *Gate House Wood Touring Park* (off Map 30; ☎ 01732-843062, 🖳 gatehousewoodtouring park.com; WI-FI; 🐾; Mar-end Oct) from £10/15 for a one-/two-man tent with use of showers, laundry facilities and a brick-built BBQ. It's really in Wrotham Heath, though

it's about a 40-minute walk from the trail. The owners are friendly.

Back in Wrotham itself, rooms are available at *The Bull Hotel* (☎ 01732-789800, 🖳 thebullhotel.com; 2T/9D, all en suite; 🛏; WI-FI; 🐾), an upmarket choice with attention to detail and décor appropriate to the historic inn. B&B rates (£39.50-79.50pp, sgl £69-139, sgl occ rates on request) vary according to the day of the week on which you wish to stay. In addition to their 'regular' **restaurant** meals (Tue-Fri noon-2.30pm & 6-9pm, Sat noon-9pm, Sun noon-8pm) they also have a US-inspired 'Smokehouse' menu (same times as above plus Mon evening) with burgers (from £12.95) and steaks (280g sirloin £27.50) featuring heavily.

Near to each other, *George & Dragon* (☎ 01732-884298, 🖳 georgeanddragon .wrotham.net; WI-FI; 🐾 bar area only) serves standard pub grub (Sun, Mon-Wed noon-3pm), though on Thursday and Friday this changes to Thai (noon-2pm & 6-9pm); note food is not served on Saturdays. *The Rose & Crown* (☎ 01732-885839, 🖳 roseandcrownwrotham.co.uk; WI-FI; 🐾 on lead) serves food (Tue-Sat noon-2.30pm & 6-9pm, Sun noon-5pm), with mains starting at £10.50 for their vegetarian beanburger.

BOROUGH GREEN [off MAP 29]

Borough Green hosts lots more facilities than its neighbour including a **Co-op supermarket** (Mon-Sat 6am-10pm, Sun 8am-10pm) next to the station with an **ATM** outside, a **pharmacy** (Mon-Fri 8.30am-7pm, Sat to 5.30pm) and plenty more places to eat too.

Borough Green & Wrotham is a stop on South Eastern Railway's **rail services**

(see box pp42-3) between London Victoria and Canterbury/Ashford International. All the **buses** serving Wrotham also call in at Borough Green; see pp45-8 for details.

A **taxi** to/from Wrotham costs £4-5 and saves an unremarkable 20-minute walk; Borough Green Taxis (☎ 01732-882020/886488) have an office at the station.

Leaving Wrotham the first obstacle to overcome is the noisy M20, though mercifully you're largely unaware it's there until you come upon it and it disappears from both your view and your conscience fairly shortly afterwards too, though its roar reminds you of its presence until – almost – the entrance to **Trosley Country Park** (Map 31). Here you'll find the welcome *Bluebell Café* (☎ 01732-820315; end Mar-end Oct Mon-Fri 9.30am-around 4pm, Sat & Sun to 5pm; rest of year Mon-Fri to 3pm, Sat & Sun to 4pm; WI-FI; 🐾 sheltered area outside only) with plenty of outside seating. Arriva's **bus** No 308 (see pp45-8)

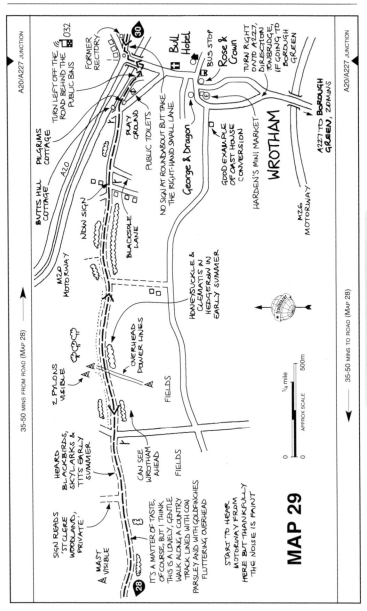

A20/A227 JUNCTION

35–50 MINS FROM ROAD (MAP 28)

FORMER RECTORY

TURN LEFT OFF THE ROAD BEHIND THE PUBLIC BINS

032

30

Bull Hotel

BUS STOP

Rose & Crown

TURN RIGHT ONTO A227, DIRECTION TONBRIDGE, (IF GOING TO BOROUGH GREEN

BUTTS HILL COTTAGE

PILGRIMS COTTAGE

A20

PLAY GROUND

PUBLIC TOILETS

NO SIGN AT ROUNDABOUT BUT TAKE THE RIGHT-HAND SMALL LANE

George & Dragon

GOOD EXAMPLE OF OAST HOUSE CONVERSION

WROTHAM

A227 TO BOROUGH GREEN, 2.0 MILES

M20 MOTORWAY

NEW SIGN

BLACKSOLE LANE

HARDEN'S MINI MARKET

M26 MOTORWAY

HONEYSUCKLE & CLEMATIS IN HEDGEROW IN EARLY SUMMER

2 PYLONS VISIBLE

OVERHEAD POWER LINES

FIELDS

HEARD BLACKBIRDS, SKYLARKS & TITS EARLY SUMMER

CAN SEE WROTHAM AHEAD

FIELDS

SIGN READS 'ST CLERE WOODLAND, PRIVATE'.

MAST VISIBLE

28

IT'S A MATTER OF TASTE, OF COURSE, BUT I THINK THIS IS A LOVELY, GENTLE WALK ALONG A COUNTRY TRACK LINED WITH COW PARSLEY AND WITH GOLDFINCHES FLUTTERING OVERHEAD

START TO HEAR MOTORWAY FROM HERE BUT THANKFULLY THE NOISE IS FAINT

MAP 29

¼ mile

APPROX SCALE

500m

0

0

35–50 MINS TO ROAD (MAP 28)

stops at Trosley Country Park. Progress through the country park is straightforward, the firm track allowing for fast walking, before the trail eventually descends sharply to meet the Pilgrims' Way. At this point a short detour to **Coldrum Barrow** (off Map 31) is in order. Owned and managed by the National Trust, this Neolithic site is a largely intact long barrow burial site or tomb. The structure dates from around 3000 years ago when agriculture was developing in Europe, stone tools were used and metal ones had yet to be invented. In the 1900s the bones of 22 people were excavated. Many visitors hang

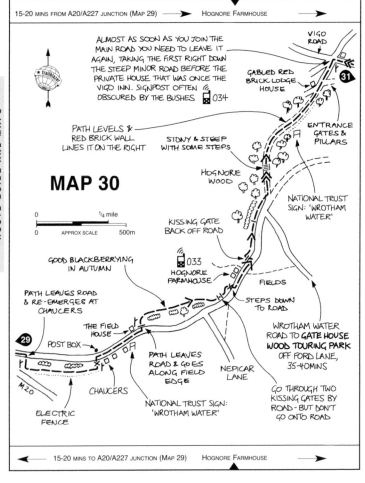

15-20 MINS FROM A20/A227 JUNCTION (MAP 29) ⟶ HOGNORE FARMHOUSE ⟶

ALMOST AS SOON AS YOU JOIN THE MAIN ROAD YOU NEED TO LEAVE IT AGAIN, TAKING THE FIRST RIGHT DOWN THE STEEP MINOR ROAD BEFORE THE PRIVATE HOUSE THAT WAS ONCE THE VIGO INN. SIGNPOST OFTEN OBSCURED BY THE BUSHES 034

VIGO ROAD

GABLED RED BRICK LODGE HOUSE

31

PATH LEVELS & RED BRICK WALL LINES IT ON THE RIGHT

STONY & STEEP WITH SOME STEPS

ENTRANCE GATES & PILLARS

HOGNORE WOOD

MAP 30

NATIONAL TRUST SIGN: 'WROTHAM WATER'

0   ¼ mile

0   APPROX SCALE   500m

KISSING GATE BACK OFF ROAD

GOOD BLACKBERRYING IN AUTUMN

033
HOGNORE FARMHOUSE

FIELDS

PATH LEAVES ROAD & RE-EMERGES AT CHAUCERS

STEPS DOWN TO ROAD

THE FIELD HOUSE

WROTHAM WATER ROAD TO GATE HOUSE WOOD TOURING PARK OFF FORD LANE, 35-40MINS

29 POST BOX

PATH LEAVES ROAD & GOES ALONG FIELD EDGE

NEPICAR LANE

M20

CHAUCERS

NATIONAL TRUST SIGN: 'WROTHAM WATER'

GO THROUGH TWO KISSING GATES BY ROAD - BUT DON'T GO ONTO ROAD

ELECTRIC FENCE

ROUTE GUIDE AND MAPS

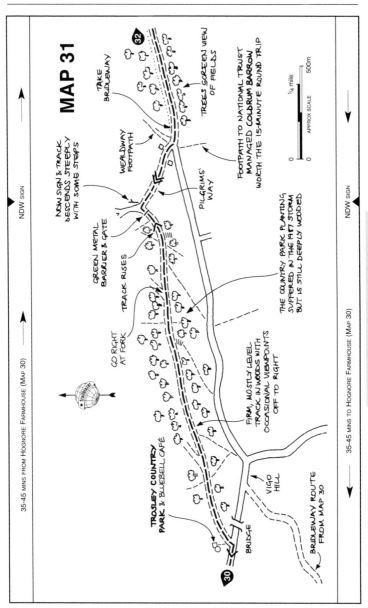

MAP 31

NDW SIGN

35-45 MINS FROM HOGNORE FARMHOUSE (MAP 30)

32

TREES SCREEN VIEW OF FIELDS

FOOTPATH TO NATIONAL TRUST MANAGED COLDRUM BARROW WORTH THE 15-MINUTE ROUND TRIP

¼ mile

0   500m

0   APPROX SCALE

NDW SIGN

TAKE BRIDLEWAY

WEALDWAY FOOTPATH

PILGRIMS' WAY

NDW SIGN & TRACK DESCENDS STEEPLY WITH SOME STEPS

GREEN METAL BARRIER & GATE

TRACK RISES

THE COUNTRY PARK PLANTING SUFFERED IN THE 1987 STORM BUT IS STILL DEEPLY WOODED

GO RIGHT AT FORK

FIRM, MOSTLY LEVEL TRACK IN WOODS WITH OCCASIONAL VIEWPOINTS OFF TO RIGHT

VIGO HILL

TROSLEY COUNTRY PARK & BLUEBELL CAFÉ

BRIDGE

BRIDLEWAY ROUTE FROM MAP 30

30

35-45 MINS TO HOGNORE FARMHOUSE (MAP 30)

lucky charms and gifts in the trees surrounding the stones and it's said that the name derives from the old Cornish word *Galdrum* or 'place of enchantments'. It's certainly a pretty location at the foot of the Downs overlooking farmland toward Blue Bell Hill and east to the Medway valley.

Back on the North Downs Way, the path continues its eastward line to the bridleway leading to Ryarsh.

RYARSH   [off Map 32]

You probably wouldn't come here unless staying at *Heavers House Farm* (☎ 01732-842074, 🖳 kentbedandbreakfast.co.uk; 1D/2T, shared facilities; ☛; WI-FI); B&B here costs £40-50pp (sgl occ from £45).

The *Duke of Wellington* (☎ 01732-842318, 🖳 dukeofwellingtonryarsh.com; food Mon-Thur noon-2pm & 6-9pm, Fri &

Sat noon-9.30pm, Sun noon-9pm; WI-FI; 🐾) pub has polished wood floors and cosy snugs and offers tapas (dishes £2.50-4.25) as well as regular pub fare.

Nu-Venture's No 58 (Maidstone to Wrotham Heath) **bus service** stops opposite the Duke of Wellington; see pp45-8 for details.

Now bending north-easterly to ascend **Holly Hill**, it feels wonderfully isolated and peaceful along this section even though the industrial towns of the Medway valley are only a couple of miles away. You get little sense of that as the trail eventually drops down through a series of undulating arable fields, through the attractive hamlet of **Upper Bush** to arrive at Cuxton.

CUXTON
               [MAP 34, p137 & MAP 35, p138]

On Bush Rd there is a **Co-op** (daily 7am-10pm).

South Eastern Railway operates **rail services** (see box pp42-3) between Strood and Paddock Wood/Tonbridge; change at Strood for services to Rochester and at Paddock Wood or Tonbridge for trains to London. Nu-Venture's **bus** No 151 (Chatham to West Malling) stops at the end of Bush Rd and the White Hart, running towards Rochester; see pp45-8.

Unless you intend staying in Rochester, which would be worth it, your only accommodation option is the luxurious *North Downs Barn* (☎ 01634-296829, 🖳 north downsbarn.co.uk; 1S private facilities, 1D

or T/1D, both en suite; ☛; WI-FI), a sympathetic barn conversion, just off the North Downs Way. B&B costs £42.50-50pp (sgl £50, sgl occ £65-70).

Further down the road there's a Chinese takeaway, *Golden River* (☎ 01634-296888; Mon-Thur 5-10pm, Fri & Sat noon-10pm), which also does fish & chips. *White Hart* (Map 35; ☎ 01634-789969, 🖳 www.whitehartcuxton.co.uk; food Mon-Thur noon-3pm & 6-9pm, Fri & Sat noon-9pm, Sun noon-6pm; WI-FI; 🐾) does filling pub grub, including such exotic delights as an ostrich burger (£11.95), and it has a pleasant beer garden (though it's marred by the noise of the traffic); also dogs are welcome.

Climbing behind Cuxton, with views over the Medway, the trail emerges to cross the Medway Bridge. There are in fact two – a road bridge carrying the M2 and another carrying the Channel Tunnel rail link. There is a dedicated pedestrian and cycle crossing running alongside the M2. It's horrible, to be sure, the scream of traffic is loud enough to shake your fillings loose and make your ears bleed, but distract yourself from the noise and fumes by looking instead at the river below and the outline of Rochester, with its cathedral and castle, in the distance.   *(cont'd on p140)*

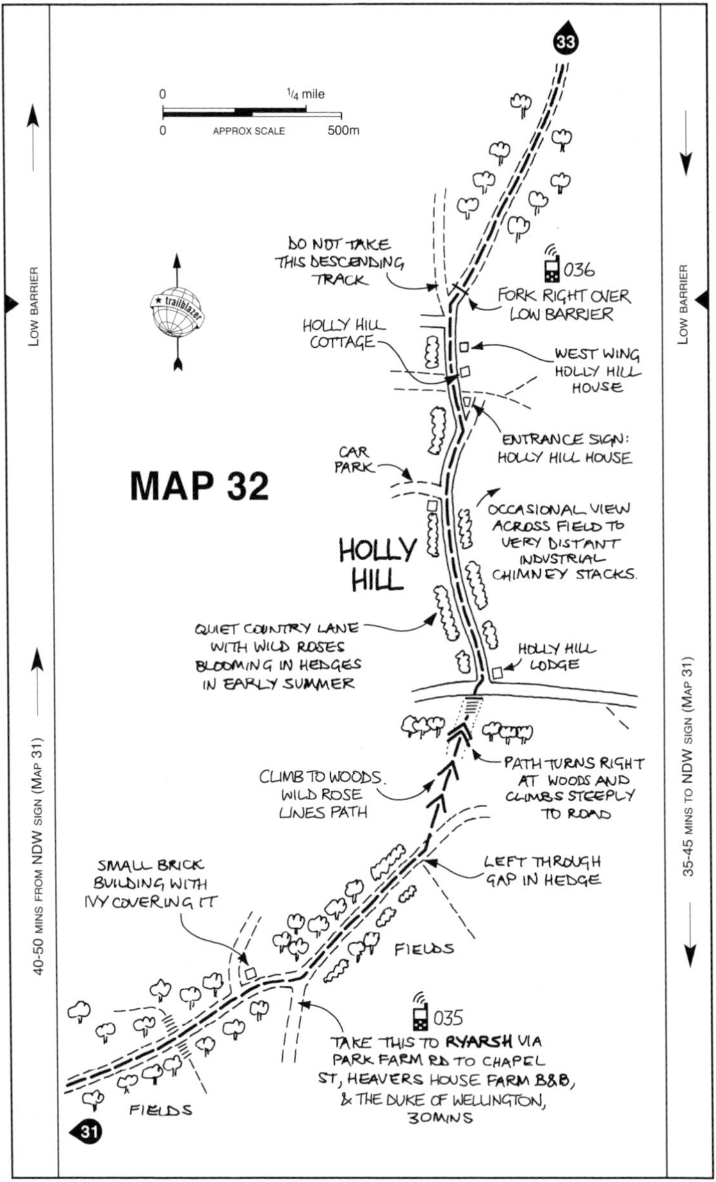

MAP 32

HOLLY HILL

0 — 1/4 mile
0 — APPROX SCALE — 500m

trailblazer

DO NOT TAKE THIS DESCENDING TRACK

036 FORK RIGHT OVER LOW BARRIER

HOLLY HILL COTTAGE

WEST WING HOLLY HILL HOUSE

ENTRANCE SIGN: HOLLY HILL HOUSE

CAR PARK

OCCASIONAL VIEW ACROSS FIELD TO VERY DISTANT INDUSTRIAL CHIMNEY STACKS.

QUIET COUNTRY LANE WITH WILD ROSES BLOOMING IN HEDGES IN EARLY SUMMER

HOLLY HILL LODGE

CLIMB TO WOODS. WILD ROSE LINES PATH

PATH TURNS RIGHT AT WOODS AND CLIMBS STEEPLY TO ROAD

SMALL BRICK BUILDING WITH IVY COVERING IT

LEFT THROUGH GAP IN HEDGE

FIELDS

035 TAKE THIS TO **RYARSH** VIA PARK FARM RD TO CHAPEL ST, HEAVERS HOUSE FARM B&B, & THE DUKE OF WELLINGTON, 30MINS

FIELDS

LOW BARRIER

LOW BARRIER

40-50 MINS FROM NDW SIGN (MAP 31)

35-45 MINS TO NDW SIGN (MAP 31)

33

31

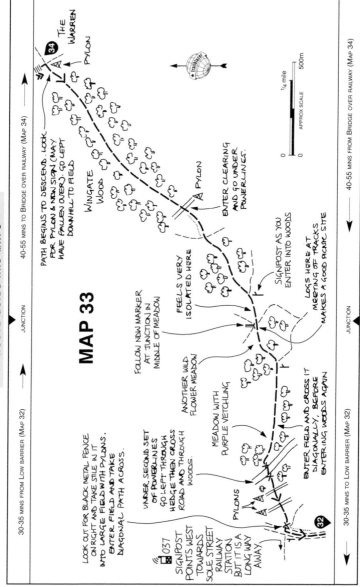

MAP 33

30-35 MINS FROM Low barrier (MAP 32) — JUNCTION — 40-55 MINS TO Bridge over railway (MAP 34)

30-35 MINS TO Low barrier (MAP 32) — JUNCTION — 40-55 MINS FROM Bridge over railway (MAP 34)

THE WARREN

34

PYLON

PATH BEGINS TO DESCEND. LOOK FOR PYLON & NEW SIGN (MAY HAVE FALLEN OVER). GO LEFT DOWNHILL TO FIELD.

WINGATE WOOD

PYLON

ENTER CLEARING AND GO UNDER POWERLINES.

SIGNPOST AS YOU ENTER INTO WOODS

FEELS VERY ISOLATED HERE

FOLLOW NDW MARKER AT JUNCTION IN MIDDLE OF MEADOW

LOGS HERE AT MEETING OF TRACKS MAKES A GOOD PICNIC SITE

ANOTHER WILD FLOWER MEADOW

MEADOW WITH PURPLE VETCHLING

ENTER FIELD AND CROSS IT DIAGONALLY, BEFORE ENTERING WOODS AGAIN

UNDER SECOND SET OF POWERLINES GO LEFT THROUGH HEDGE THEN CROSS ROAD AND THROUGH WOODS.

PYLONS

LOOK OUT FOR BLACK METAL FENCE ON RIGHT AND TAKE STILE IN IT INTO LARGE FIELD WITH PYLONS. ENTER FIELD AND TAKE DIAGONAL PATH ACROSS.

037 SIGNPOST POINTS WEST TOWARDS SOLE STREET RAILWAY STATION BUT IT IS A LONG WAY AWAY

32

¼ mile

500m

0   0

APPROX SCALE

★ trailblazer

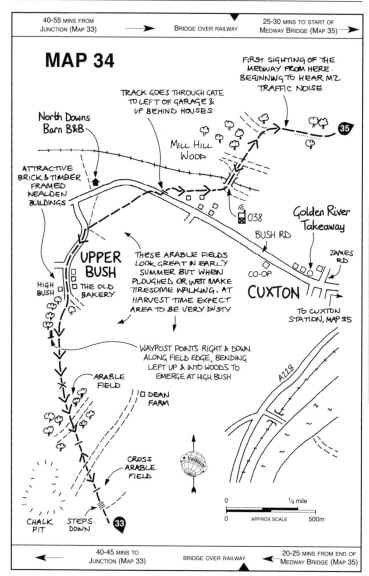

MAP 34

FIRST SIGHTING OF THE MEDWAY FROM HERE. BEGINNING TO HEAR M2 TRAFFIC NOISE

TRACK GOES THROUGH GATE TO LEFT OF GARAGE & UP BEHIND HOUSES

North Downs Barn B&B

MILL HILL WOOD

35

ATTRACTIVE BRICK & TIMBER FRAMED WEALDEN BUILDINGS

038

Golden River Takeaway

BUSH RD

UPPER BUSH

JAMES RD

CO-OP

HIGH BUSH

THE OLD BAKERY

THESE ARABLE FIELDS LOOK GREAT IN EARLY SUMMER BUT WHEN PLOUGHED OR WET MAKE TIRESOME WALKING. AT HARVEST TIME EXPECT AREA TO BE VERY DUSTY

CUXTON

TO CUXTON STATION, MAP 35

WAYPOST POINTS RIGHT & DOWN ALONG FIELD EDGE, BENDING LEFT UP & INTO WOODS TO EMERGE AT HIGH BUSH

A228

ARABLE FIELD

DEAN FARM

★ trailblazer

CROSS ARABLE FIELD

CHALK PIT

STEPS DOWN

33

0   ¼ mile

0   APPROX SCALE   500m

ROUTE GUIDE AND MAPS

ROUTE GUIDE AND MAPS

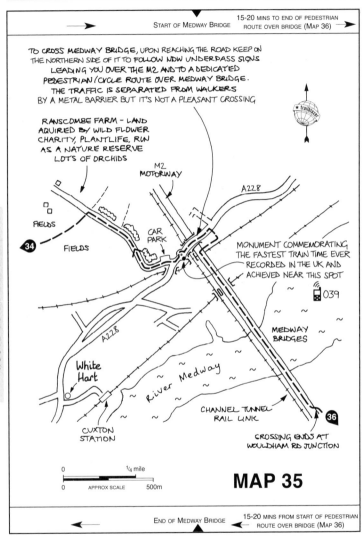

START OF MEDWAY BRIDGE

15-20 MINS TO END OF PEDESTRIAN
ROUTE OVER BRIDGE (MAP 36)

TO CROSS MEDWAY BRIDGE, UPON REACHING THE ROAD KEEP ON
THE NORTHERN SIDE OF IT TO FOLLOW NOW UNDERPASS SIGNS
LEADING YOU OVER THE M2 AND TO A DEDICATED
PEDESTRIAN/CYCLE ROUTE OVER MEDWAY BRIDGE.
THE TRAFFIC IS SEPARATED FROM WALKERS
BY A METAL BARRIER BUT IT'S NOT A PLEASANT CROSSING

RANSCOMBE FARM — LAND
AQUIRED BY WILD FLOWER
CHARITY, PLANTLIFE, RUN
AS A NATURE RESERVE
LOTS OF ORCHIDS

M2
MOTORWAY

A228

FIELDS

34

FIELDS

CAR
PARK

MONUMENT COMMEMORATING
THE FASTEST TRAIN TIME EVER
RECORDED IN THE UK AND
ACHIEVED NEAR THIS SPOT

039

A228

MEDWAY
BRIDGES

White
Hart

River Medway

CHANNEL TUNNEL
RAIL LINK

36

CUXTON
STATION

CROSSING ENDS AT
WOULDHAM RD JUNCTION

0   ¼ mile
0   APPROX SCALE   500m

MAP 35

END OF MEDWAY BRIDGE

15-20 MINS FROM START OF PEDESTRIAN
ROUTE OVER BRIDGE (MAP 36)

❏ **Kentish Men or Men of Kent**
The Medway divides Kent in two at Rochester. People to the east were known as Men
of Kent and those to the west including Canterbury were known as Kentish Men.

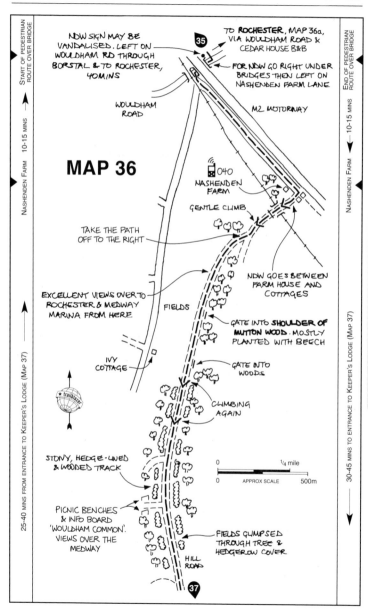

Start of Pedestrian route over bridge

Nashenden Farm 10-15 mins

25-40 mins from entrance to Keeper's Lodge (Map 37)

NDW SIGN MAY BE VANDALISED. LEFT ON WOULDHAM RD THROUGH BORSTAL & TO ROCHESTER, 40MINS

TO **ROCHESTER**, MAP 36a, VIA WOULDHAM ROAD & CEDAR HOUSE B&B

FOR NDW GO RIGHT UNDER BRIDGES THEN LEFT ON NASHENDEN FARM LANE

35

WOULDHAM ROAD

M2 MOTORWAY

MAP 36

040 NASHENDEN FARM

GENTLE CLIMB

TAKE THE PATH OFF TO THE RIGHT

NDW GOES BETWEEN FARM HOUSE AND COTTAGES

EXCELLENT VIEWS OVER TO ROCHESTER & MEDWAY MARINA FROM HERE

FIELDS

GATE INTO **SHOULDER OF MUTTON WOOD**. MOSTLY PLANTED WITH BEECH

IVY COTTAGE

GATE INTO WOODS

CLIMBING AGAIN

trailblazer

STONY, HEDGE-LINED & WOODED TRACK

0   1/4 mile

0   APPROX SCALE   500m

PICNIC BENCHES & INFO BOARD 'WOULDHAM COMMON'. VIEWS OVER THE MEDWAY

FIELDS GLIMPSED THROUGH TREE & HEDGEROW COVER

HILL ROAD

37

End of Pedestrian route over bridge

Nashenden Farm 10-15 mins

30-45 mins to entrance to Keeper's Lodge (Map 37)

ROUTE GUIDE AND MAPS

ROCHESTER [MAP 36a]

'On the left of the spectator lay the ruined wall, broken in many places, and in some overhanging the narrow beach below in rude and heavy masses. ... Behind it rose the ancient castle, its towers roofless, and its massive walls crumbling away, but telling us proudly of its old might and strength ... On either side the banks of the Medway, covered with cornfields and pastures, with here and there a windmill or a distant church, stretched away as far as the eye could see, presenting a rich and varied landscape, rendered more beautiful by the changing shadows which passed swiftly across it, as the thin and half-formed clouds skimmed away in the light of the morning sun.' **Charles Dickens**, *Pickwick Papers*

As you've just passed the halfway point – and have also reached the most northerly point on the trail – it's a good excuse to visit Rochester, a 40-minute walk off the path, and perhaps celebrate with a day off and a good meal.

Sometimes referred to as the city of Great Expectations, the great Victorian novelist, **Charles Dickens**, is to Rochester what Mickey Mouse is to Disney. Growing up in nearby Chatham, he used local settings in his novels such as *The Mystery of Edwin Drood*, *The Uncommercial Traveller* and *Pickwick Papers*. Indeed, Dickens also asked to be buried in the moat of Rochester Castle! (Incidentally, Dickens' associations with the North Downs Way are not confined to Rochester; Canterbury was the setting of one of his classic works, *David Copperfield*, and he described the walk from Maidstone to Rochester – a track that would follow a pretty similar course to the North Downs Way from Rochester over Blue Bell Hill (see p146) – as one of the

most beautiful walks in England.) With two Dickens' festivals a year, one in July and one in December, accommodation goes fast. But this commercialism aside there's plenty to see including a Norman castle, England's second oldest cathedral, a wonderful Restoration house and a fascinating almshouse for poor travellers 'not being rogues or proctors'.

What to see and do

Rochester Cathedral (🖳 rochestercathed ral.org; Mon-Fri 7.30am-6pm, from Sat 8.30am-5pm, Sun 7.30am-5pm; free but a donation is suggested) celebrated its 1400th year in 2004 and is the second oldest cathedral in England; Canterbury Cathedral claims the title as the oldest.

Rochester Castle (🖳 english-heri tage.org.uk; daily Apr-Sep 10am-6pm, Oct-Mar to 4pm; £6.40, free to English Heritage members) is the other obvious site and reckoned to be one of the country's best-preserved Norman castles. Started in the 11th century by Bishop Gundolf there are excellent views from the top of the 113ft tower over the Medway and the cathedral.

Guildhall Museum (☎ 01634-332900, 🖳 www.visitmedway.org/destina tions/rochester; Tue-Sun & Bank Hols 10am-5pm, daily in school holidays) is strong on local Medway history and it's free.

Well worth seeing is the **Restoration House & Gardens** (☎ 01634-848520, 🖳 restorationhouse.co.uk; Jun-Sep Thur & Fri only; £8.50, guided tour £11, garden only £4). The house, a 17th-century mansion house, takes its name from King Charles II's stay there on the eve of the Restoration. It's privately owned and superbly maintained, filled with period furniture and a

---

❏ **Borstal – what's in a name?**
Borstal was the name given to young offender institutions after the prison of the same name in Rochester where imprisoned men were first separated from young boys. Troublesome youths were sent to borstal to benefit from military-style discipline and learn a workshop trade. Sounds familiar? Brendan Behan's novel, *Borstal Boy*, 1958, subsequently dramatised, is based on his experience of a spell in borstal during WWII.

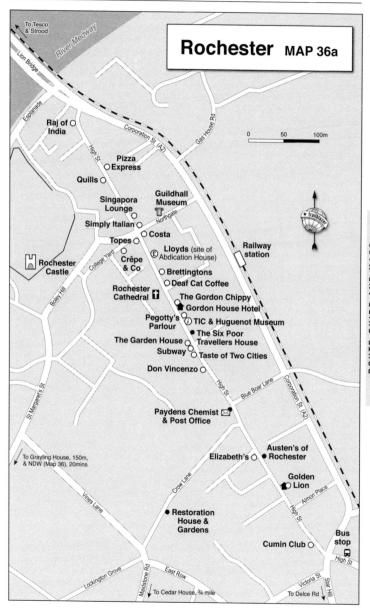

Rochester **MAP 36a**

To Tesco & Strood

River Medway

Lion Bridge

Esplanade

Corporation St (A2)

Gas House Rd

0   50   100m

Raj of India

High St

Pizza Express

Quills

Singapora Lounge

Guildhall Museum

Northgate

Simply Italian

Costa

Topes

Railway station

Crêpe & Co

Lloyds (site of Abdication House)

College Yard

Rochester Castle

Brettingtons

Deaf Cat Coffee

Boley Hill

Rochester Cathedral

The Gordon Chippy

Gordon House Hotel

Pegotty's Parlour

TIC & Huguenot Museum

The Six Poor Travellers House

The Garden House

Subway

Taste of Two Cities

Don Vincenzo

High St

Blue Boar Lane

Corporation St (A2)

St Margaret's St

To Grayling House, 150m, & NDW (Map 36), 20mins

Paydens Chemist & Post Office

Elizabeth's

Austen's of Rochester

Crow Lane

Golden Lion

Vines Lane

Almon Place

High St

Restoration House & Gardens

Bus stop

Cumin Club

High St

Lookington Grove

Maidstone Rd

East Row

To Cedar House, ¾ mile

Victoria St

Star Hill

To Delce Rd

trailblazer

good collection of English portraits. It is said to have been Dickens' inspiration for Satis House in *Great Expectations*.

In a different class, the other delight is **The Six Poor Travellers House** (☎ 01634-823117; Easter-Oct Wed-Sun 11am-1pm & 2-4pm; free), taking its name from the poor travellers 'not being rogues or proctors' who were given one night's lodging in the six bedrooms at the rear of the 16th-century almshouse. They were also provided with a supper of meat, bread and a pint of ale, a pretty generous allowance even by today's standards.

There's a **Huguenot Museum** (☎ 01634-789347, 🖳 huguenotmuseum.org; Wed-Sat 10am-5pm, Bank Hol Mons 10am-4pm; £4) above the TIC.

Services

The **tourist information centre** (TIC; ☎ 01634-843666, 🖳 www.visitmedway.org/destinations/rochester; Mon-Sat 10am-5pm, Apr-end Sep Sun 10.30am-5pm) is at 95 High St. There's a Huguenot Museum (see above) upstairs and details of accommodation nearby is stuck to the windows. There are two **ATMs** nearby; the Lloyds machine is at the site of the **Abdication House**, where King James stayed before leaving for France in 1688. For any ailments there is **Paydens Chemists** (☎ 01634-842838) which also has a **post office** counter (both are open Mon-Sat 9am-5.30pm).

For **food provisions**, Austen's of Rochester (Tue-Fri 8.30am-7pm, Sat & Mon 8.30am-5pm) is a traditional greengrocer's; while in Strood, over the ornate 'Lion Bridge' at the northern end of the High St, is a Tesco (Mon-Sat 6am-midnight, Sun 10am-4pm) and an Iceland (Mon-Sat 8am-7pm, Sun 10am-4pm).

The Blue Boar Lane car park hosts the monthly **Farmers' Market**, on the third Sunday of each month; see box p22.

Transport

The **railway station** has regular services (operated by South Eastern Railway) to several London stations including Victoria, Charing Cross and St Pancras International, as well as to Canterbury East and Dover Priory; see public transport box pp42-3 for details.

Arriva's **bus** No 155 (Chatham to Maidstone) calls at Warden Rd & Star Hill. Nu-Venture's No 142 stops on Delce Rd and their 151, 172 & 173, which also serve Chatham, stop at the railway station. See pp45-8 for details

For a taxi call **Vokes** (☎ 01634-222222, or ☎ 01634-777777, 🖳 vokes taximedway.co .uk).

Where to stay

At 66 Priestfields, *Cedar House* (☎ 01634-324175, 🖳 cedarhouserochester.co.uk; 2D, both en suite; ☛; WI-FI) charges £45-47.50pp (sgl occ £75-85) for B&B, though note there is a minimum two-night stay at weekends. It's one of the more convenient B&Bs for the North Downs Way. At the end of the motorway bridge turn left instead of right on Wouldham Rd. This turns into Borstal St which in turn transforms into Priestfields. Cedar House is about 1.5km from the bridge.

Borstal Rd meets St Margaret's St about five minutes from the Cathedral where *Grayling House* (☎ 01634-826593, 🖳 graylinghousebandbrochester.co.uk; 1D or T/1Tr both en suite, 1S private facilities, 2S/4D or T shared facilities; ☛; WI-FI) offers B&B for £32.50-40pp (sgl £35-40, sgl occ rates on request).

In the centre of Rochester there's *Gordon House Hotel* (☎ 01634-831000, 🖳 www.gordonhousehotel.net; 10D/3Qd, all en suite; ☛; WI-FI some rooms). B&B costs £37.50-44.50pp (sgl occ from £65).

There's also a Wetherspoons pub, *Golden Lion* (☎ 01634-880521, 🖳 jd wetherspoon.com; 6D/3D or T, all en suite; ☛; WI-FI), further along the High St at 147-151; note that breakfast is available (£2-6) but not included in the rate. The rates (£24.50-42.50pp, sgl occ room rate) are OK given the central location.

Where to eat and drink

There are several good independent cafés in town in addition to the usual *Costa* outlet (Mon-Sat 6.30am-8pm, Sun 8am-7pm). *Deaf Cat Coffee* (Mon-Sat 9am-5pm, Sun

10am-5pm) doesn't offer much in the way of food except a few pre-made sandwiches and other snacks but what it does, it does well, namely some first-rate coffees and teas.

Around the corner from the High St in an enviable location near the cathedral and with outside seating, *Crêpe & Co* (☎ 01634-780645, 🖳 crepeandco.co.uk; daily 9am-7.30pm, takeaway only for orders after 7pm) offers sweet and savoury crêpes and waffles, juices and smoothies, starting at £3.50 for the basic lemon and sugar crêpe.

For something more substantial, *The Garden House* (☎ 01634-842460; Sun-Mon 10.30am-3.30pm, Tue-Sat 10.30am-4pm) offers a fine range of home-made cooking and daily specials (eg cold poached salmon & salad with new potatoes, £7.50) as well as sandwiches (from £4.45).

Try the traditional *Pegotty's Parlour* (☎ 01634-847941; Mon-Sat 9.30am-5pm, Sun 11am-4pm, winter Mon-Sat 10am-4.30pm, Sun 11am-4pm); it's easy to miss, being located on the first floor, but does some lovely lunches and great full English breakfasts (£4.95).

As for smarter and more substantial fare, *Elizabeth's* (☎ 01634-843472, 🖳 elizabethsrestaurant.co.uk; Tue-Sun noon-2pm, Tue-Thur 6.30-9pm, Fri & Sat to 9.30pm) has a cosy feel to it with a twist of Spanish in the menu. Starters are £9 on the à la carte menu, mains from £16.50 for the Jerusalem artichoke, tomato & shallot pithivier though there are better-value set menus (two/three courses £19.95/25). The 16th-century building was the setting for the home of Uncle Pumblechoock in Dickens's *Great Expectations*.

Topes (☎ 01634-845270, 🖳 topes-restaurant.com; Wed-Sun noon-3pm, Wed, Thur & Sat 6.30-10pm, also breakfast Sat 9.30-11.30am, coffee & cake Wed-Sun from 11am), 60 High St, offers set-menu British cuisine (two courses from £19.50, three for £25, rising to £28/35 on Sat) in a restaurant combining the exposed brick-and-beam look with crisp linen tablecloths. On Friday evening their restaurant turns into Rochester's first and only gin palace, with over 40 different gins on offer along with simple bar meals (eg £3 for venison scotch eggs, or fishcakes). Coffee and cake and a Saturday breakfast are also served up.

Quills (☎ 01634-407402, 🖳 thequills .co.uk; Mon-Tue 8.30am-4pm, Wed & Thur 8.30am-9.30pm, Fri & Sat to 10pm, Sun 8.30am-5pm), towards the northern end of the High St, lists some great burgers on its menu starting at £9.95 for its mushroom, bean chilli & avocado burger.

For a meaty slap-up meal, *Brettingtons* (☎ 01634-400192, 🖳 brettingtons.com; Mon-Thur noon-3pm & 6-9pm, Fri noon-3pm & 5-10pm, Sat noon-10.30pm, Sun noon-9pm) is a steak and lobster bar with steaks from £20.25 for 250g rare-breed sirloin, up to £80 for 350g wagyu fillet.

Looking for food from beyond these shores? For **Italian food**, in addition to a branch of the national chain *Pizza Express* (☎ 01634-812171, 🖳 pizzaexpress.com; Mon-Sat 11.30am-11pm, Sun noon-10.30pm) and one of the regional chain *Simply Italian* (☎ 01634-408077; Mon-Sat noon-9.30pm, Sun noon-9pm), there is also the independent *Don Vincenzo* (☎ 01634-408373, 🖳 donvincenzo.co.uk; Mon-Fri noon-3pm & 6-10pm, Sat noon-4pm & 6-10.30pm, Sun noon-8.30pm) which does a decent line in risotto (from £11.50).

Looking further east, to Asia, *Singapora Lounge* (☎ 01634-842178, 🖳 www.singaporalounge.co.uk; daily noon to midnight), 51 High St, attracts a crowd offering a fusion of Malaysian, Thai, and Chinese cuisine. A spicy beef *rendang* is £11.95. And there are a few good **Indian** restaurants including the sophisticated *Cumin Club* (☎ 01634-400880, 🖳 cuminclub.com; daily noon-2pm & 6-11.30pm), *Taste of Two Cities* (☎ 01634-841327, 🖳 tasteoftwocities.co.uk; daily 6-11.30pm) and, at the northern end of the High St, *Raj of India* (☎ 01634-844489, 🖳 rajofindia-rochester.co.uk; daily noon-2pm & 6pm-midnight).

For **takeaway** food there's *The Gordon Chippy* (Mon-Thur noon-11pm, Fri & Sat to midnight, Sun to 10pm), and a branch of *Subway* (Mon-Thur 7am-8pm, Fri & Sat 7am-1pm, Sun 10am-8pm).

ROUTE GUIDE AND MAPS

ROCHESTER TO HOLLINGBOURNE   [MAPS 36-42]

There's a lot of interest on this **14.8-mile/23.8km (4hrs 35mins to 6hrs 5mins)** section including several Neolithic sites, Kent's oldest village, the chance to stay with monks at Aylesford Friary and visit the ruins of a motte-and-bailey castle at Thurnham. The walking is seldom strenuous and occasionally blissful, and after the traumas of walking alongside the M2 yesterday, you'll be pleased to know that there are only two A roads to cross today (the A229 and A249), both easily negotiated via underpass and bridge respectively. And though their distant roar remains audible for several miles, it's the beauty of the Kent countryside – and the ancient stone constructions that lie hidden within – that lingers in the memory long after you've taken off your boots at the end of the day. Refreshments directly on (or very near) the trail can be found at: the Robin Hood pub, just an hour or so into the stage; at the petrol station shop by the A229 (open 24 hours); and then at Detling, nearly nine miles into the day.

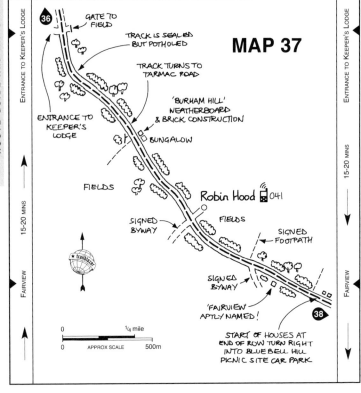

MAP 37

36

GATE TO FIELD

TRACK IS SEALED BUT POTHOLED

TRACK TURNS TO TARMAC ROAD

'BURHAM HILL' WEATHERBOARD & BRICK CONSTRUCTION

ENTRANCE TO KEEPER'S LODGE

BUNGALOW

FIELDS

Robin Hood 041

SIGNED BYWAY

FIELDS

SIGNED FOOTPATH

★ trailblazer

SIGNED BYWAY

'FAIRVIEW' APTLY NAMED!

38

0   ¼ mile
0   APPROX SCALE   500m

START OF HOUSES AT END OF ROW TURN RIGHT INTO BLUEBELL HILL PICNIC SITE CAR PARK

ENTRANCE TO KEEPER'S LODGE

15-20 MINS

FAIRVIEW

ENTRANCE TO KEEPER'S LODGE

15-20 MINS

FAIRVIEW

ROUTE GUIDE AND MAPS

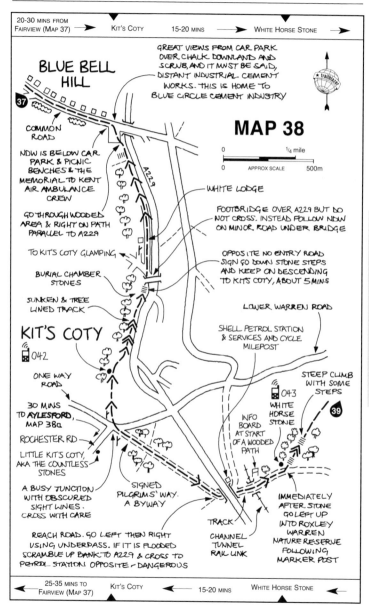

GREAT VIEWS FROM CAR PARK OVER CHALK DOWNLAND AND SCRUB, AND IT MUST BE SAID, DISTANT INDUSTRIAL CEMENT WORKS. THIS IS HOME TO BLUE CIRCLE CEMENT INDUSTRY

BLUE BELL HILL

MAP 38

0   1/4 mile

0   APPROX SCALE   500m

COMMON ROAD

NDW IS BELOW CAR PARK & PICNIC BENCHES & THE MEMORIAL TO KENT AIR AMBULANCE CREW

WHITE LODGE

FOOTBRIDGE OVER A229 BUT DO NOT CROSS. INSTEAD FOLLOW NDW ON MINOR ROAD UNDER BRIDGE

GO THROUGH WOODED AREA & RIGHT ON PATH PARALLEL TO A229

TO KIT'S COTY GLAMPING

OPPOSITE NO ENTRY ROAD SIGN GO DOWN STONE STEPS AND KEEP ON DESCENDING TO KITS COTY, ABOUT 5 MINS

BURIAL CHAMBER STONES

SUNKEN & TREE LINED TRACK

LOWER WARREN ROAD

SHELL PETROL STATION & SERVICES AND CYCLE MILEPOST

KIT'S COTY

042

STEEP CLIMB WITH SOME STEPS

ONE WAY ROAD

043

WHITE HORSE STONE

39

30 MINS TO **AYLESFORD**, MAP 38a

ROCHESTER RD

INFO BOARD AT START OF A WOODED PATH

LITTLE KIT'S COTY, AKA THE COUNTLESS STONES

A BUSY JUNCTION WITH OBSCURED SIGHT LINES. CROSS WITH CARE

SIGNED PILGRIMS' WAY. A BYWAY

IMMEDIATELY AFTER STONE GO LEFT UP INTO ROXLEY WARREN NATURE RESERVE FOLLOWING MARKER POST

TRACK

REACH ROAD. GO LEFT THEN RIGHT USING UNDERPASS. IF IT IS FLOODED SCRAMBLE UP BANK TO A229 & CROSS TO PETROL STATION OPPOSITE - DANGEROUS

CHANNEL TUNNEL RAIL LINK

ROUTE GUIDE AND MAPS

What's more, after Kit's Coty walkers can detour to Aylesford along the Rochester Rd where a tearoom and a couple of pubs lie in wait.

The day begins with a climb along the edge of **Shoulder of Mutton Wood**, eventually emerging on a tarmac road to pass within view of the *Robin Hood* pub (Map 37; ☎ 01634-861500, 💻 robinhood-pub.co.uk; food served Mon-Thur noon-2.30pm & 6-9pm, Fri & Sat noon-9.30pm, Sun noon-9pm; WI-FI; 🐾). This section of the Way is popular with cyclists, most of whom are pleasant and civil but, as with life in general, you'll always get one or two who think the path is for their own personal use only. Just smile sweetly. Continuing on the same path eventually brings you out at **Blue Bell Hill** picnic site, from where you drop down along a surfaced bridleway to pass **Kit's Coty** (see box below).

If you're worn out already you can divert off to *Kit's Coty Glamping* (☎ 01634-685862, 💻 kitscotyglamping.co.uk; WI-FI; Apr-end Sep) which offers a cabin, a shepherd's hut and three bell tents for weary, wealthy walkers. One of the **tents** sleeps two people (rates start at £85) and the others sleep four/six people (£95-110/105-20); the **shepherd's hut** sleeps two in a double bed (£85-100), and the **cabin** sleeps two adults, or two adults and two children (from £120). They also offer cream tea on arrival, breakfast hampers and local takeaways deliver to them which is ideal for walkers. To get there, having left the minor road off the A229, turn right at the end of the large wooden fence and walk straight along Collingwood Rd for approximately 600m to the end.

At the bottom of the lane, the modern world crashes back into yours as you have to negotiate a crossing of the busy Rochester Road. If you're feeling peckish (or just plain knackered) continue right down Rochester Road, past **Little Kit's Coty** (see box below) to Aylesford.

❑ Medway burial tombs

Kit's Coty is a Neolithic burial site built between 3500BC and 2500BC near Aylesford consisting of three upright stones and a capstone across the top standing about 15ft high. The structure is thought to have been at the entrance to a long barrow burial chamber about 200ft long running east to west. The site is now railed off and managed by English Heritage.

The **White Horse Stone** (see Map 38), further along the trail, is also thought to be a Neolithic burial site. Between the two and just off the trail – is **Little Kit's Coty** (Map 38) – also known as the **Countless Stones**. The latter name derives from the legend that, if you were to try to count how many there are, you'd end up with a different figure each time. That said, another superstition associated with them is that those who do try to count them will endure bad luck afterwards. The stones lie a couple of hundred metres off the path. Those diverting down to Aylesford will actually walk past them – they are in the field on the left-hand side as you walk down the hill, though the sign pointing to them is often obscured by the vegetation. For those who aren't visiting Aylesford, having passed Kit's Coty and crossed the busy road to join the wooded byway, look to your right through the trees and the stones lie beyond the first pylon, though the fence that surrounds them is often overgrown so you may not be able to see much.

AYLESFORD   [MAP 38a]

Pronounced 'ales ford' and reputedly one of
the oldest villages in Kent, with the buildings along the narrow High St stacked
tightly together above the River Medway.

The **village store** (Mon-Sat 7am-
5.30pm, Sun 8am-12.30pm) has a range of
snacks, drinks and groceries, but there are
few other amenities for walkers save for a
few places to eat and a couple of accommodation options.

Transport

South Eastern Railway's services (see box
pp42-3) between Strood and Paddock
Wood/Tonbridge) call here; change at
Strood for services to Rochester and at
Paddock Wood or Tonbridge for trains to
London. Arriva's **bus** No 155 (see pp45-8)
heads to Chatham in one direction,
Maidstone in the other.

Where to stay

The Carmelite Friary at Aylesford was
founded in 1242, subsequently dissolved by
Henry VIII and then re-established in 1949.
The Friars (☎ 01622-717272, 🖳 thefriars
.org.uk; 27S/31D/7Tr/1Qd, shared facilities
but three en suite; 🛏; WI-FI) offer a great
welcome with simple rooms and communal

facilities. Rates are from £35pp (sgl/sgl occ
from £42) for B&B, or it's from £58pp
(sgl/sgl occ from £65) including breakfast,
lunch and dinner; spiritual sustenance is
free. It's a large and busy complex complete with tea room, chapels and shrines.
Judging by the calendar of events they've
cornered the market in retreats and pilgrimage. The monks are also called Whitefriars
because of the colour of their robes. Non
residents can eat here if booked at least
48hrs in advance (£8.75 for a light supper
or £16 for three-course lunch and £6.75 for
breakfast).

The other accommodation option in
town is the friendly and helpful *Aylesford
B&B* (☎ 01622-717208, 🖳 aylesfordbed
andbreakfast.co.uk; 4D or T, all en suite;
WI-FI; 🐾), at 29a Forstal Cottages on
Forstal Rd, about 10-15 minutes east from
the High St. Rates are a very reasonable
£20-30pp, with single occupancy £32-36.

Where to eat and drink

For basic fare there's *The Village Pantry*
(Mon-Sat 8.30am-4pm).

Filling pub grub is available at *The
Bush* (☎ 01622-430331; food Mon-Sat
noon-3pm Wed-Sat 6-9pm, Sun noon-4pm;

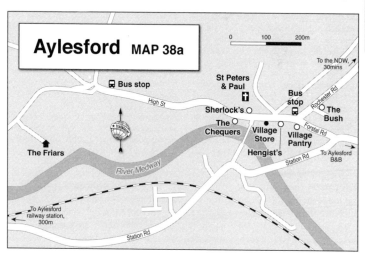

WI-FI; 🐾 on a lead) the first eatery you come to; they have an extensive menu including an all-day breakfast, rogan josh with rice, and lasagne for around £8.50 and steak & chips from £11.50; sandwiches cost from £3.50.

The Chequers (☎ 01622-717286, 💻 chequersaylesford.com; food Tue-Sat noon-3pm & 6-9pm, Sun & Mon noon-3pm only; WI-FI; 🐾 on lead) offers similar fare, with most mains £8.95.

Across the road, the themed restaurant *Sherlock's* (☎ 01622-710649, 💻 sherlocks restaurantkent.com; Thur-Sat 7-10pm) eliminated the impossible and is left with the improbable, to paraphrase the great sleuth. Paté de foie gras 'inspired by

Mycroft's travels' costs £6.95 and 'Mrs Hudson's Salmon', with a lime sauce, is £13.05.

For upmarket cuisine there is *Hengist's* (☎ 01622-885800, 💻 hengistres taurant.co.uk; Mon-Thur noon-3pm & 6-10pm, Fri & Sat noon-10pm, Sun noon-5pm) but unless you carry stylish glad rags in your pack you'll probably feel out of place at this elegant restaurant. At lunch it's a set menu only – £15 for two courses, £19 for three – while in the evening mains start at £12 for the fish & chips – though most dishes are above £15. Still, they also offer a coffee and cake during the day (10am-5pm) for £3.50.

Back at Rochester Road and the trail, a tree-shrouded bridleway takes you to an underpass under the A229. Note that this is prone to **flooding**, year-round, and diversion signs may be in place at Blue Bell Hill; see the note on Map 38, p145. Nu-Venture's **bus** No 142 operates from Chatham to Kit's Coty via Rochester and Blue Bell Hill Village; see pp45-8 for details.

At the end of the underpass (or the flood diversion route), the trail passes the 24-hour Shell petrol station **shop** with snacks and drinks, before climbing via the insignificant-looking **White Horse Stone** (easily missed) and into **Roxley Warren Nature Reserve**, remaining substantially in woodland until emerging above Detling.

DETLING   [MAP 40, p151]

Detling is one of the several villages on the North Downs Way that, it must be said, feels like it's slowly dying. The post office and stores have been shut for a long while now.

Thank Heavens, then, for *Cock Horse Inn* (☎ 01622-730144, 💻 cockhorsedetling .co.uk; food Mon 6-8.30pm, Tue-Sat noon-4pm & 6-8.30pm, Sun noon-4pm; WI-FI; 🐾 bar area only and on lead), a friendly place and one that, delightfully, is right on the trail. The food is good, with evening mains

starting at £9.95 and including seared duck breast & mash for £16.95. There is also somewhere to stay: *Wealden Hall B&B* (☎ 01622-739622, 💻 wealdenhall.co.uk; 1D/1D or T, both en suite; 💧; WI-FI; 🐾) is a super-smart B&B with a heated outdoor pool (May-Sep) right on the path, charging from £55pp (sgl occ from £90).

Arriva's **bus** Nos 333 and 334 still operate to Maidstone; see pp45-8 for details. The Detling Shopper bus (Mon-Fri 3/day) heads to the same destination.

Regaining the ridgeline the trail strikes out for the overgrown **ruins of Thurnham Castle**. It's known as a 'motte and bailey' fortification, basically a mound surrounded by an enclosure, and dates from the Norman period. Souvenir hunters pilfered most of the stone work and quarrying damaged what remains but it was once a large garrison – about 70 metres in diameter – and remains a nice place to sit and have a picnic lunch and admire the scenery below.

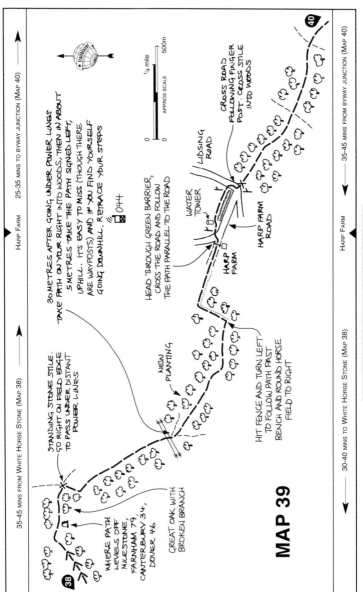

MAP 39

THURNHAM [MAP 40]

Accommodation and food are available at *The Black Horse Inn* (☎ 01622-737185, 🖳 blackhorsekent.co.uk; 20D/4T/3Qd, all en suite; 🛁; WI-FI; 🐾 £6), a very attractive dark-beamed, candle-strewn country pub just off the trail. B&B rates are from £47.50pp (sgl occ from £75), with a slight increase at weekends.

Their kitchen (Mon-Sat noon-10pm, Sun to 9.30pm) serves a range of mains, including several dishes that you seldom see on other pub menus (pan-fried squid with a tomato & jalapeno chutney with a squid-ink dressing for £8.50), starting from £8.

If you feel like really spoiling yourself *Thurnham Keep* (☎ 01622-734149, 🖳 thurnhamkeep.co.uk; 3D, all en suite; 🛁; WI-FI) is a luxury B&B, also just off the trail. The Edwardian country house is set in seven acres and rates are £70-80pp (sgl occ £60-70), though for advance bookings there's a two-night minimum stay over Friday and Saturday nights but nearer the time a single-night stay may be OK if they have availability.

Following the fence line up through fields the trail crosses Coldblow Lane from where it is a 15-minute walk uphill to *Coldblow Farm* (Map 41; ☎ 01622-730439, 🖳 coldblow-camping.co.uk; WI-FI intermittent; May-Sep but weather dependent). It's so named after the Saxon for 'crossing of the ways' though it's hard not to credit the sometimes chill wind whipping across the Downs ridge for the name. They offer **camping** at £9/14 per pitch for one/two people (🐾 free).

Shortly afterwards the path divides for a short while; the lower route is the classic North Downs Way, but the upper route takes you past a viewpoint with a wooden sculpture and picnic benches. With the latter now the popular route (and deservedly so), the official North Downs Way is actually becoming a little underused and overgrown; given this, we advise that you take the 'Viewpoint' route; the two trails meet back again about fifteen minutes later.

After crossing mostly open fields on a fairly well-defined track the Way drops down to Hollingbourne. The path passes the wonderfully named *Dirty Habit* (Map 42; ☎ 01622-880880, 🖳 elitepubs.com/the_dirtyhabit; food Mon-Thur noon-3pm & 5.30-9pm, Fri & Sat noon-9.30pm, Sun noon-8.30pm; WI-FI; 🐾 bar area), which has a decent and imaginative menu including Moroccan lamb burger, lime & feta yogurt, pickled courgette, pepper, harissa, hummus & chips (£14.95). This is the most convenient eating place for the path, but not the only one in the village (see below).

HOLLINGBOURNE
[off MAP 42, p153]

Hollingbourne is an attractive little village, more vibrant than some, though you've got a long walk from the trail to reach its heart. The church is 300m from the trail; the station is at least 1000m beyond that, and the village itself is about 400m beyond the turn-off to the station. Take the path by the church for the prettiest and shortest route.

In the village you'll find **Christopher's** (Mon-Fri 8.30am-5.30pm, Sat to 12.30pm, Sun to 11.30pm), the village store which also houses the **post office** (Mon, Tue, Thur & Fri 8.30am-5.30pm, Wed to 1pm, Sat to 12.30pm, Sun to 11.30pm).

For **food** there's *Sugar Loaves* (☎ 01622-880220, 🖳 sugarloaveshollingbourne.co.uk; food Mon-Fri noon-3pm & 6-9pm, Sat noon-9pm, Sun noon-6pm; WI-FI; 🐾) pub and *The Windmill* (☎ 01622-889000, 🖳 thewindmillhollingbourne.co.uk; food

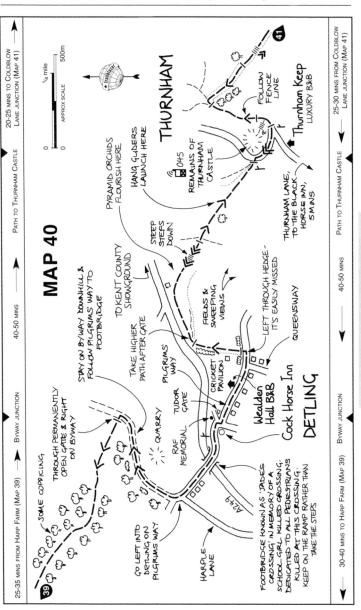

MAP 40

25-35 MINS FROM HARP FARM (MAP 39) → BYWAY JUNCTION → 40-50 MINS → PATH TO THURNHAM CASTLE → 20-25 MINS TO COLDBLOW LANE JUNCTION (MAP 41)

30-40 MINS TO HARP FARM (MAP 39) ← BYWAY JUNCTION ← 40-50 MINS ← PATH TO THURNHAM CASTLE ← 25-30 MINS FROM COLDBLOW LANE JUNCTION (MAP 41)

39

41

THURNHAM

Thurnham Keep
LUXURY B&B

¼ mile
APPROX SCALE
0   500m

SOME COPPICING

THROUGH PERMANENTLY OPEN GATE & RIGHT ON BYWAY

STAY ON BYWAY DOWNHILL & FOLLOW PILGRIMS' WAY TO FOOTBRIDGE

PYRAMID ORCHIDS FLOURISH HERE

HANG GLIDERS LAUNCH HERE

TO KENT COUNTY SHOWGROUND

045
REMAINS OF THURNHAM CASTLE

FOLLOW FENCE LINE

STEEP STEPS DOWN

TAKE HIGHER PATH AFTER GATE

PILGRIMS' WAY

QUARRY

TUDOR GATE

RAF MEMORIAL

CRICKET PAVILION

FIELDS & SWEEPING VIEWS

LEFT THROUGH HEDGE – IT'S EASILY MISSED

QUEENSWAY

THURNHAM LANE, TO THE BLACK HORSE INN, 5 MINS

Wealden Hall B&B

Cock Horse Inn

DETLING

A249

GO LEFT INTO DETLING ON PILGRIMS' WAY

FOOTBRIDGE KNOWN AS 'JADE'S CROSSING,' IN MEMORY OF A SCHOOL-GIRL KILLED CROSSING. DEDICATED TO ALL PEDESTRIANS KILLED AT THIS CROSSING. KEEP ON THE RAMP RATHER THAN TAKE THE STEPS

HARPLE LANE

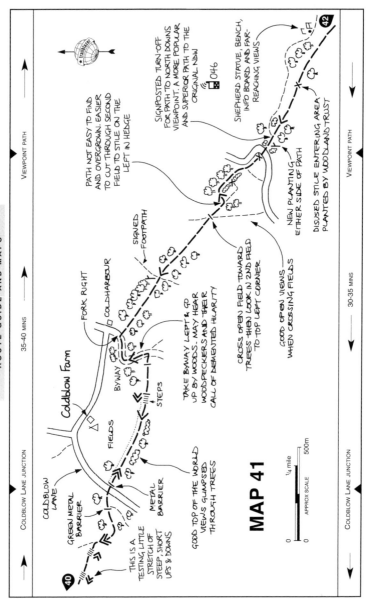

COLDBLOW LANE JUNCTION — 35-40 MINS — VIEWPOINT PATH

VIEWPOINT PATH — 30-35 MINS — COLDBLOW LANE JUNCTION

MAP 41

¼ mile
0 .... 500m
0
APPROX SCALE

THIS IS A TESTING LITTLE STRETCH OF STEEP, SHORT UPS & DOWNS

GREEN METAL BARRIER

COLDBLOW LANE

GOOD TOP OF THE WORLD VIEWS GLIMPSED THROUGH TREES

METAL BARRIER

FIELDS

Coldblow Farm

FORK RIGHT

COLDHARBOUR

BYWAY

STEPS

SIGNED FOOTPATH

TAKE BYWAY LEFT & GO UP BY WOODS. MAY HEAR WOODPECKERS AND THEIR CALL OF DEMENTED HILARITY

CROSS OPEN FIELD TOWARD TREES, THEN LOOK IN 2ND FIELD TO TOP LEFT CORNER

GOOD OPEN VIEWS WHEN CROSSING FIELDS

PATH NOT EASY TO FIND AND OVERGROWN. EASIER TO CUT THROUGH SECOND FIELD TO STILE ON THE LEFT IN HEDGE

SIGNPOSTED TURN-OFF FOR PATH TO NORTH DOWNS VIEWPOINT. A MORE POPULAR AND SUPERIOR PATH TO THE ORIGINAL NDW

SHEPHERD STATUE, BENCH, INFO BOARD AND FAR-REACHING VIEWS

NEW PLANTING EITHER SIDE OF PATH

DISUSED STILE ENTERING AREA PLANTED BY WOODLAND TRUST

40

42

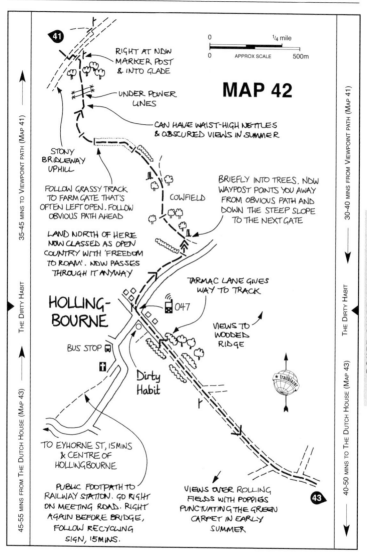

MAP 42

41

RIGHT AT NDW MARKER POST & INTO GLADE

UNDER POWER LINES

CAN HAVE WAIST-HIGH NETTLES & OBSCURED VIEWS IN SUMMER

STONY BRIDLEWAY UPHILL

FOLLOW GRASSY TRACK TO FARM GATE THAT'S OFTEN LEFT OPEN. FOLLOW OBVIOUS PATH AHEAD

COWFIELD

BRIEFLY INTO TREES. NDW WAYPOST POINTS YOU AWAY FROM OBVIOUS PATH AND DOWN THE STEEP SLOPE TO THE NEXT GATE

LAND NORTH OF HERE NOW CLASSED AS OPEN COUNTRY WITH 'FREEDOM TO ROAM'. NDW PASSES THROUGH IT ANYWAY

TARMAC LANE GIVES WAY TO TRACK

HOLLING-BOURNE

047

VIEWS TO WOODED RIDGE

BUS STOP

Dirty Habit

TO EYHORNE ST, 15 MINS & CENTRE OF HOLLINGBOURNE

PUBLIC FOOTPATH TO RAILWAY STATION. GO RIGHT ON MEETING ROAD. RIGHT AGAIN BEFORE BRIDGE, FOLLOW RECYCLING SIGN, 15 MINS.

VIEWS OVER ROLLING FIELDS WITH POPPIES PUNCTUATING THE GREEN CARPET IN EARLY SUMMER

43

0   ¼ mile
0   APPROX SCALE   500m

35-45 MINS TO VIEWPOINT PATH (MAP 41)

THE DIRTY HABIT

45-55 MINS FROM THE DUTCH HOUSE (MAP 43)

30-40 MINS FROM VIEWPOINT PATH (MAP 41)

THE DIRTY HABIT

40-50 MINS TO THE DUTCH HOUSE (MAP 43)

ROUTE GUIDE AND MAPS

Mon-Sat noon-2.30pm & 5.30-9.30pm, Sun noon-6pm; WI-FI; bar area only), a smarter place with mains around the £14-17 mark, though £24 and beyond for a steak.

Hollingbourne **railway station**, on Eyhorne St, is a stop on South Eastern Railway's London Victoria to Canterbury West service (see box pp42-3).

Arriva and Nu-Venture operate the No 13 **bus service**; buses depart from the church and it is a useful service stopping on Eyhorne St at the post office and at Leeds Castle's main entrance on its way to Maidstone. Stagecoach's No 10X (Maidstone to Ashford) also stops in Hollingbourne; see pp45-8 for details.

HOLLINGBOURNE TO BOUGHTON LEES [MAPS 42-49]

A long-ish stage of **12.6 miles/20.3km (3hrs 35mins to 5hrs 10mins)**, necessarily so due to the lack of any accommodation in Charing. Campers can reduce the length of this stage by stopping in Westwell at the campsite there (see p161; for a total of 10.6 miles/17.1km); while those with unlimited funds may want to stop at Eastwell and stay at the Manor Hotel there (see p162; for a total of 11.8 miles/19km). Otherwise, Boughton Lees is a sensible place to end the stage: it's right on the trail, it's got a B&B, a pub and a campsite – which all happen to be the same place – and there's a bus to Ashford too, for those who want to escape back to London. It is also the nearest village to the point where the North Downs Way divides – see p164 for details.

As for the walking itself on this stage – well it's very pleasant and straightforward. If you weren't feeling like a pilgrim before now, you certainly will once you join this route. For today you pass plenty of evidence that this route has been used by pilgrims for centuries. Setting off from Dirty Habit – a reference, of course, to the clothes of monks who would have made up a large proportion of those walking to Canterbury for their faith – on the way you also pass Pilgrim Lodge and Pilgrim Cottage on a path that's been officially called Pilgrims' Way (see box p173). Indeed, there's a rather good wooden sculpture of a pilgrim sitting on a bench just after the Harrietsham turn-off! And just to emphasise the spiritual purpose of this path, each of the several ancient villages that line the Pilgrims' Way have their own centuries-old church, that would once have served the pilgrims as they made their way to Canterbury – and which still perform this function to a degree today; the first is at Harrietsham, home to the 12th-century St John the Baptist Church.

HARRIETSHAM [off MAP 43]

Though not as charming as many of its neighbouring villages, Harrietsham does have a few amenities including a **Village Store** (Mon-Sat 7am-9pm, Sun 7.30am-8pm), at the far end of the village from the North Downs Way, and a **post office** (Mon-Fri 9am-1pm), where you can get money out.

For accommodation and dining *The Roebuck* (☎ 01622-858388, 🖥 roebuckinn .relaxinnz.co.uk; 1S/5T/3D/1Tr, all en suite; 🛇; WI-FI; 🐾 bar only) is a likeable-enough place with B&B from £34.50pp

(sgl £59, sgl occ rates on request; room rate only also available). **Food** is served (Tue-Fri noon-1.45pm & 6-8.45pm, Sat noon-2.45pm & 6-8.45pm, Sun noon-3pm; no food on Mon), with mains from their simple menu starting at £8.95 for chilli and rice.

South Eastern Railway's London Victoria to Canterbury West service (see box pp42-3) stops at the **railway station**. Stagecoach's **bus** service No 10X (Maidstone to Ashford) stops by The Roebuck; see pp45-8.

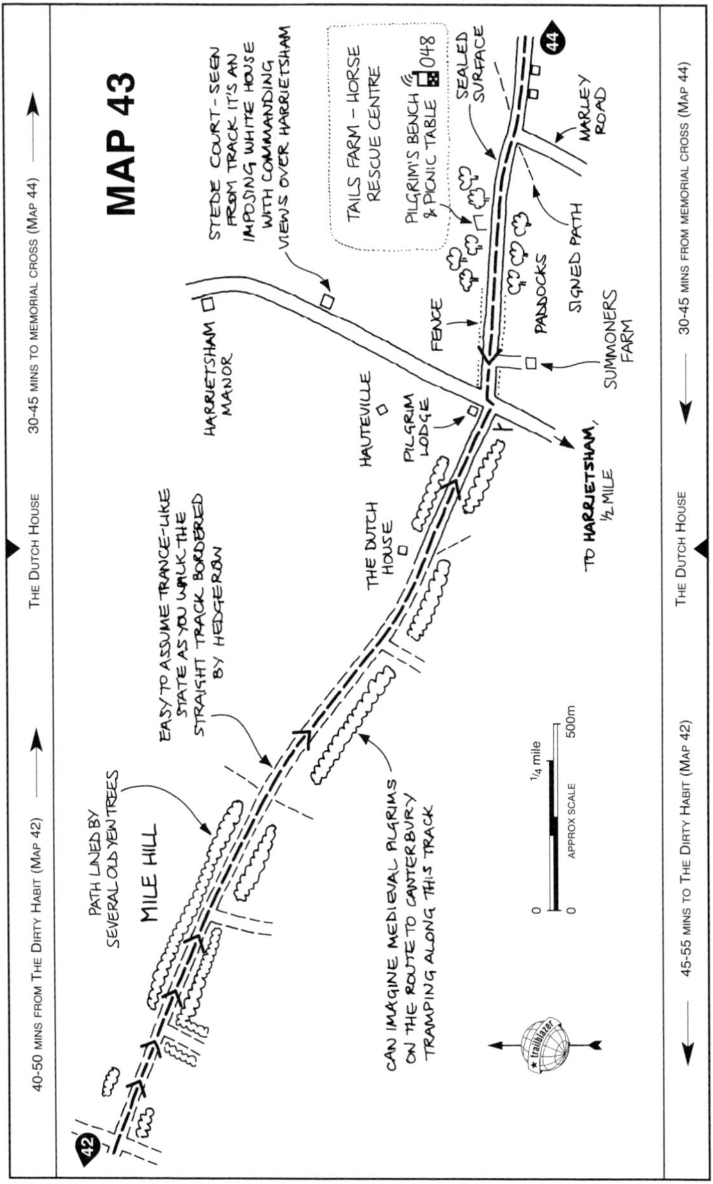
MAP 43
30-45 MINS TO MEMORIAL CROSS (MAP 44)
THE DUTCH HOUSE
40-50 MINS FROM THE DIRTY HABIT (MAP 42)
STEDE COURT - SEEN FROM TRACK. IT'S AN IMPOSING WHITE HOUSE WITH COMMANDING VIEWS OVER HARRIETSHAM
TAILS FARM - HORSE RESCUE CENTRE
PILGRIM'S BENCH & PICNIC TABLE
048
SEALED SURFACE
44
MARLEY ROAD
SIGNED PATH
PADDOCKS
FENCE
SUMMONERS FARM
HARRIETSHAM MANOR
HAUTEVILLE
PILGRIM LODGE
TO HARRIETSHAM, ½ MILE
THE DUTCH HOUSE
EASY TO ASSUME TRANCE-LIKE STATE AS YOU WALK THE STRAIGHT TRACK BORDERED BY HEDGEROW
PATH LINED BY SEVERAL OLD YEW TREES
MILE HILL
CAN IMAGINE MEDIEVAL PILGRIMS ON THE ROUTE TO CANTERBURY TRAMPING ALONG THIS TRACK
42
0
¼ mile
0
APPROX SCALE
500m
trailblazer
45-55 MINS TO THE DIRTY HABIT (MAP 42)
THE DUTCH HOUSE
30-45 MINS FROM MEMORIAL CROSS (MAP 44)

By now you will have come to the conclusion that the Pilgrims' Way itself is really rather a straight and level track, mostly bordered by hedges with occasional views over vast arable fields. This makes for fast walking on a mostly firm track below the ridge line and at times it's all too easy to drift into a trance-like state as the miles slip by – until before you know it, Lenham, where there's a greater degree of choice of accommodation and dining options – all of them huddled around the main village square.

LENHAM   [MAP 44a]

In many ways Lenham is your typical North Downs Way settlement. A handsome village with a long history, filled with venerable, vernacular buildings and enough eateries, accommodation and other services to lure the trekker off the trail.

The first shop you come to is a *Co-op supermarket* (daily 7am-10pm), though there's a **Village Store** (Mon-Thur 8am-8pm, Fri & Sat to 9pm, Sun 10am-6pm) in town with more local produce and an **ATM** (£1.75 withdrawal fee). You can also get money out from the **post office** (Mon-Tue, Thur & Fri 8.30am-5.45pm, Wed to 5.30pm, Sat to 1.30pm). Opposite you'll find a **pharmacy** (🖳 saxonwarriorpharmacy.com; Mon-Fri 9am-5.30pm, Sat 9am-1pm). On the second Sunday of every month in the main square there's a **farmers' market** (see box p22).

The **railway station** is a stop on South Eastern Railway's London Victoria to Canterbury West service (see box pp42-3). Stagecoach's **bus** No 10X (Maidstone to Ashford) stops by The Square; see pp45-8 for details.

Where to stay & eat

Dog and Bear Hotel (☎ 01622-858219, 🖳 dogandbearlenham.co.uk; 1S/12D/8D or T/1Tr/2Qd, all en suite; 🛏; WI-FI; 🐕) started life as a 15th-century coaching inn. B&B costs £40-50pp (sgl from £60) in this friendly establishment. One room has a four-poster bed.

The first eatery you come to when leaving the North Downs Way is *The Bow Window* (☎ 01622-850802, 🖳 thebowwindowlenham.co.uk; Mon-Wed 9am-5pm, Thur-Sat 9am-10pm, Sun 10am-3pm; WI-FI; 🐕), which has pretty much everything a walker requires including a welcoming

attitude towards dogs and some tasty offerings, with toasted and doorstop sarnies from £5.25. They also offer tapas in the evenings (tapas platter £12.95).

Pippa's (Mon-Sat 10am-5pm, Sun 11am-4pm) is a popular tearoom on the square with a few hot dishes (eg fish pie £8.95) as well as sandwiches and cakes. On the opposite side, *Home Bake* (Mon-Fri 8am-5pm, Sat 7.30am-2pm) is the best option for takeaway grub at lunchtimes, with pasties for £2.

Chequers Fish Bar (Mon-Fri 8am-2.30pm & 4-10.30pm, Sat 8am-10.30pm, Sun & Bank Hols 10am-9pm) works long hours to keep its punters fed with fish and kebabs (cod & chips £6.40).

Take-away Chinese food is available from *Chopsticks & Bowl* (☎ 01622-858416; Sun-Thur noon-2pm & 5-11.30pm, Fri & Sat noon-2.30pm & 5-11.45pm), offering good-value dishes including a portion of spicy Singapore Special Fried Rice (£4.80).

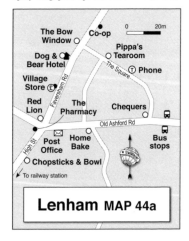

Lenham MAP 44a

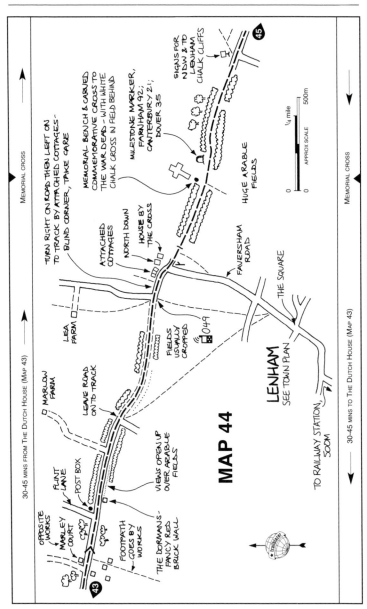

MEMORIAL CROSS

MEMORIAL CROSS

30-45 MINS FROM THE DUTCH HOUSE (MAP 43)

30-45 MINS TO THE DUTCH HOUSE (MAP 43)

MAP 44

LENHAM
SEE TOWN PLAN

TO RAILWAY STATION,
500M

THE SQUARE

FAVERSHAM ROAD

FIELDS
USUALLY
CROPPED

NORTH DOWN
HOUSE BY
THE CROSS

ATTACHED
COTTAGES

TURN RIGHT ON ROAD THEN LEFT ON
TO TRACK BY ATTACHED COTTAGES -
BLIND CORNER, TAKE CARE

MEMORIAL BENCH & CARVED
COMMEMORATIVE CROSS TO
THE WAR DEAD - WITH WHITE
CHALK CROSS IN FIELD BEHIND

MILESTONE MARKER,
FARNHAM 92;
CANTERBURY 21;
DOVER 35

SIGNS FOR
NDW & TO
LENHAM
CHALK CLIFFS

HUGE ARABLE
FIELDS

LEA
FARM

MARLOW
FARM

LEAVE ROAD
ON TO TRACK

VIEWS OPEN UP
OVER ARABLE
FIELDS

FLINT
LANE

POST BOX

OPPOSITE
WORKS

MARLEY
COURT

FOOTPATH
GOES BY
WORKS

THE DORMANS -
FANCY RED
BRICK WALL

0   1/4 mile

0   500m
APPROX SCALE

45

43

For good pub grub try *The Red Lion* (☎ 01622-858531, 🖳 redlionlenham.co.uk; food Mon-Fri noon-2.30pm & 6-9pm, Sat & Sun noon-9pm; WI-FI; 🐾) with set lunchtime menus (Mon-Thur noon-3pm) consisting largely of pub standards at £11.95 for two courses, or £13.95 for three. The food is just as good at the *Dog and Bear* (see p156; Mon-Sat noon-9.30pm, Sun noon-9pm) with sausages and mash for £9.95.

If all the accommodation in Lenham is booked up *The Harrow Hill Hotel* (also known as *The Harrow Inn*; ☎ 01622-859846, 🖳 harrowhillhotel.com; 1T/5D/1Tr/three rooms sleeping up to five, all en suite; ➠; WI-FI; 🐾) is 20 minutes off the trail (see Map 45). It's a very efficient and friendly country pub with a variety of rooms including one with a Jacuzzi and one with a four-poster bed. **B&B** costs £32.50-47.50pp (sgl occ £45-95). **Food** is served daily noon-2.30pm & 6.30-9pm (to 9.30pm on Fri & Sat); the bar is closed 3-6pm and lunch is not available in winter.

After Lenham the North Downs Way passes under a large chalk cross (which may feel like it's another example of the Christian pilgrimage nature of this walk, though it's actually been put there as a memorial to local soldiers who died in WWII), before following a byway with little evidence of much vehicle use. With views over large arable fields the trail passes through woodland and descends to the A252, with Charing just a short distance away.

CHARING   [MAP 46, p160]

'Charing again was the last convenient halt in any rich man's journey...It is something under 16 miles from Canterbury, following the track of the Old Road and eve the poor upon the pilgrimages would have halted there... Charing, therefore, was designed by its every character to be a place of some importance, and was a very conscious little town.' **Hilaire Belloc,** *The Old Road*

Even today you can tell just what an important village Charing must have been. Many of the buildings are rather grand, a few are half timbered and the **church** (St Peter & St Paul) has a fine tower. Right next to it and just off the High St there are also the **ruins** of a former archbishop's palace, which are well worth a look. Unfortunately, like so many villages around here, Charing is suffering from decline. Where once there were five pubs, for example, today there is just the one, newly opened micro-pub (*The Bookmakers Arms*; ☎ 07885-252001; bar Tue-Sat 6-11pm, Sun 1-4pm; food is not served; 🐾).

Of those establishments that remain open, **GM & M John's** (Mon-Thur 8am-4.30pm, Fri to 5pm, Sat to 1pm) is both butcher and baker. Next door is the **post office** (Mon-Fri 9am-5.30pm, Sat 9am-12.30pm) where you can get **money** out using your debit card. Across the road is Way & Brett, the **local village store** (Mon-Sat 7am-8pm, Sun 9am-6pm).

Thankfully there's still a tea room, *Mulberry's* (☎ 01233-714171, 🖳 mulber rys.co; Mon-Sat 10am-4pm), with a good range of scones and cakes. There are no B&Bs left but should you need to find somewhere to eat in the evening, *Jasmine House* (☎ 01233-714988, 🖳 jasminehouse kent.com; Mon & Wed-Thur 3-10.30pm, Fri & Sat to 11pm, Sun 1.30-10pm) is a smart and cavernous Chinese restaurant about 600m west of the High St just past the main roundabout on the A20. Meals are reasonably priced (starting at about £6.40 for a main) and they have a built a fine reputation for their hot pots (from £7.40 up to £9.50 for the mixed seafood & tofu hot pot).

South Eastern Railway operates services (see box pp42-3) to London Victoria, Ashford International and Canterbury West from the **railway station**. Stagecoach's **bus** No 10X (Maidstone to Ashford) stops here; see pp45-8.

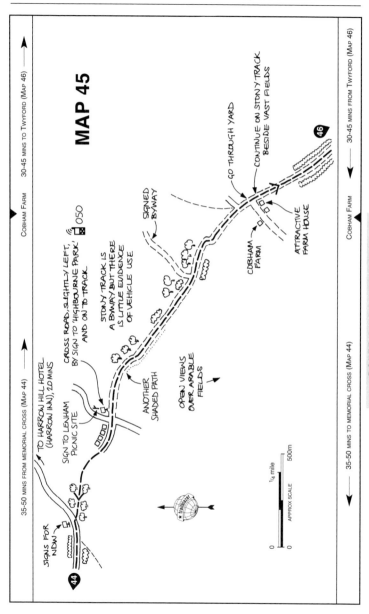

MAP 45

SIGNS FOR
NDW

TO HARROW HILL HOTEL
(HARROW INN), 20 MINS

SIGN TO LENHAM
PICNIC SITE

CROSS ROAD, SLIGHTLY LEFT,
BY SIGN TO 'HIGHBOURNE PARK'
AND ON TO TRACK

050

STONY TRACK IS
A BYWAY BUT THERE
IS LITTLE EVIDENCE
OF VEHICLE USE

ANOTHER
SHADED PATH

OPEN VIEWS
OVER ARABLE
FIELDS

SIGNED
BYWAY

GO THROUGH YARD

CONTINUE ON STONY TRACK
BESIDE VAST FIELDS

COBHAM
FARM

ATTRACTIVE
FARM HOUSE

¼ mile
500m
APPROX SCALE
0
0

ROUTE GUIDE AND MAPS

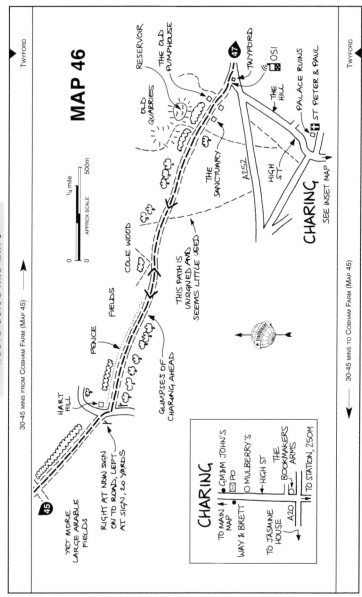

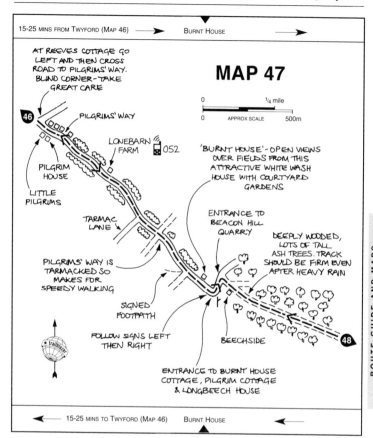

AT REEVES COTTAGE GO LEFT AND THEN CROSS ROAD TO PILGRIMS' WAY. BLIND CORNER – TAKE GREAT CARE

MAP 47

46

PILGRIMS' WAY

0   1/4 mile

0   APPROX SCALE   500m

LONEBARN FARM 052

'BURNT HOUSE' – OPEN VIEWS OVER FIELDS FROM THIS ATTRACTIVE WHITE WASH HOUSE WITH COURTYARD GARDENS

PILGRIM HOUSE

LITTLE PILGRIMS

TARMAC LANE

ENTRANCE TO BEACON HILL QUARRY

DEEPLY WOODED, LOTS OF TALL ASH TREES. TRACK SHOULD BE FIRM EVEN AFTER HEAVY RAIN

PILGRIMS' WAY IS TARMACKED SO MAKES FOR SPEEDY WALKING

SIGNED FOOTPATH

FOLLOW SIGNS LEFT THEN RIGHT

BEECHSIDE

48

trailblazer

ENTRANCE TO BURNT HOUSE COTTAGE, PILGRIM COTTAGE & LONGBEECH HOUSE

ROUTE GUIDE AND MAPS

After Charing the path continues to follow the route of the Pilgrims' Way, now hurtling headlong into the dense woods of Westwell Downs, before arriving at the village that shares its name.

WESTWELL [MAP 48, p163]

There's not much here but **campers** will find pitches for £7.50pp at the fair and friendly ***Dunn Street Farm*** (🖥 dunnstreet farm.co.uk, bookings preferred especially if out of the main season 🖥 dunnstreetfarm @gmail.com; 🐕 on leads and well behaved as it is a livestock farm); the route passes in front of the farm gates.

The **campsite** has a just a fridge, freezer, washing machine (£2 per load) and kettle when it comes to kitchen facilities, so if you're cooking for yourself you'll need to bring some sort of stove. Nevertheless, it's a lovely friendly place with free showers and drinking water taps – and it's so refreshing to find a campsite positioned

right on the trail. If you don't have the facilities or desire to cook for yourself, *The
Wheel* (☎ 01233-712223, 🖳 thewheelin-
nwestwell .uk; food Mon-Fri noon-3pm &
6-9.30pm, Sat noon-9.30pm, Sun noon-
4.30pm; WI-FI; 🐾) has been taken over by
new people and is now open and serving
food.

From Westwell a fairly lengthy crossing of a couple of vast arable fields follows as you make your way to the tranquil park landscape of **Eastwell**. Don't
miss the 30-second diversion to the **ruined church of St Mary's** (Map 49 and
see box below) and its lakeside setting – truly one of the most magical locations
on the entire path. The church was actually destroyed by a V2 bomber in WWII,
but is still consecrated ground and holds the grave of the last of the Plantagenets.

From here, it's a straightforward amble through the grounds of *Eastwell
Manor Hotel* (☎ 01233-213000, 🖳 eastwellmanor.co.uk; 23D or T, all en suite;
🍷; WI-FI). This is top-hole, glossy brochure stuff, carved panelled rooms with
baronial-stone fireplaces. You'll pay from £62.50pp (sgl occ rates on request)
for B&B. Some of the rooms have four posters. There's a **restaurant** here too.

The path cuts across the driveway of the hotel before crossing one more
field on its way to Boughton Lees and its large village green.

BOUGHTON LEES   [MAP 49, p165]

Leaving the grounds of the hotel, you find
yourself in the village of Boughton Lees
and the wonderful *Flying Horse Inn* (☎
01233-620914, 🖳 theflyinghorse-kent.uk;
food Mon-Fri noon-3pm & 6-8.30pm, Sat
noon-9pm, Sun noon-5pm; 🐾 bar area
only) is a lovely spot. Marvellously, they
also buck the downward trend of the North

❑ **St Mary's Church, Eastwell, and the tomb of Richard Plantagenet**
Though today the church is closed to the public, inside it is said to be the tomb of
Richard Plantagenet, the man who claimed to be the illegitimate son of Richard III
(reigned 1452-1485). Though the king refused to officially recognise Richard as his
own, the boy, who was raised by teachers who taught in Latin, received regular
amounts of money from an anonymous donor. At the time the boy had no idea who
his father was and the king and his son remained strangers throughout Richard's
childhood. All that changed on the eve of the Battle of Bosworth, when the king sum-
moned Richard, then 16, to tell him of his royal lineage and to say that, should the
battle be won, the king would acknowledge Richard as his son; but if he lost, the son
should flee for his own safety.

The king, of course, was defeated and ended up interred beneath a car park in
Leicester. His son, Richard, taking his father's advice, chose to live anonymously as
a bricklayer and mason. His identity was only discovered by Sir Thomas Moyle, who
had hired him to build his manor at Eastwell and who found him reading a book in
Latin. Though Sir Thomas offered Richard the chance to live at his manor once it was
completed, Richard, by then nearly 70, refused, instead building a one-room cottage
in the grounds. (A building called Plantagenet Cottage still stands on the site of the
original; the manor, incidentally, was demolished in the 1920s.) There he resided until
his death at the age of 81 – the last of the Plantagenet dynasty that had ruled England
for over 300 years.

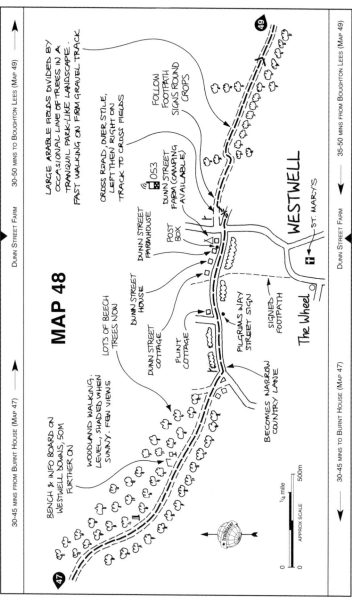

MAP 48

LARGE ARABLE FIELDS DIVIDED BY OCCASIONAL LINE OF TREES IN A TRANQUIL PARK-LIKE LANDSCAPE. FAST WALKING ON FARM GRAVEL TRACK

CROSS ROAD, OVER STILE, LEFT THEN RIGHT ON TRACK TO CROSS FIELDS

FOLLOW FOOTPATH SIGNS ROUND CROPS

DUNN STREET FARM (CAMPING AVAILABLE)

053

DUNN STREET FARMHOUSE

POST BOX

DUNN STREET HOUSE

LOTS OF BEECH TREES NOW

DUNN STREET COTTAGE

FLINT COTTAGE

PILGRIMS WAY STREET SIGN

SIGNED FOOTPATH

WESTWELL

ST. MARY'S

The Wheel

BECOMES NARROW COUNTRY LANE

BENCH & INFO BOARD ON WESTWELL DOWNS, 50M FURTHER ON

WOODLAND WALKING. LEVEL, SHADED WHEN SUNNY. FEW VIEWS

¼ mile

APPROX SCALE

500m

0

0

47

49

Downs Way when it comes to accommodation by *opening* a **B&B** (4D, all en suite; ☎; WI-FI; £35-45pp, sgl occ £60-80) – *and* a basic **campsite** (🌢) too, which is free as long as you book to eat in the restaurant.

Try to avoid the room directly above the bar, however – it gets very noisy.

Stagecoach's No **666** **bus** between Ashford and Faversham calls at the village green; see pp45-8.

BOUGHTON LEES TO CHILHAM [MAPS 49-52]

'I walk'd along a stream, for pureness rare,
  Brighter than sunshine; for it did acquaint
The dullest sight with all glorious prey
  That in the pebble-paved channel lay'
Christopher Marlowe, *The Stream*, about the River Stour.

The path divides not long after you leave Boughton Lees on this short-but-sweet stage of **5.9 miles/9.5km (1¾hrs to 2hrs 20 mins)**. Having marched along the tarmac for about half a mile you come to a signpost, where a choice needs to be made: continue on the tarmac for the shorter route, via Wye and the outskirts of Folkestone, to Dover (a total distance of around 25 miles according to the signpost); or take a left and head off into a tree tunnel for a longer (30 miles according to the signpost), prettier and more interesting saunter via Canterbury and its World Heritage cathedral. In this section we take the longer northern route, though there is much to recommend this southern trail, which we describe beginning on p195.

The main path leaves the tarmac and heads through a tree tunnel to the lovely little church at **Boughton Aluph** (see Map 50), from where the trail cuts through the yard of Soakham Farm, in a lovely setting with uninterrupted views over the Great Stour Valley. The trail climbs steeply on to **Soakham Downs** and then through an attractive beech and chestnut forest, for the next hour or so before following a quiet tarmac road past Chilham Place and into the village overlooked by it.

❏ Oast-houses and hop gardens

Oast-houses are basically huge ovens used to dry hops, an ingredient in beer production. Now most have been converted into houses and occasionally B&Bs. Usually consisting of four rooms, the oven and the store room downstairs, the drying room and the cooling room upstairs, when converted they make a spacious living area. The characteristic conical roof and pointed chimneys were designed to draw extra air through the kiln, increasing the amount of hops that could be dried in one go. Often oast-houses were built near ponds – combining fire and wood is a risky business.

The hop is a climbing plant and was traditionally grown on a system of poles and strings up to 20ft high. The female flower, or cone, is what gives beer a 'hoppy' bitter taste. At the height of the Kent hop industry up to 80,000 pickers would descend on the county for the September harvest but modern plants grow as 8ft hedges and now the crop is easily harvested by machine.

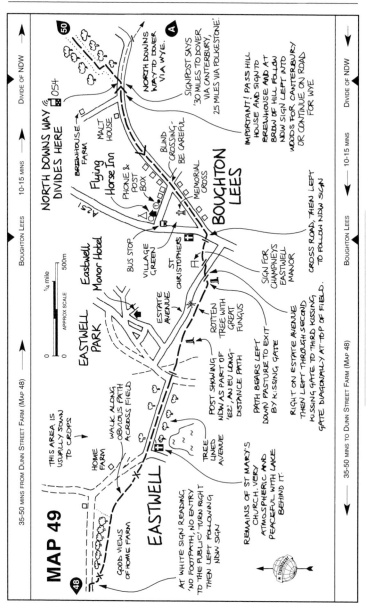

MAP 49

35-50 MINS FROM DUNN STREET FARM (MAP 48)

48

NORTH DOWNS WAY DIVIDES HERE

50

A

NORTH DOWNS WAY TO DOVER VIA WYE.

SIGNPOST SAYS '30 MILES TO DOVER VIA CANTERBURY, 25 MILES VIA FOLKESTONE'.

IMPORTANT! PASS HILL HOUSE AND SIGN TO BREWHOUSE AND AT BROW OF HILL FOLLOW NDW SIGN LEFT INTO WOODS FOR CANTERBURY OR CONTINUE ON ROAD FOR WYE

BREWHOUSE FARM

MALT HOUSE

Flying Horse Inn

PHONE & POST BOX

BLIND CROSSING- BE CAREFUL

BOUGHTON LEES

MEMORIAL CROSS

A251

EASTWELL PARK

Eastwell Manor Hotel

BUS STOP

VILLAGE GREEN

ST CHRISTOPHERS

CROSS ROAD, THEN LEFT TO FOLLOW NDW SIGN

SIGN FOR CHAMPNEYS EASTWELL MANOR

ESTATE AVENUE

ROTTEN TREE WITH GREAT FUNGUS

POST SHOWING NDW AS PART OF 'E2', AN EU LONG-DISTANCE PATH

PATH BEARS LEFT DOWN PASTURE TO EXIT BY KISSING GATE

RIGHT ON ESTATE AVENUE THEN LEFT THROUGH SECOND KISSING GATE TO THIRD KISSING GATE DIAGONALLY AT TOP OF FIELD.

HOME FARM

THIS AREA IS USUALLY SOWN TO CROPS

WALK ALONG OBVIOUS PATH ACROSS FIELD

TREE LINED AVENUE

EASTWELL

GOOD VIEWS OF HOME FARM

AT WHITE SIGN READING, 'NO FOOTPATH, NO ENTRY TO THE PUBLIC' TURN RIGHT THEN LEFT FOLLOWING NDW SIGN

REMAINS OF ST MARY'S CHURCH. VERY ATMOSPHERIC AND PEACEFUL WITH LAKE BEHIND IT.

0   1/4 mile

0   500m

APPROX SCALE

trailblazer

35-50 MINS TO DUNN STREET FARM (MAP 48) • BOUGHTON LEES • 10-15 MINS • DIVIDE OF NDW

← 35-50 MINS FROM DUNN STREET FARM (MAP 48) • BOUGHTON LEES • 10-15 MINS • 10-15 MINS • DIVIDE OF NDW →

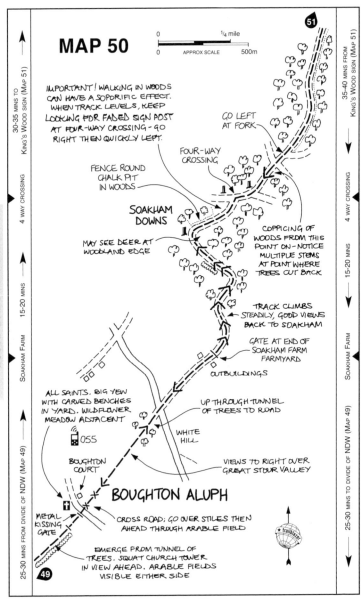

MAP 50

0   ¼ mile
APPROX SCALE
0   500m

51

35-40 MINS FROM
KING'S WOOD SIGN (MAP 51)

30-35 MINS TO
KING'S WOOD SIGN (MAP 51)

IMPORTANT! WALKING IN WOODS
CAN HAVE A SOPORIFIC EFFECT.
WHEN TRACK LEVELS, KEEP
LOOKING FOR FADED SIGN POST
AT FOUR-WAY CROSSING - GO
RIGHT THEN QUICKLY LEFT.

GO LEFT
AT FORK

FOUR-WAY
CROSSING

FENCE ROUND
CHALK PIT
IN WOODS

SOAKHAM
DOWNS

COPPICING OF
WOODS FROM THIS
POINT ON - NOTICE
MULTIPLE STEMS
AT POINT WHERE
TREES CUT BACK

MAY SEE DEER AT
WOODLAND EDGE

4 WAY CROSSING

4 WAY CROSSING

15-20 MINS

15-20 MINS

TRACK CLIMBS
STEADILY, GOOD VIEWS
BACK TO SOAKHAM

GATE AT END OF
SOAKHAM FARM
FARMYARD

OUTBUILDINGS

SOAKHAM FARM

SOAKHAM FARM

ALL SAINTS. BIG YEW
WITH CARVED BENCHES
IN YARD. WILDFLOWER
MEADOW ADJACENT

UP THROUGH TUNNEL
OF TREES TO ROAD

WHITE
HILL

055

BOUGHTON
COURT

VIEWS TO RIGHT OVER
GREAT STOUR VALLEY

BOUGHTON ALUPH

25-30 MINS FROM DIVIDE OF NDW (MAP 49)

25-30 MINS TO DIVIDE OF NDW (MAP 49)

METAL
KISSING
GATE

CROSS ROAD; GO OVER STILES THEN
AHEAD THROUGH ARABLE FIELD

trailblazer

EMERGE FROM TUNNEL OF
TREES. SQUAT CHURCH TOWER
IN VIEW AHEAD. ARABLE FIELDS
VISIBLE EITHER SIDE

49

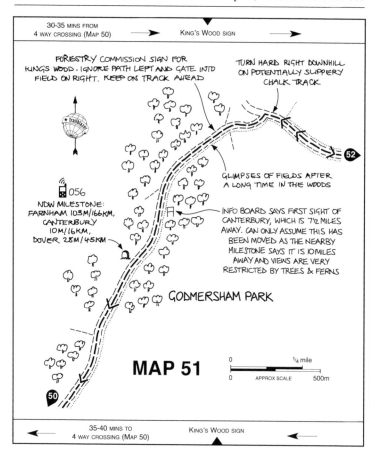

FORESTRY COMMISSION SIGN FOR KING'S WOOD. IGNORE PATH LEFT AND GATE INTO FIELD ON RIGHT. KEEP ON TRACK AHEAD

TURN HARD RIGHT DOWNHILL ON POTENTIALLY SLIPPERY CHALK TRACK

★ trailblazer

52

GLIMPSES OF FIELDS AFTER A LONG TIME IN THE WOODS

056

NOW MILESTONE:
FARNHAM 103M/166KM,
CANTERBURY
10M/16KM,
DOVER 28M/45KM

INFO BOARD SAYS FIRST SIGHT OF CANTERBURY, WHICH IS 7½ MILES AWAY. CAN ONLY ASSUME THIS HAS BEEN MOVED AS THE NEARBY MILESTONE SAYS IT IS 10 MILES AWAY AND VIEWS ARE VERY RESTRICTED BY TREES & FERNS

GODMERSHAM PARK

MAP 51

0   ¼ mile

0   APPROX SCALE   500m

50

ROUTE GUIDE AND MAPS

CHILHAM   [MAP 52, p169]

Chilham is a very pretty village overlooked by a Jacobean castle, now a private residence. A previous owner replaced the brick wall with railings opening a pleasing view for the public. At the heart of the village is the medieval square bordered by black and white half-timbered buildings some of them faced with brick.

The friendly **post office shop** (Mon, Tue, Thur-Fri 8.30am-1pm & 2-5.30pm, Wed & Sat 8.30am-1pm, Sun 8.30-10am) has snacks and drinks.

Chilham **railway station** is a stop on South Eastern Railway's services between Canterbury West and London Charing Cross/Victoria; see box pp42-3. Stagecoach's **bus** No 1/1A/1X (Ashford to Canterbury) calls here; see pp45-8.

The Old Alma Inn (☎ 01227-731913, 🖥 theoldalma.co.uk; 4D/1T, all en suite; WI-FI; 🐾), a former pub now a **B&B**, charges £35-37.50pp (sgl occ from £50). It's the closest to the railway station and on the A28.

Probably the most historic place is the ivy-clad *Bagham Farmhouse* (☎ 01227-730306; 2D/2T, all en suite; WI-FI), built in 1460 and now standing off the A28. B&B costs from £39pp, or from £50 for single occupancy.

Woolpack Inn (☎ 01227-730351, ⌨ woolpackinnchilham.co.uk; 1S/7D/3T/1Tr/1Qd/one room for up to five people, all en suite or with private facilities; ▾; WI-FI; 🐾) is an excellent pub with very comfortable rooms. If you're on your own and lucky enough to get the single it'll set you back from about £55; otherwise the rooms start at about £42.50pp (sgl occ room rate).

The **food** at the *Woolpack* (daily noon-9.30pm) is top notch both in the bar (mains from £8.95 for the small cod & chips) and in the pricier restaurant (mains from £12.95).

The *White Horse Inn* (☎ 01227-730355, ⌨ thewhitehorsechilham.uk; food Mon-Thur noon-3pm & 5-9pm, Fri & Sat noon-10pm, Sun noon-8pm; WI-FI; 🐾) also does bar food and has regular music nights.

Shelly's Tea Room (⌨ shellystearooms.com; daily 10am-6pm), on The Square, knows what it's doing with a cream tea (£7.35).

CHILHAM TO CANTERBURY   [MAPS 52-55]

Oast-houses and orchards, history and hops, apples and inns – today's **6.4-mile/10.3km walk (2hrs 20mins to 3hrs)** from the prettiest village on the North Downs Way to its largest and most fascinating city is a showcase for much of the clichéd glories of Kent – and it's quite delightful.

Leaving Chilham through the grounds and graveyard of St Mary's (where the oldest grave dates from 1638) the trail climbs gently but purposefully past orderly orchards to the curiously named **Old Wives Lees** (Map 53). A sharp right turn at the junction leads you out of the village (eventually) past oast-houses and yet another orchard – this one run on a more industrial scale, with the workers' accommodation forming its own mobile-home village by the railway bridge – and onto the village of **Chartham Hatch**, though this no longer has any services.

If you need to get away from all this bucolic beauty, a 20-minute walk down Hatch Lane will bring you to the railway station at Chartham.

CHARTHAM   [MAP 54, p171]

For food in the evening your only option lies beyond the railway station at *The Artichoke* (☎ 01227-738316, ⌨ artichokechartham.co.uk; food Mon-Sat noon-3pm & 5.30-8.30pm, Sun noon-5pm; WI-FI; 🐾) a handsome timber-framed pub.

Chartham **railway station** is a stop on South Eastern Railway's services (see box pp42-3) between Canterbury West and London Charing Cross/Victoria. Stagecoach's **bus** Nos 1/1A/1X (Ashford to Canterbury) call here from opposite the railway station (Mon-Sat 1/hr); see pp45-8.

Back on the trail, the final stretch of your pilgrimage for this stage is a pleasant stroll through **No Man's Orchard** (see box p173) followed by a lengthy schlep through woodland, before a crossing of the A2 signals the start of the suburbs of Canterbury, gaining entrance to the city centre via the West Gate to arrive at its revered and venerable cathedral.   (cont'd on p173)

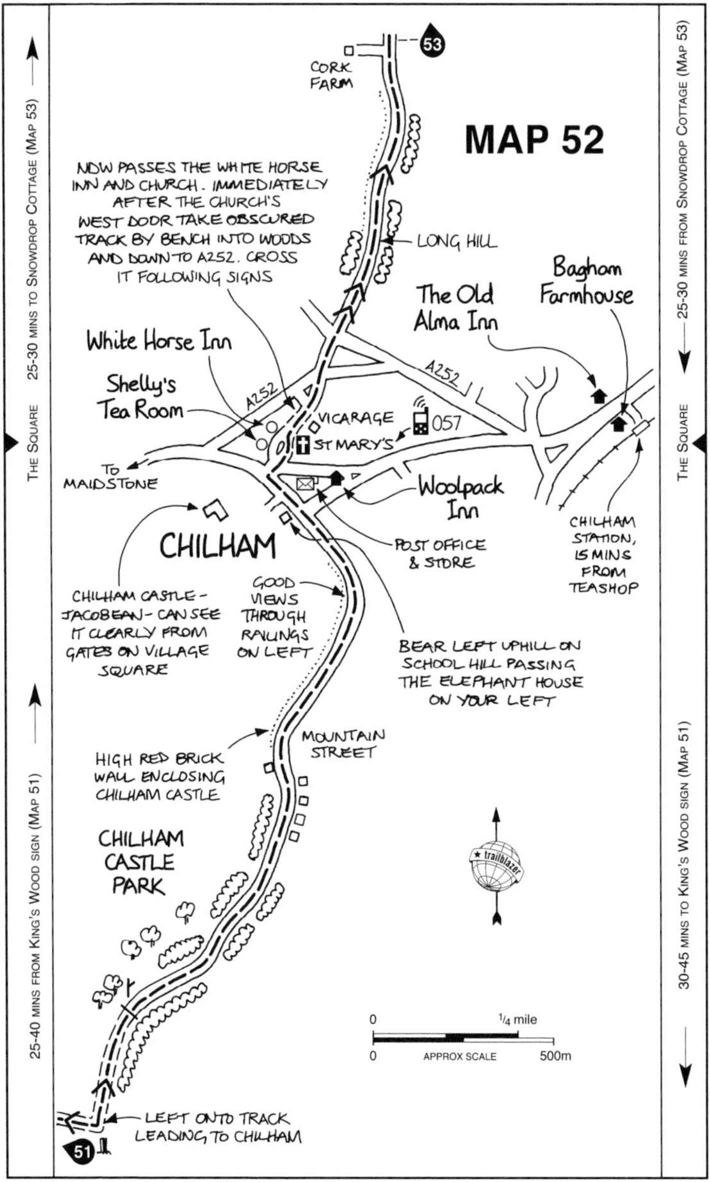

MAP 52

CORK FARM

53

NOW PASSES THE WHITE HORSE INN AND CHURCH. IMMEDIATELY AFTER THE CHURCH'S WEST DOOR TAKE OBSCURED TRACK BY BENCH INTO WOODS AND DOWN TO A252. CROSS IT FOLLOWING SIGNS

LONG HILL

Bagham Farmhouse

The Old Alma Inn

A252

White Horse Inn

Shelly's Tea Room

A252

VICARAGE

057

☩ ST MARY'S

TO MAIDSTONE

CHILHAM

POST OFFICE & STORE

Woolpack Inn

CHILHAM STATION, 15 MINS FROM TEASHOP

CHILHAM CASTLE - JACOBEAN - CAN SEE IT CLEARLY FROM GATES ON VILLAGE SQUARE

GOOD VIEWS THROUGH RAILINGS ON LEFT

BEAR LEFT UPHILL ON SCHOOL HILL PASSING THE ELEPHANT HOUSE ON YOUR LEFT

HIGH RED BRICK WALL ENCLOSING CHILHAM CASTLE

MOUNTAIN STREET

CHILHAM CASTLE PARK

trailblazer

0   ¼ mile

0   500m

APPROX SCALE

51

LEFT ONTO TRACK LEADING TO CHILHAM

25-30 MINS TO SNOWDROP COTTAGE (MAP 53)

THE SQUARE

25-40 MINS FROM KING'S WOOD SIGN (MAP 51)

25-30 MINS FROM SNOWDROP COTTAGE (MAP 53)

THE SQUARE

30-45 MINS TO KING'S WOOD SIGN (MAP 51)

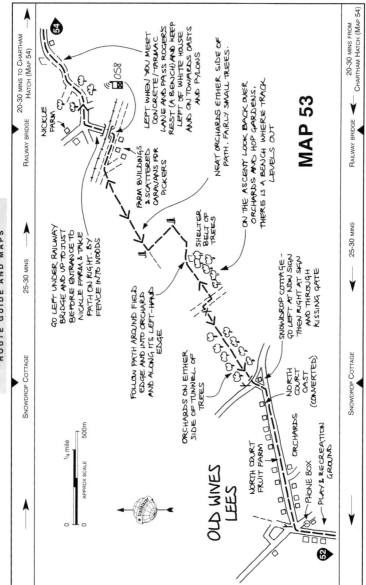

ROUTE GUIDE AND MAPS

MAP 53

SNOWDROP COTTAGE — 25-30 MINS — RAILWAY BRIDGE — 20-30 MINS TO CHARTHAM HATCH (MAP 54)

SNOWDROP COTTAGE — 25-30 MINS — RAILWAY BRIDGE — 20-30 MINS FROM CHARTHAM HATCH (MAP 54)

1/4 mile
500m
0
0
APPROX SCALE

★ trailblazer

54

NICKLE FARM

058

LEFT WHEN YOU MEET CONCRETE/TARMAC LANE AND PASS ROGERS REST (A BENCH) AND KEEP LEFT OF WHITE HOUSE AND ON TOWARDS OASTS AND PYLONS

FARM BUILDINGS & SCATTERED CARAVANS FOR PICKERS

NEAT ORCHARDS EITHER SIDE OF PATH. FAIRLY SMALL TREES.

ON THE ASCENT LOOK BACK OVER ORCHARDS AND HOP GARDENS. THERE IS A BENCH WHERE TRACK LEVELS OUT

GO LEFT UNDER RAILWAY BRIDGE AND UP TO JUST BEFORE ENTRANCE TO NICKLE FARM & TAKE PATH ON RIGHT. BY FENCE INTO WOODS

SHELTER BELT OF TREES

FOLLOW PATH AROUND FIELD EDGE AND INTO ORCHARD AND ALONG ITS LEFT-HAND EDGE

ORCHARDS ON EITHER SIDE OF TUNNEL OF TREES

SNOWDROP COTTAGE - GO LEFT AT NEW SIGN THEN RIGHT AT SIGN AND THROUGH KISSING GATE

NORTH COURT OAST (CONVERTED)

OLD WIVES LEES

NORTH COURT FRUIT FARM

ORCHARDS

PHONE BOX

PLAY & RECREATION GROUND

52

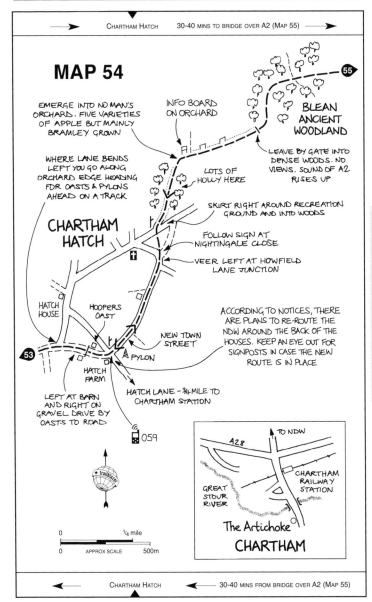

MAP 54

EMERGE INTO NO MAN'S ORCHARD. FIVE VARIETIES OF APPLE BUT MAINLY BRAMLEY GROWN

INFO BOARD ON ORCHARD

BLEAN ANCIENT WOODLAND

WHERE LANE BENDS LEFT YOU GO ALONG ORCHARD EDGE HEADING FOR OASTS & PYLONS AHEAD ON A TRACK

LOTS OF HOLLY HERE

LEAVE BY GATE INTO DENSE WOODS. NO VIEWS, SOUND OF A2 RISES UP

CHARTHAM HATCH

SKIRT RIGHT AROUND RECREATION GROUND AND INTO WOODS

FOLLOW SIGN AT NIGHTINGALE CLOSE

VEER LEFT AT HOWFIELD LANE JUNCTION

HATCH HOUSE

HOOPERS OAST

NEW TOWN STREET

A PYLON

ACCORDING TO NOTICES, THERE ARE PLANS TO RE-ROUTE THE NDW AROUND THE BACK OF THE HOUSES. KEEP AN EYE OUT FOR SIGNPOSTS IN CASE THE NEW ROUTE IS IN PLACE

HATCH FARM

LEFT AT BARN AND RIGHT ON GRAVEL DRIVE BY OASTS TO ROAD

HATCH LANE – ¾ MILE TO CHARTHAM STATION

☎ 059

★ trailblazer

0   ¼ mile
0   APPROX SCALE   500m

TO NDW

A28

CHARTHAM RAILWAY STATION

GREAT STOUR RIVER

The Artichoke

CHARTHAM

ROUTE GUIDE AND MAPS

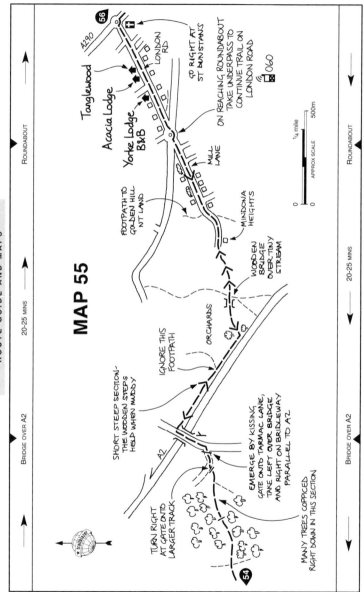

ROUNDABOUT   20-25 MINS   BRIDGE OVER A2   20-25 MINS   ROUNDABOUT   BRIDGE OVER A2

MAP 55

Tanglewood

Acacia Lodge

Yorke Lodge B&B

56

A290

LONDON RD

GO RIGHT AT ST DUNSTANS

ON REACHING ROUNDABOUT TAKE UNDERPASS TO CONTINUE TRAIL ON LONDON ROAD

060

MILL LANE

FOOTPATH TO GOLDEN HILL NT LAND

MINDONA HEIGHTS

WOODEN BRIDGE OVER TINY STREAM

SHORT STEEP SECTION- THE WOODEN STEPS HELP WHEN MUDDY

IGNORE THIS FOOTPATH

ORCHARDS

A2

EMERGE BY KISSING GATE ONTO TARMAC LANE, TAKE LEFT OVER BRIDGE AND RIGHT ON BRIDLEWAY PARALLEL TO A2

TURN RIGHT AT GATE ONTO LARGER TRACK

MANY TREES COPPICED RIGHT DOWN IN THIS SECTION

54

APPROX SCALE

0   500m

0   ¼ mile

❏ No Man's Orchard – a community orchard
This orchard (see Map 54) was planted in 1947 and purchased by Chartham and Harbledown parish councils becoming a community orchard in 1995. Orchards and fruit farms featured prominently in the landscape of Kent; with its mild climate and rich, deep soils the county came to be known as the garden of England. But experts reckon that 90% of its orchards have been lost in the last 50 years. No Man's Orchard is a traditional orchard planted with tall stemmed, large trees in contrast to modern dwarf varieties which are easier to harvest mechanically. The orchard is managed to attract birds with trees left to blossom and windfall fruit left on the ground to attract wildlife.

CANTERBURY   [MAP 56, pp176-7]
'*And specially from every shire's end*
Of England they to Canterbury went,
The holy blessed martyr there to seek
Who helped them when they lay so ill and
weak'
Geoffrey Chaucer, *The Canterbury Tales*

Canterbury, home of the Mother Church for Anglicans, shrine of the martyr St Thomas à Becket and the destination of Chaucer's bawdy pilgrims, is worth at least a full day's visit and makes an ideal stop-over before the final leg to Dover. As one of England's top visitor attractions the demand for rooms is always high so it's best to book ahead.

The centre is car-free with a **medieval street pattern** surrounded by a ring road.

What to see and do
Many visitors will be aghast to discover that they have to pay to even enter the precincts of their own mother church, but others will argue that at least **Canterbury Cathedral** (☎ 01227-762862, 🖥 www.canterbury-cathedral.org; Mon-Sat 9am-5.30pm, to 5pm in winter, Sun 12.30-2.30pm; £12.50) is worth the money. It was founded in AD597 by St Augustine, a Catholic and the cathedral's first archbishop. It's now the seat of the Mother Church of the Anglican Communion, or to give it its formal title 'The Cathedral and Metropolitical Church of Christ at Canterbury'. On 29 December 1170 four knights burst through Canterbury Cathedral's doors and murdered the then

❏ The Pilgrims' Way
On 29 December 1170, Archbishop Thomas à Becket was murdered in Canterbury Cathedral by four knights, their swords scattering his brains on the floor. The spot where he was killed went on to become a shrine drawing thousands of pilgrims following Becket's swift elevation by the Pope to sainthood in 1173 and for the remainder of the Middle Ages it was one of the most popular and wealthiest of shrines.

It's doubtful that there was ever only one route by which pilgrims came to venerate at the cathedral and it was only after 1860 that the name 'Pilgrims' Way' appeared on Ordnance Survey maps. The pilgrimages reached their height of popularity towards the end of the 14th century, at a time when Geoffrey Chaucer wrote *Canterbury Tales*. The North Downs Way coincides with the so-called Pilgrims' Way for much of its length in Kent. At Detling (Map 40, p151) the Way is also marked by the traditional symbol of pilgrimage, the scallop shell, and behind the Tudor gate is thought to have been a pilgrim hospital or shelter for medieval pilgrims on their journey to Canterbury.

Archbishop, Thomas à Becket (see box p173); he had been appointed by Henry II to bring the Church under the influence of the monarchy but set about defending its rights and paid the price.

The cathedral, the ruins of St Augustine's Abbey (see below) and St Martin's church (see below) make up the city's **UNESCO World Heritage site**. The cathedral has a wonderful Romanesque crypt, 12th-century quire and stained glass and of course the site and shrine of St Thomas à Becket's martyrdom. The best way to appreciate all that is there is to take a guided tour (Mon-Fri 10.30am, noon & 2.30pm, but 2pm in winter, Sat 10.30am, noon & 1pm; £5) lasting about an hour. Tickets are available from the cathedral's Welcome Centre on the day: there are no tours on Sunday nor at 10.30am in January.

English Heritage (EH) manages the **ruins of St Augustine's Abbey** (☎ 01227-767345; daily summer 10am-6pm, to 5pm in Oct, Nov-Mar Sat & Sun 10am-4pm; £6.20, free to EH members); founded in AD598, it was thoroughly smashed by Henry VIII on the dissolution of the monasteries. There's a good audio tour.

Off Longport lies England's oldest parish church and the oldest church in continuous use in the English-speaking world, **St Martin's** (☎ 01227-768072, ☐ www .martinpaul.org/stmartins; Tue, Thur & Fri 11am-3pm, Sat 11am-4pm).

Greyfriars (Easter to end Sep Mon-Sat 2-4pm; free), in the gardens off Stour St, was the first Franciscan chapel and was founded in 1267; it is so named for the colour of the monks' habits.

Today the private areas of **Eastbridge Hospital** (☎ 01227-471688, ☐ eastbridge hospital.org.uk; Mar to end Oct Mon-Sat 10.30am-5pm, winter 11am-4pm; £2), on St Peter's St, provide warden-assisted accommodation for Canterbury elderly. Originally a hospital for pilgrims, the Chantry chapel, the Pilgrims' Chapel and the medieval undercroft are fascinating.

For tales of medieval misadventure and humour **The Canterbury Tales Visitor Attraction** (☎ 01227-696001, ☐ canter burytales.org.uk; Apr-Aug daily 10am-5pm,

Sep & Oct to 4pm, Nov-Mar Wed-Sun 10am-4pm; £9.95) brings to life Chaucer's larger than life characters with animated exhibits.

The 1000-year-old **St Dunstan's Church** (open daily) is the first church passed on the way into Canterbury before West Gate. Reputedly the head of Sir Thomas More lies in a lead vault in this church. More, a Catholic and Lord Chancellor of England, refused to swear an oath of supremacy recognising Henry VIII as head of the church in England. In 1535 on the orders of Henry he was charged with treason and beheaded.

Canterbury Guided Tours (☎ 01227-459779, ☐ canterburyguidedtours.com) offer daily walking tours (Easter to Oct; £7.50/7/25 adult/concessions/family ticket) lasting 90 minutes, departing from the Buttermarket at 11am and 2pm (11am only for the rest of the year).

Services
The **tourist information centre** (TIC; ☎ 01227-862162, ☐ canterbury.co.uk; Mon-Wed & Fri 9am-6pm, Sat 9am-5pm, Thur to 8pm, Sun 10am-5pm) resides in The Beaney House of Art & Knowledge at 18 High St.

There are several banks with **ATMs** on the High St, particularly clustered near the corner of St Margaret's St, and a **post office** (Mon-Sat 9am-5.30pm, Sun 10.30am-2.30pm) in the branch of WH Smith on St George's St.

There are three **outdoor shops**: Blacks (Mon-Sat 9am-6pm, Sun 10.30am-4.30pm), 44 Burgate St; Cotswold Outdoors (Mon-Sat 9am-6pm, Sun 10.30am-4.30pm), at 15-16 Guildhall St; and Mountain Warehouse (Mon-Sat 9am-6pm, Sun 11am-5pm) on The Parade. You'll also find an **army-surplus store**, Golding Surplus Limited (☎ 01227-787899, ☐ goldingsurplus.co.uk; Mon-Sat 9am-5.30pm, Sun 11am-4pm) at 25 Palace St (aka King's Mile).

Boots **chemist** (Mon-Sat 8am-6pm, Sun 11am-5pm) is on Whitefriars opposite the bus station. Just next to it is a **supermarket**, Tesco (Mon-Sat 7am-10pm, Sun

11am-5pm), while opposite that is a Marks & Spencer (Mon-Sat 8am-7pm, Sun 11am-5pm).

A general **market** is held every Wednesday and Friday at St George's St and a farmers market is held every third Saturday in Westgate Hall (see box p22); see also The Good Shed p179.

Transport
There are two **railway stations**: **Canterbury West** is a stop on South Eastern Railways' services to London Victoria & Charing Cross as well as between St Pancras International and Ramsgate; **Canterbury East** is a stop on the London Victoria to Dover Priory line. See box pp42-3 for details.

The **bus station** is on St George's Lane – as you'd expect, there are many buses serving many destinations from here; perhaps most useful are Stagecoach's bus Nos 16 & 17 (to Folkestone); the Nos 1/1A/1X (to Ashford via Chartham & Chilham); and the 15 (to Dover). See pp45-8 for more information.

Canterbury is a stop on **National Express** coach services (see p44) between London Victoria Coach Station and Dover/Deal (NX007) and Ramsgate (NX022).

You can pick up a **taxi** from the southern end of the High St, or call Galaxy Taxis (☎ 01227-464232).

Where to stay
There is a campsite serving Canterbury but it's about a mile east of town. *Canterbury Camping and Caravanning Club Site* (☎ 01227-463216, 🖥 campingandcaravanning club.co.uk; WI-FI; 🐾 on lead) never turns away a backpacker (it's the Caravan Club rules); prices change according to the season and whether you arrive at a weekend or not, but make sure you ask for their backpacker rate; expect to pay £7-11.45pp. To reach it, continue along the North Downs Way out of the city, but instead of dropping down Spring Lane carry on along the A257 (see Map 56) for three-quarters of a mile, turning right onto Bekesbourne Lane. It's about a 20-minute walk from the city walls to the site. Or you can catch Stagecoach's No 43 bus service (to Sandwich; daily 1/hr) from the bus station which will drop you at the top of Bekesbourne Lane, from where it's just a 100m stroll.

Non-camping budget travellers have a couple of choices. To the south-east of the city is *YHA Canterbury* (☎ 0345-371 9010, 🖥 yha.org.uk/hostel/canterbury; 1 x 3-/6 x 4-/1 x 5-/6 x 6-bed dorms plus 1T; some rooms en suite; WI-FI communal area), 54 New Dover Rd. The rates are variable but start from about £13pp for members, and £29-69 for a private room, though an en suite one may cost up to £89.

(cont'd on p178)

ROUTE GUIDE AND MAPS

❏ The North Downs Way route through Canterbury   [Map 56, pp176-7]
The path enters the city by West Gate and after the river keeps straight on to the pedestrianised High St. After passing the tourist office look out for Mercery Lane on your left, take it towards the cathedral, then turn right when you reach the cathedral entrance to cross over Lower Bridge St, part of the busy 'ring road' surrounding the old city. Keep straight on till you can turn right onto Monastery St then left along Burgate and on to Longport St.

Turn left at the roundabout onto the A257 (the direction marked is Littlebourne), keeping the ruins of St Augustine's Abbey on your left. Walk up the road and then turn right down Spring Lane past the sign to St Martin's, then right again onto Pilgrims' Way, opposite Hadlow College.

Follow the North Downs Way marker post and pass the playing fields. Turn right over the railway bridge and follow the road (still called the Pilgrims' Way) as it bends left. The road becomes a rough track at the end of the row of houses and continues bordered by hedges to Barton Farm Business Park.

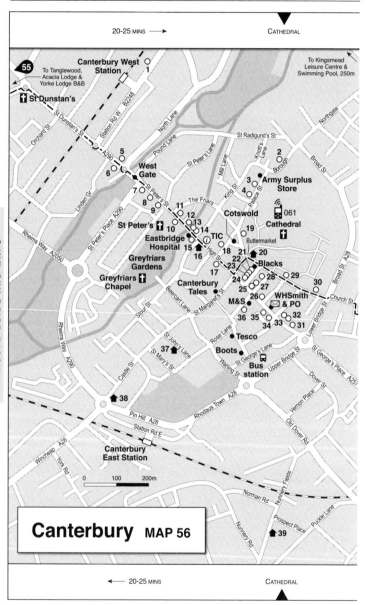

20-25 MINS ⟶

CATHEDRAL

To Kingsmead
Leisure Centre &
Swimming Pool, 250m

55

To Tanglewood,
Acacia Lodge &
Yorke Lodge B&B

Canterbury West
Station

1

St Dunstan's

St Radigund's St

5

West
Gate

6

7

8

9

St Peter's

10

11

12

13

14

The Friars

Cotswold

2

Borough

Army Surplus
Store

3

4

061

Cathedral

19

Eastbridge
Hospital 15

16

TIC

17

18 21 20

22

23

24

25

26

27

Blacks

28 29

30

WHSmith
& PO

32

31

Greyfriars
Gardens

Greyfriars
Chapel

Canterbury
Tales

M&S

36 35

33

34

37

Tesco

Boots

Bus
station

38

Pin Hill A28

Station Rd E

Canterbury
East Station

0   100   200m

Canterbury MAP 56

39

⟵ 20-25 MINS

CATHEDRAL

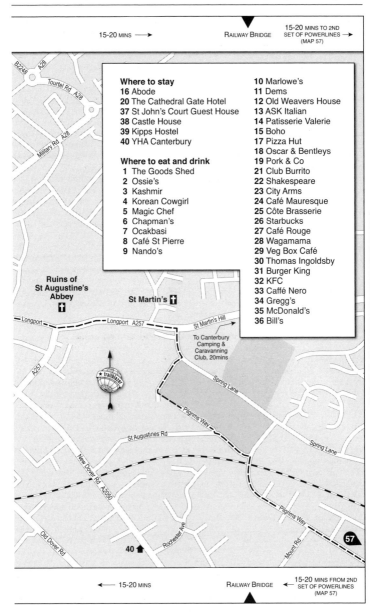

(cont'd from p175) They also have three 'hobbit houses' in their back garden – well-appointed wooden **cabins** (sleeping up to five people; £59-115; 🐕) furnished with a kitchenette area that houses a fridge, microwave, sink, kettle and crockery and shower/toilet facilities; they also provide bedding and, best of all, it's one of the few places in the city where your dog is allowed to stay. There is a self-catering kitchen but meals are available in the hostel.

Convenient to Canterbury East station is ***Kipps Hostel*** (☎ 01227-786121, 🖳 kipps-hostel.com; 2S/3D or T shared facilities, 1 x 4-/1 x 6-/2 x 8-/1 x 9-dorm-bed rooms all with private facilities; WI-FI), 40 Nunnery Fields. Room rates are £27.50-33.50pp (sgl/sgl occ £32-50), while dorm beds vary in price according to the time of year and size of the dorm but are between £14.50 and £28.50. There's a good atmosphere, free wi-fi and a clean, well-equipped kitchen.

Arriving in the city the trail passes a few **B&Bs** on London Rd (Map 55), which is convenient for Canterbury West station (see p175). Two that stand out are ***Acacia Lodge*** (☎ 01227-769955, 🖳 acacialodge.co.uk; 2D/1T en suite or private bathroom; WI-FI), 39 London Rd, and ***Tanglewood*** (contact via Acacia; 2D/1T en suite; WI-FI), 30 London Rd. Both are under the same ownership and immaculately kept; B&B at both costs from £37.50pp (sgl occ from £70).

Down the road at No 50, luxurious ***Yorke Lodge*** (☎ 01227-451243, 🖳 yorkelodge.com; 1S/1T/4D/1Tr/1Qd, all en suite; 🥣; WI-FI; 🐕) one of the very few B&Bs in Canterbury to allow dogs to stay (and free of charge too). Well appointed and immaculately clean and tidy, rates in this relaxing B&B are £45-57.50pp (sgl/sgl occ from £68/75).

Part of ***Castle House*** (☎ 01227-761897, 🖳 castlehousehotel.co.uk; 7D/2D or T/1Tr/5Qd, all en suite; 🥣; WI-FI), 28 Castle St, formed the medieval city walls, now near the busy Wincheap roundabout. Large rooms start at £42.50pp and rise to £70pp (sgl occ £80), with a two-night minimum stay at weekends in the high season.

And there's good value at the modest ***St John's Court Guest House*** (☎ 01227-456425, 🖳 stjohnscourtguesthouse.co.uk; 2S/3D or T/1T/1Tr, shared bathroom; 🥣; WI-FI), St John's Lane, charging from £35pp (sgl/sgl occ £55).

The Cathedral Gate Hotel (☎ 01227-464381, 🖳 cathgate.co.uk; 6S/4T/12D/1Tr, some en suite; 🥣; WI-FI) next to the Cathedral has a real medieval feel to it with sloping floors, low doorways and the hustle and bustle from the street below. Continental breakfast is included (a full English breakfast costs an extra £7.50pp) and the rates are £40.75-60pp (sgl/sgl occ from £50).

The former County Hotel has now been transformed into a luxurious designer hotel, ***Abode Canterbury*** (☎ 01227-766266, 🖳 abodecanterbury.co.uk; 63D/9T, all en suite; 🥣; WI-FI), 30 High St. B&B costs £40-62.50pp (sgl occ room rate) for the cosy rooms and up to £175-250pp (sgl occ room rate) for those labelled 'fabulous' by the hotel. Note that rates vary and the best rates are for advance booking; if a room only rate is chosen breakfast costs £10-15pp extra.

Where to eat and drink

There are some quirky little cafés on the main drag and around the Cathedral. For unpretentious, honest French fare look no further than the long-established ***Café St Pierre*** (☎ 01227-456791; Mon-Sat 8am-6pm, Sun 9am-5.30pm) at the northern end of the main road running through the heart of the old city (known, at this end, as St Peter's St). All baguettes are £5.40.

Further along, at 27 High St, ***Boho*** (☎ 01227-458931, 🖳 bohocanterbury.co.uk; Mon-Thur 9am-6pm, Fri & Sat to 9pm, Sun 10am-5pm) is a colourful little place with great outdoor seating area and a constantly changing menu in which you may see such mouthwatering items as a pulled pig & chip bap (£8.95), or smoked salmon & home-made potato cake with crème fraîche and beetroot chutney (£8.95).

For vegetarians and their ilk there's ***Veg Box Café*** (☎ 01227-456654, 🖳 thevegboxcafe.co.uk; Mon-Sat 8.30am-5pm, Sun 9.30am-4pm), where they try to use only local, organic and Fairtrade produce in their meals. They also offer free tea or coffee with their breakfasts (which start at £4 for their granola or 'eggs in purgatory', an organic egg poached in a spicy tomato sauce, topped with a sprinkle of cheese and fresh herbs).

Veg Box isn't the only place using locally sourced ingredients. *The Goods Shed* (☎ 01227-459153, ☐ thegoodsshed .co.uk; Tue-Fri 8-10.30am & noon-2.30pm, Sat to 3pm & 6-9.30pm, Sun 9-10.30am & noon-3pm; WI-FI) is England's first full-time farmers' market restaurant, housed in a revamped Victorian engine shed with high oak-beamed ceilings and huge windows. Bringing the kitchen to the market, the menu constantly changes (dinner mains for £14-20) using the produce available on the day so you can get the likes of guinea fowl, lentils, spinach & black pudding (£17.50) though in the morning they offer a build-your-own-breakfast (50p-£1 per item).

Back within the city walls, *Oscar & Bentleys* (☎ 01227-454544, ☐ oscar-bent leys.co.uk; Sun-Tue 10.30am-4pm, Wed-Sat 10.30am-9pm) is a handsome little place on Guildhall, struggling for attention behind the mighty Costa next door but able to thrive thanks to an imaginative menu of well-cooked food with mains mostly around the £12.50 mark, though the delicious braised steak chilli con carne is £15.25.

As you'd expect from a major city, Canterbury is awash with the big brands of cafés, fast-food outlets and restaurants. There's a whole slew of them at the southern end of the main street (known as St George's St), including *Caffè Nero* (Mon-Fri 7am-6.30pm, Sat & Sun from 7.30am), *Starbucks* (Mon-Sat 6.30am-8.30pm, Sun 7am-7.30pm), and *Costa* (actually south-west of the main drag on Rose Lane; Mon-Sat 7.30am-7pm, Sun 9am-6pm).

The fast-food restaurant chains have also infested this same St George's St, including *McDonald's* (24 hours), *Burger King* (Mon-Sat 8am-10pm, Sun 9am-9pm), *KFC* (daily 10am-11pm), *Subway* (Mon-Sat 7am-6pm, Sun 10am-6pm) and *Gregg's* (Mon-Wed 7am-6pm, Thur & Fri to 7pm, Sun 9am-4.30pm).

There are also branches of the more 'upmarket' eateries such as *Côte Brasserie* (☎ 01227-786386, ☐ cote.co.uk; Mon-Fri 8am-11pm, Sat from 9am, Sun 9am-10.30pm), where mains cost from £9.95, though do try the Breton fish stew for £13.50; and, behind it, *Café Rouge* (☎ 01227-784984, ☐ caferouge.com; Mon-Fri 9am-10pm, Sat 9am-10.30pm, Sun 9.30am-9.30pm) whose menu includes mains (from £11.95) such as baked crêpe filled with Portobello & chestnut mushrooms. *Wagamama* (☎ 01227-454307, ☐ wagamama.com; Sun-Thur 11.30am-10pm, Fri & Sat to 11pm; gyoza dumplings from £5.75), is just behind them on Longmarket; *Patisserie Valerie* (☎ 01227-760450, ☐ patisserie-valerie.co.uk; Sun-Thur 8.30am-7pm, Fri & Sat to 7.30pm), at 23 High St, specialises in cakes, with afternoon tea for £25 for two; *Nando's* (☎ 01227-766261, ☐ nandos.co.uk; Sun-Thur 11.30am-10pm, Fri & Sat to 10.30pm), at 46 St Peter's St, serves peri peri chicken from £3.95 for a quarter of a chicken, and up to £12.95 for the whole bird!; and *Bill's* (☎ 01227-479552, ☐ bills-website.co.uk; Mon-Sat 8am-11pm, Sun 9am-10.30pm) on the way to Tesco on Rose Lane, with mains from £9.95 for the macaroni cheese.

There are also, on the main drag, two branches of those well-known Italian/pizzeria joints, *Ask Italian* (☎ 01227-767617, ☐ askitalian.co.uk; Sun-Thur 11am-10pm, Fri & Sat 11am-11pm; pizzas from £10.20) at 24 High St and *Pizza Hut* (☎ 01227-451049, ☐ pizzahut.co.uk; Mon-Thur 11am-10pm, Fri & Sat to 11pm, Sun 11am-9pm; pizzas from £9.55) at No 39.

For more interesting independent places check out *Pork & Co* (☎ 01227 764430, ☐ porkandco.co.uk; Mon-Sat 11am-9pm, Sun 11am-8pm), which does pretty much what it says on the shop-front, serving pork rolls (£8.50 with crackling & chips) and other porcine-related food products from its store on Sun St, just down from the Cathedral gates.

For exotic fare we like the following: *Café Mauresque* (☎ 01227-464300, ☐ cafemauresque.co.uk; daily noon-10pm), tucked down narrow Butchery Lane, serves

North African fare with everybody's favourite Moroccan dish, tagine (a slow-cooked stew) from £16.45 (for one with chicken and homemade merguez sausages).

Down the same lane is *Club Burrito* (☎ 01227-652401, 🖳 clubburrito.com; Sun-Tue 11.30am-9pm, Wed-Sat 11.30am-midnight), in our opinion the best of several Mexican places in the city, with a burrito bowl from £7.90.

While over on King's Mile at 13 Palace St is *Korean Cowgirl* (☎ 01227-788006, 🖳 thekoreancowgirl.com; Mon-Sat noon-10pm, Sun noon-9pm), a curious Asian fusion smokehouse with some delicious food: for a complete blow-out, try the Dirty Cowgirl – a half-pound of brisket, a half-pound of pulled pork, a quarter rack of ribs and three pieces of Korean fried chicken, plus two sides of your choice, for £25.95!

If that all sounds a bit too, well, foreign, more familiar fare can be found at *Marlowe's* (☎ 01227-462194, 🖳 marlowes restaurant.co.uk; daily 11.30am-10pm), one of the best-value eateries on the High St, with mains from £10.95 though it's £15.95 for the pan-seared tuna steak with a salmon & dill potato cake. Nearby, *Old Weavers House* (☎ 01227-464660, 🖳 weavers restaurant.co.uk; Mon-Sat 9am-11.30pm, Sun to 10.30pm), just before the bridge on St Peter's St, deserves a mention for its pleasant riverside seating and its 'punt & dine' offer: £16.99 for a main course plus a 45-minute punting tour of the city's waterways.

For **pub food**, Butchery Lane has a couple of decent options including *City Arms* (☎ 01227-458081, 🖳 thecityarmspub .co.uk; food daily noon-4pm; WI-FI), with roasts for £7.95), and *Shakespeare* (☎ 01227-463252, 🖳 shakespearecanterbury .com; food Sun-Thur noon-8.30pm, Fri & Sat to 8pm; WI-FI) – more a restaurant and wine bar than a proper boozer, though they do some great gourmet burgers from £10.95. There's also the Wetherspoons-owned *Thomas Ingoldsby* (☎ 01227-463339; food daily 8am-11pm; WI-FI) with their usual good-value menu, right on the trail at the end of Burgate.

Smarter, more formal dining options include *Dems* (☎ 01227-769018, 🖳 dems brasserie.co.uk; Sun & Tue-Thur 7.30am-9.30pm, Fri & Sat to 10.30pm), at 10 St Peter's St, with mains from £12 for the vegetarian roasted gnocchi; *Chapman's* (☎ 01227-780749, 🖳 chapmansofsevenoaks .co.uk; Mon 6-9pm, Tue-Thur noon-2pm & 6-9pm, Fri to 9.30pm, Sat noon-9.30pm), just outside the city walls on St Dunstan's. The slap-up option here is the seafood platter, including crabmeat, half a lobster, mussels, tiger prawns, whelks, cockles, oysters and a bread basket – £34 per person.

Takeaway outlets tend to be gathered around West Gate, including the kebab house *Ocakbasi* (☎ 01227-784019; Sun-Thur noon-3am, Fri & Sat to 3.30am) and the Chinese takeaway *Magic Chef* (☎ 01227-462108; Mon & Wed-Thur 5-11.30pm, Fri & Sat to midnight, Sun to 11pm). Over on the series of contiguous streets that were called The Parade and Borough (but which have all been rebranded as 'the King's Mile') there's a chippy, *Ossie's* (☎ 01227-462187; Mon-Wed 11am-10pm, Thur-Sat to 11pm) and an Indian, *Kashmir* (☎ 01227-462050, 🖳 kash mirtandoori.co.uk; Mon-Sat noon-2pm & 5-11.30pm, Sun noon-11.30pm).

CANTERBURY TO SHEPHERDSWELL [MAPS 56-62]

After leaving Canterbury along Pilgrims' Way you spend a long time crossing very large arable fields on this **10.8-mile/17.4km (2hrs 40 mins to 3hrs 25 mins)** stage. Not the most fascinating part of the North Downs Way, for a large stretch of this trek the A2 is an unwelcome, noisy companion. Walkers should thus find pleasure where they can to distract themselves from the constant blast of traffic, be it in the tiny yet gorgeous hamlets of Patrixbourne and

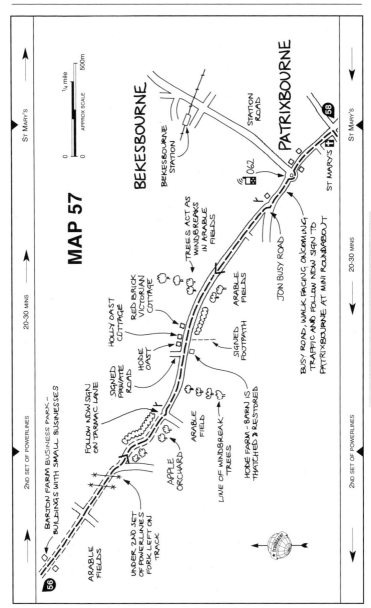

Womenswold, the lovely wildflower meadows that spring up where the farmer leaves the ground untouched, and the butterflies that flit above them, including the **marble white butterfly** – common in these fields but not encountered elsewhere on the trail.

Note that at the time of research there were no B&Bs in Shepherdswell so be prepared to march on to Dover.

Having negotiated your way through Canterbury it's not long before you come to the quaint village of **Patrixbourne** (see Map 57), a huddle of houses built higgledy-piggledy around handsome St Mary's Church. At the village's end you should turn off the road to walk parallel to the A2, or continue along the road to Bridge.

BRIDGE   [MAP 58]

Bridge has a Londis **supermarket** with a **post office** (both Mon-Sat 7am-7.30pm, Sun 8am-6pm) and an outdoor **ATM** (£1.85 for withdrawals), a **chemist** (Mon-Fri 9am-1pm, 2-6pm, Sat 9am-12.30pm), a **grocer-cum-butchers**, Greenhill's (Tue-Fri 8am-6pm, Sat 8am-5pm) and three pubs, two of which do food.

Stagecoach's **bus services** No 17 (Canterbury to Folkestone) and 89/89A (Canterbury to Dover) stop by the White Horse; see pp45-8 for details.

There are fine rooms at **Renville Oast** (☎ 07754-243819, 🖳 renvilleoast.co.uk; 3D, all en suite; WI-FI), where **B&B** costs in the £40-50pp range (sgl occ rates on request), but it's a good 15-minute walk uphill north of the post office and off the A2 slip road. The 16th-century *White Horse Inn* (☎ 01227-833830, 🖳 www.whitehorse bridge.co.uk; food Mon-Fri noon-3pm & 5.30-9pm, Sat noon-9pm, Sun noon-7pm; WI-FI; 🐾 bar area) has the best food, with mains starting at £7.95 for the sausage & mash; they serve roasts only on Sundays.

The *Red Lion* (☎ 01227-832213, 🖳 redlionbridge.co.uk; food served Mon-Sat noon-2.30pm & 6-8.30pm, Sun noon-5pm, to 4pm in winter; WI-FI; 🐾) also does pub grub with steak night on a Thursday (eg 8oz rump steak £12.50).

The third pub, the *Plough & Harrow* (Mon-Fri 11am-3pm, Sat 11am-11pm, Sun noon-10pm) doesn't serve food.

The path passes the entrance to **Higham Park and Gardens** (see box below and Map 58), before crossing huge arable fields to arrive at the quaint village of **Womenswold** (Map 60).

❑ Chitty Chitty Bang Bang

The fine Palladian house at **Higham Park and Gardens** (see Map 58) is glimpsed from the North Downs Way and visitors come for the Italianate gardens designed by Harold Peto. But it was here in the 1920s that Polish count and dashing racing-car driver Louis Zborowski built three racing cars powered by aero engines and all called Chitty Chitty Bang Bang.

Inspired by the count and his cars, Ian Fleming, who at the time lived at nearby Bekesbourne, wrote the children's story *Chitty Chitty Bang Bang* in 1964 and Roland Emett, sculptor and cartoonist, worked up the model of the car in the 1968 movie of the same name adapted from Roald Dahl's screenplay. One of the count's cars is displayed at the National Motor Museum, Beaulieu, Hampshire.

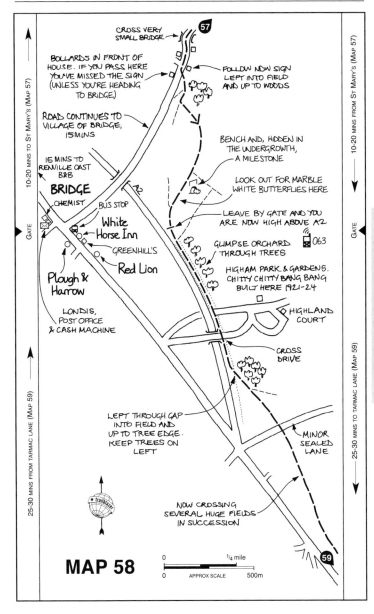

MAP 58

A further march through fields will take you to **Woolage Village**, built for colliery workers on the Kent coalfields. (If, instead of turning right along the road to follow the trail, you instead turned left, you would reach the grounds of Fredville Park in Nonington, home to several ancient trees including the massive 'Majestic' pedunculate oak that featured in the Channel 4 programme on the North Downs Way presented by Tony Robinson. Unfortunately, what Channel 4 didn't tell its viewers was that Fredville Park is private and you can't actually visit the oak, which various estimates have put as being between 450 and 795 years old, without trespassing!).

After Woolage the trail climbs through a **tunnel of trees and hedgerows** (Map 61), before dropping along a country lane and farm track to arrive in Shepherdswell. *(cont'd on p188)*

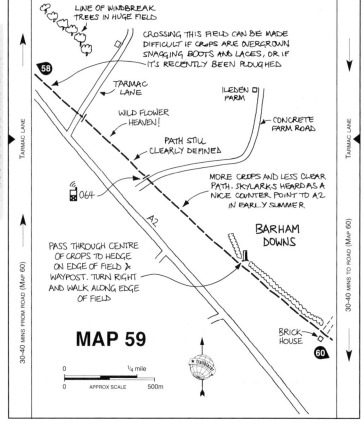

ROUTE GUIDE AND MAPS

LINE OF WINDBREAK TREES IN HUGE FIELD

CROSSING THIS FIELD CAN BE MADE DIFFICULT IF CROPS ARE OVERGROWN, SNAGGING BOOTS AND LACES, OR IF IT'S RECENTLY BEEN PLOUGHED

58

TARMAC LANE

ILEDEN FARM

WILD FLOWER HEAVEN!

CONCRETE FARM ROAD

PATH STILL CLEARLY DEFINED

MORE CROPS AND LESS CLEAR PATH. SKYLARKS HEARD AS A NICE COUNTER POINT TO A2 IN EARLY SUMMER

064

A2

BARHAM DOWNS

PASS THROUGH CENTRE OF CROPS TO HEDGE ON EDGE OF FIELD & WAYPOST. TURN RIGHT AND WALK ALONG EDGE OF FIELD

MAP 59

BRICK HOUSE

60

TARMAC LANE

TARMAC LANE

30-40 MINS FROM ROAD (MAP 60)

30-40 MINS TO ROAD (MAP 60)

0 ¼ mile

0 APPROX SCALE 500m

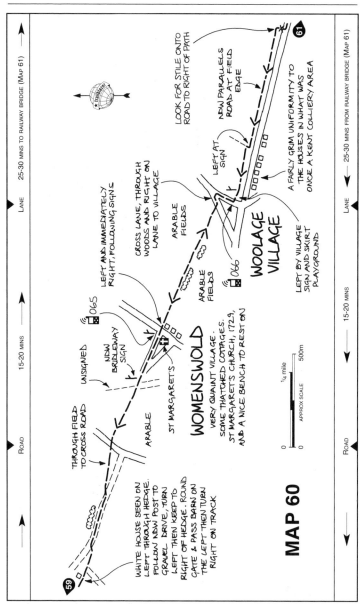

MAP 60

ROAD ⟶ 15-20 MINS ⟶ LANE ⟶ 25-30 MINS FROM RAILWAY BRIDGE (MAP 61) ⟶

ROAD ⟵ 15-20 MINS ⟶ LANE ⟵ 25-30 MINS TO RAILWAY BRIDGE (MAP 61) ⟶

59

WHITE HOUSE SEEN ON LEFT THROUGH HEDGE. FOLLOW NEW POST TO GRAVEL DRIVE, TURN LEFT THEN KEEP TO RIGHT OF HEDGE. ROUND GATE & PASS BARN ON THE LEFT THEN TURN RIGHT ON TRACK

THROUGH FIELD TO CROSS ROAD

ARABLE

UNSIGNED

NEW BRIDLEWAY SIGN

065

ST MARGARET'S

WOMENSWOLD

VERY QUAINT VILLAGE. SOME THATCHED COTTAGES. ST MARGARET'S CHURCH, 1729, AND A NICE BENCH TO REST ON

LEFT AND IMMEDIATELY RIGHT, FOLLOWING SIGNS

CROSS LANE, THROUGH WOODS AND RIGHT ON LANE TO VILLAGE

ARABLE FIELDS

ARABLE FIELDS

066

WOOLAGE VILLAGE

LEFT BY VILLAGE SIGN AND SKIRT PLAYGROUND

LEFT AT SIGN

A FAIRLY GRIM UNIFORMITY TO THE HOUSES IN WHAT WAS ONCE A KENT COLLIERY AREA

LOOK FOR STILE ONTO ROAD TO RIGHT OF PATH

NOW PARALLELS ROAD AT FIELD EDGE

61

trailblazer

¼ mile
APPROX SCALE
0   500m

ROUTE GUIDE AND MAPS

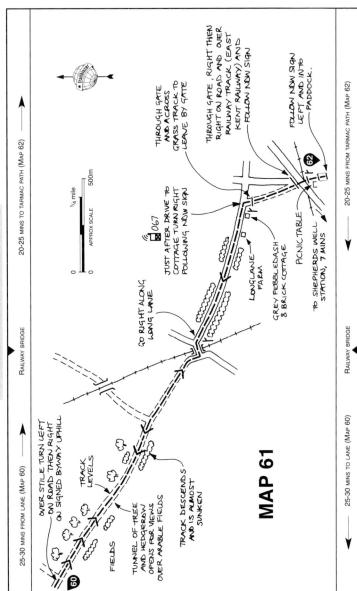

MAP 61

25-30 MINS FROM LANE (MAP 60) →

20-25 MINS TO TARMAC PATH (MAP 62) →

RAILWAY BRIDGE

RAILWAY BRIDGE

25-30 MINS TO LANE (MAP 60)

20-25 MINS FROM TARMAC PATH (MAP 62)

OVER STILE TURN LEFT ON ROAD THEN RIGHT ON SIGNED BYWAY UPHILL

TRACK LEVELS

FIELDS

TUNNEL OF TREE AND HEDGEROW OPENS FOR VIEWS OVER ARABLE FIELDS

TRACK DESCENDS AND IS ALMOST SUNKEN

GO RIGHT ALONG LONG LANE

JUST AFTER DRIVE TO COTTAGE TURN RIGHT FOLLOWING NDW SIGN

067

THROUGH GATE AND ACROSS GRASS TRACK TO LEAVE BY GATE

THROUGH GATE, RIGHT THEN RIGHT ON ROAD AND OVER RAILWAY TRACK (EAST KENT RAILWAY) AND FOLLOW NDW SIGN

FOLLOW NDW SIGN LEFT AND INTO PADDOCK.

LONGLANE FARM

GREY PEBBLEDASH & BRICK COTTAGE

PICNIC TABLE

TO SHEPHERDS WELL STATION, 7 MINS

62

¼ mile

APPROX SCALE

0   500m

0

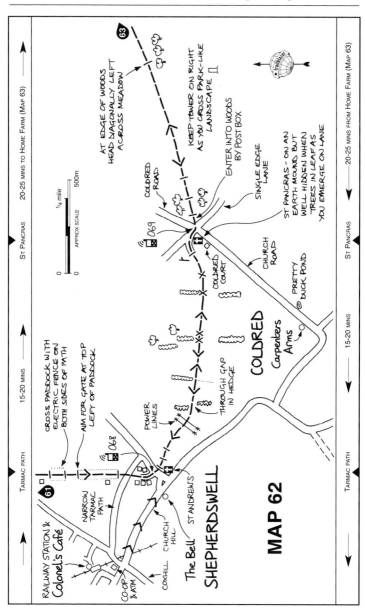

63

20-25 MINS TO HOME FARM (MAP 63)

St PANCRAS

20-25 MINS FROM HOME FARM (MAP 63)

AT EDGE OF WOODS
HEAD DIAGONALLY LEFT
ACROSS MEADOW

KEEP TOWER ON RIGHT
AS YOU CROSS PARK-LIKE
LANDSCAPE

ENTER INTO WOODS
BY POST BOX

COLDRED
ROAD

SINGLE EDGE
LANE

069

St PANCRAS - ON AN
EARTH MOUND BUT
WELL HIDDEN WHEN
TREES IN LEAF AS
YOU EMERGE ON LANE

CHURCH
ROAD

COLDRED
COURT

PRETTY
DUCK POND

COLDRED

Carpenters
Arms

15-20 MINS

1/4 mile

500m

APPROX SCALE

0

0

15-20 MINS

CROSS PADDOCK WITH
ELECTRIC FENCE ON
BOTH SIDES OF PATH

AIM FOR GATE AT TOP
LEFT OF PADDOCK

THROUGH GAP
IN HEDGE

POWER
LINES

068

TARMAC PATH

61

RAILWAY STATION &
Colonel's Cafe

NARROW
TARMAC
PATH

CO-OP
& ATM

COXHILL

CHURCH HILL

St ANDREW'S

The Bell

SHEPHERDSWELL

MAP 62

TARMAC PATH

ROUTE GUIDE AND MAPS

SHEPHERDSWELL [MAP 62, p187]

As the biggest stop between Canterbury and Dover, Shepherdswell is a welcome spot for walkers striving to finish the trail in one day and there are just enough facilities to warrant a brief stop here.

The **Co-op** (Mon-Sat 6am-10pm, Sun 7am-10pm) has snacks and food for meals on the go and there is an **ATM**. For food during the day, East Kent Railway Station, next to the main Shepherds Well station (see below), has *Colonel's Café* (☎ 01304-832042; Tue-Fri 8.30am-4pm, Sat & Sun 9am-5pm) where you can enjoy a jacket potato while watching the heritage trains chug by.

Note that the **railway station** is called Shepherds Well – ie two words – so bear that in mind if you are struggling to find mention of it online; it is a stop on South Eastern Railway's London Victoria to Dover Priory service (see box pp42-3).

Stagecoach **bus** No 89/89A calls in near The Bell on its way between Canterbury/Aylesham and Dover; see pp45-8.

The only pub remaining in the village is *The Bell* (☎ 01304-830661; bar Mon-Thur 12.30-10.30pm, Fri & Sat to 11.30pm, Sun to 10pm); at the time of research new owners had just taken over and the only food available was bar snacks and cakes but they hope to serve meals and plan to start with Sunday lunch.

SHEPHERDSWELL TO DOVER [MAPS 62-66]

This last **8.6-mile/13.8km (2hrs 35 mins to 3¼hrs)** section is easy walking through park landscape and pockets of woodland with no villages en route until, before you know it, the trail descends the Roman road into Dover. Not especially thrilling, these last few miles of the North Downs Way do tend to 'dribble on' a bit but there are a couple of highlights to make the walk worthwhile, including a crossing of attractive Waldershare Park and, at its end, a lovely overgrown graveyard by an abandoned church. Glimpsing the flag flying proudly above Dover Castle for the first time is always a bit of a thrill too, as well as a sure sign that you are approaching one of the country's most historic ports – and the finale of your North Downs Way adventure.

Beginning at Shepherdswell, the trail weaves its way through undulating fields to **Coldred** where it's easy to miss the Church of St Pancras. Nearby, the *Carpenters Arms* (bar Mon-Sat 11am-3pm & 6-11pm, Sun noon-2pm & 6-10pm) across the village green – complete with 'slow ducks crossing sign' – is a true local pub, drinks only no food, but worth a quick look at least. Stagecoach **bus** Nos 89/89A (see pp45-8) stops here en route between Canterbury/Aylesham and Dover.

From **Waldershare Park** (Map 63) the trail climbs through **Ashley** (Map 64) to rise again to the A2 beyond **Pineham** (Map 65). A little detour ensures a safe crossing of the A2 to start shortly a descent along the Roman road to Dover. There'll probably be no marker, signboard, klaxon or bunting to greet your arrival, and the good citizens of Dover will doubtless be milling about the Market Square (formerly the Way's official end) shopping, mooching and completely unaware of your achievement. But don't be disappointed or downcast: just put your head down and plough on through the crowds of dawdlers, dotards

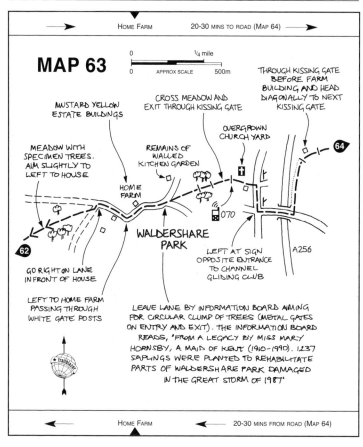

HOME FARM   20-30 MINS TO ROAD (MAP 64) →

MAP 63

0   ¼ mile
0   APPROX SCALE   500m

MUSTARD YELLOW
ESTATE BUILDINGS

THROUGH KISSING GATE
BEFORE FARM
BUILDING AND HEAD
DIAGONALLY TO NEXT
KISSING GATE

CROSS MEADOW AND
EXIT THROUGH KISSING GATE

OVERGROWN
CHURCH YARD

MEADOW WITH
SPECIMEN TREES.
AIM SLIGHTLY TO
LEFT TO HOUSE

REMAINS OF
WALLED
KITCHEN GARDEN

64

HOME
FARM

WALDERSHARE
PARK

62

LEFT AT SIGN
OPPOSITE ENTRANCE
TO CHANNEL
GLIDING CLUB

A256

GO RIGHT ON LANE
IN FRONT OF HOUSE

LEFT TO HOME FARM
PASSING THROUGH
WHITE GATE POSTS

070

LEAVE LANE BY INFORMATION BOARD AIMING
FOR CIRCULAR CLUMP OF TREES (METAL GATES
ON ENTRY AND EXIT). THE INFORMATION BOARD
READS, 'FROM A LEGACY BY MISS MARY
HORNSBY, A MAID OF KENT (1910-1990). 1237
SAPLINGS WERE PLANTED TO REHABILITATE
PARTS OF WALDERSHARE PARK DAMAGED
IN THE GREAT STORM OF 1987'

trailblazer

← HOME FARM   20-30 MINS FROM ROAD (MAP 64)

ROUTE GUIDE AND MAPS

and drunks, down King St and its continuation, Bench St, through the underpass to emerge at the seafront, where you'll find a monument to mark the official end of the North Downs Way. Nearby is a bench where you can sit surrounded by three local icons – James Bond creator Ian Fleming, who had a house further down the coast, WWII forces' sweetheart and singer, Dame Vera Lynn, and 2012 Olympic torchbearer Jamie Clark – each rendered in rusting steel. It's as good a spot as any to sit awhile and contemplate your achievement. After all, it's no small feat to have walked over 131 miles across the south-eastern corner of England – and you should feel mighty proud that you've done so.

(cont'd on p192)

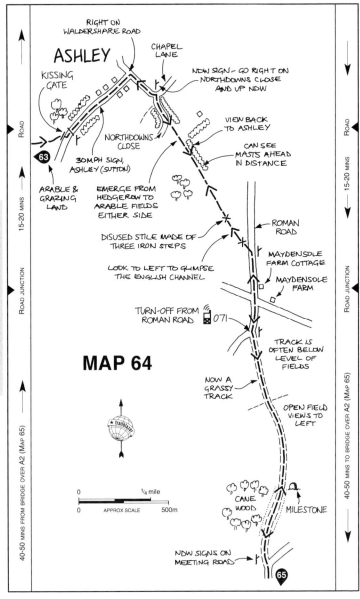

RIGHT ON
WALDERSHARE ROAD

CHAPEL
LANE

ASHLEY

KISSING
GATE

NDW SIGN - GO RIGHT ON
NORTHDOWNS CLOSE
AND UP NDW

VIEW BACK
TO ASHLEY

NORTHDOWNS
CLOSE

CAN SEE
MASTS AHEAD
IN DISTANCE

30 MPH SIGN,
ASHLEY (SUTTON)

63

ARABLE &
GRAZING
LAND

EMERGE FROM
HEDGEROW TO
ARABLE FIELDS
EITHER SIDE

ROMAN
ROAD

DISUSED STILE MADE OF
THREE IRON STEPS

MAYDENSOLE
FARM COTTAGE

LOOK TO LEFT TO GLIMPSE
THE ENGLISH CHANNEL

MAYDENSOLE
FARM

TURN-OFF FROM
ROMAN ROAD   071

MAP 64

TRACK IS
OFTEN BELOW
LEVEL OF
FIELDS

NOW A
GRASSY
TRACK

OPEN FIELD
VIEWS TO
LEFT

★ trailblazer

0   ¼ mile

0   500m
APPROX SCALE

CANE
WOOD

MILESTONE

NDW SIGNS ON
MEETING ROADS

65

ROAD

15-20 MINS

ROAD JUNCTION

ROUTE GUIDE AND MAPS

15-20 MINS

40-50 MINS FROM BRIDGE OVER A2 (MAP 65)

ROAD

15-20 MINS

ROAD JUNCTION

40-50 MINS TO BRIDGE OVER A2 (MAP 65)

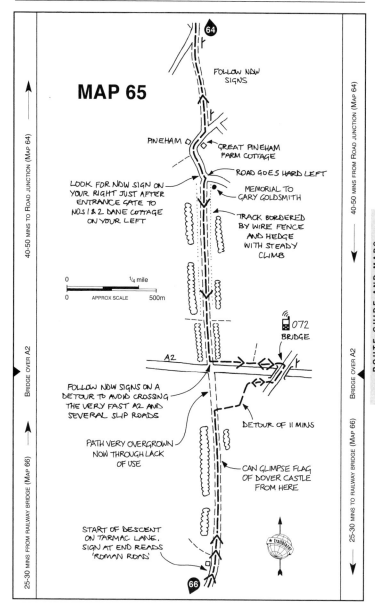

ROUTE GUIDE AND MAPS

MAP 65

64

FOLLOW NDW SIGNS

PINEHAM

GREAT PINEHAM FARM COTTAGE

ROAD GOES HARD LEFT

MEMORIAL TO GARY GOLDSMITH

LOOK FOR NDW SIGN ON YOUR RIGHT JUST AFTER ENTRANCE GATE TO NOS 1 & 2 DANE COTTAGE ON YOUR LEFT

TRACK BORDERED BY WIRE FENCE AND HEDGE WITH STEADY CLIMB

0   1/4 mile
0   APPROX SCALE   500m

072 BRIDGE

A2

FOLLOW NDW SIGNS ON A DETOUR TO AVOID CROSSING THE VERY FAST A2 AND SEVERAL SLIP ROADS

DETOUR OF 11 MINS

PATH VERY OVERGROWN NOW THROUGH LACK OF USE

CAN GLIMPSE FLAG OF DOVER CASTLE FROM HERE

START OF DESCENT ON TARMAC LANE. SIGN AT END READS 'ROMAN ROADS'

66

40-50 MINS TO ROAD JUNCTION (MAP 64)

BRIDGE OVER A2

25-30 MINS FROM RAILWAY BRIDGE (MAP 66)

40-50 MINS FROM ROAD JUNCTION (MAP 64)

BRIDGE OVER A2

25-30 MINS TO RAILWAY BRIDGE (MAP 66)

trailblazer

DOVER   [MAP 66]

*'Neither Dover nor its Castle has anything
of note to be said of them… and has it self
an ill repaired, dangerous, and good for little harbour and peir, very chargeable and
little worth.'* **Daniel Defoe**, writing in 1724
in *A Tour thro' the Whole Island of Great
Britain* [note: the spelling 'mistakes' are all
Defoe's!]

*'[Dover is] like other sea-port towns; but
really much more clean, and with less
blackguard people in it than I ever
observed in any sea-port before. It is a most
picturesque place, to be sure'* **William
Cobbett**, writing in 1823 in *Rural Rides*.

Dover struggles as a destination. People
either pass through on the way to the
Continent or use it as a gateway to somewhere else in England. As with any busy
port town it has its fair share of life's flot-
sam and jetsam and after the cultural high
point of Canterbury it's a disappointment.
There's an impressive castle, a museum, a
fine Roman house and a view of the White
Cliffs but little else to keep you here long.

What to see and do

Dover Museum (💻 dovermuseum.co.uk;
free; same phone and opening hours as the
TIC, see Services), on Market Square in the
tourist information centre, has extensive
exhibits on the town's history since 1066 as
well as the Bronze Age Boat Gallery, where
you can see the remains of the oldest seago-
ing vessel, dating back to 1500BC.

Dover Castle (☎ 01304-211067, 💻
english-heritage.org; Apr-Sep 10am-6pm,
Oct 10am-5pm, Nov & Mar 10am-4pm
though check on website as closed on certain days; £19.40) 'guardian of the gateway
to England' is strategically placed on the
White Cliffs of Dover. It's a prime site for
English Heritage and the tours of the secret

tunnels used in the Napoleonic Wars and
WWII are fascinating.

The **Roman Painted House** (☎
01304-203279, 💻 theromanpaintedhouse.
org.uk; Jun-Sep Tue-Sat 10am-5pm, Sun 1-
5pm, Apr-May Tue-Sat only; £3) was discovered in 1970 and reckoned to be one of
the best-preserved Roman buildings in
England largely because it was buried to
make way for a new building in AD270. Over
400 sq metres of painted plaster survive.

Finally, a good view of the **White
Cliffs of Dover** is free from the Prince of
Wales pier by the Hoverport.

Services

The **tourist information centre** (TIC; ☎
01304-201066, 💻 whitecliffscountry.org
.uk; Mon-Sat 9.30am-5pm, Easter-Sep Sun
10am-3pm) is on Market Square.

The **chemists** Boots (Mon-Thur 9am-
5.30pm, Fri & Sat 8.45am-5.30pm, Sun
10am-4pm) and Superdrug (Mon-Sat
8.30am-5.30pm, Sun 10am-4pm) are on
Cannon St, above Market Sq, and there are
two banks (Barclays and Lloyds) with
ATMs on Market Sq conveniently located
in the heart of town and right on the trail.

There is a **post office** on Pencester Rd
in a Costcutter (Mon-Sat 7am-10pm, Sun
8am-8pm) and a Londis **supermarket**
(Mon-Thur 6am-10pm, Fri-Sun to 11pm)
on the southern side of Market Square.

Transport

Trains operated by SE Railway (see box
pp42-3) go from Dover Priory to London
Victoria, Charing Cross and St Pancras.

National Express coach service
NX007 (see p44) operates to London via
Canterbury from Pencester Rd **bus station**.

Stagecoach's **bus services** No 89/89A
(to Canterbury/Aylesham) and 15 (to Canterbury) also call at Pencester Rd; see pp45-8.

(Opposite) **Top**: In Dover, by the end of the North Downs Way (see p189) is a bench with
metal silhouettes of three local icons – James Bond creator Ian Fleming, Dame Vera Lynn,
and 2012 Olympic torchbearer Jamie Clark. **Middle**: A former owner of Chilham Castle
(see p169) replaced some of the high brick wall with railings, thereby allowing walkers
glimpses of this splendid Jacobean home. **Bottom**: Many of the buildings in the centre of
Canterbury are several hundred years old, such as this house, now a restaurant (see p180).

(Overleaf) Dating back to the 11th century, Dover Castle overlooks the town centre.

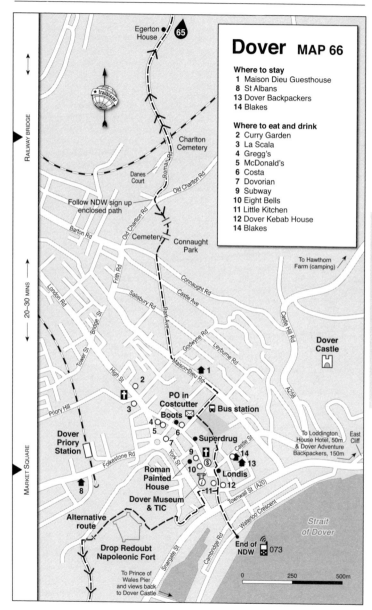

Where to stay

Campers will find the closest pitch is over three miles away at *Hawthorn Farm* (☎ 01304-852658, 🖳 keatfarm.co.uk/holiday-park-homes/hawthorn-farm; Mar-Nov; WI-FI; 🐾), situated at Martin Mill, off the A258. To get there it's best to take the train to Martin Mill station (8 mins; 1-2/hr) and walk about 400m from there. Now part of the Keat Farm network of campsites, a pitch for a one-/two-man tent for walkers costs £16-17.

Dover Backpackers (☎ 01304-202108, 🖳 doverbackpackers.wordpress .com; 2 x 2-/2 x 3-/1 x 4-/1 x 5-/1 x 6-bed rooms, some en suite; WI-FI; 🐾) is part of Castle Inn on Dolphin Lane which claims to be the 'last bar in Britain' and, as such, boasts that it has had three of The Beatles, Sir Cliff Richard and the actor Hugh Grant as guests! What they'd make of the place these days is anyone's guess for it's fair to say that the bar doesn't seem to attract quite the same calibre of customer. Online reviews are decidedly mixed, though it is cheap enough, with dorm beds starting at around £15pp, private rooms from £46. They also have a branch called *Dover Adventure Backpackers* (☎ 01304-215563; 1 x 6- / 1 x 10-bed dorm; one/two rooms sleeping four/five people; shared shower block) on East Cliff down by the ferry port; a dorm bed costs from £16pp, private rooms from £36. Use of kitchen facilities.

Walking into town on the trail, when turning left into Maison Dieu Rd, there is the walker friendly *Maison Dieu Guesthouse* (☎ 01304-204033, 🖳 maison-dieu.co.uk; 1S/2D/1T/1D or T/1Qd, all en suite or with private facilities; WI-FI; Mar-Dec) charges £27.50-42.50pp (sgl from £40, sgl occ room rate). Breakfast is £7 extra.

St Albans (☎ 01304-206308, 🖳 accommodation-dover.co.uk; 2S/4D, all en suite; WI-FI) is closest to the railway station. Room rates are £22.50-50pp (sgl £35-80, sgl occ room rate). Breakfast is only served in the main season and is an extra cost.

Out on East Cliff, at No 14, on the seafront below the Castle is *Loddington House Hotel* (☎ 01304-201947, 🖳 loddingtonhousehotel.co.uk; 2T en suite, 3D private facilities; 🍷; WI-FI) which is really an upmarket B&B. They charge £27.50-39.50pp (sgl occ rates on request).

Blakes (☎ 01304-202194, 🖳 blakesof dover.com; 1D/2Qd, all en suite; WI-FI), at 52 Castle St, charges £32.50pp (sgl occ room rate) for room only. A continental/cooked breakfast costs £3.95/7.95.

Where to eat and drink

Dover is not a culinary centre. The town does have its fair share of representatives of the international and national chains, including *Costa* (Mon-Sat 7am-6.30pm, Sun 8.30am-5pm), *Subway* (Mon-Sat 7am-8pm, Sun 10am-6pm), *McDonald's* (daily 6am-9pm) and *Greggs* (Mon-Sat 7am-9.30pm, Sun 10am-6pm). Wetherspoon's also have a representative, *The Eight Bells* (☎ 01304-205030; food daily 8am-11pm) with good-value food served throughout the day and evening – though dogs are not allowed inside the pub.

For simple no frills cafeteria-style food supplied by a local outlet, try the spotless *Dovorian* (Mon-Fri 9am-6pm, Sat 9am-5.30pm) on Worthington St. The Formica-topped tables fill up fast at lunch-time when the blue-rinse brigade descend for large portions of their all-day breakfast (£5.95). They also run a chippy where haddock costs £7.50.

Curry Garden (☎ 01304-206357, 🖳 currygardendover.co.uk; Mon-Wed & Fri 5.3-11pm, Sat & Sun noon-2.15pm & 5-11.30pm), on High St, dishes out the standard repertoire of curries (tandoori chicken from £6.99) and *La Scala* (☎ 01304-208044, 🖳 lascalarestaurant.org.uk; Mon-Sat 6-10pm) is a friendly Italian restaurant where a bowl of pasta cooked with swordfish, onions tomatoes basil & white wine costs £10.95.

Little Kitchen (☎ 01304-201111; Mon-Sat 8am-3.30pm) is a fast-food restaurant and café just west of Market Square on King St. Across the road, for **takeaway** foods *Dover Kebab House* (☎ 01304-205676; daily 5pm-midnight) is the most convenient for Market Square.

And if it's a glass of wine you're after try *Blakes* (see Where to stay) which serves food (Mon-Sat noon-11pm, Sun noon-9pm) and has good beer and a cellar bar (🐾).

APPENDIX A: ALTERNATIVE ROUTE

BOUGHTON LEES TO DOVER VIA WYE

Look at a geological map of Kent and you'll notice that the chalk swathe of the North Downs that cuts through the county becomes slightly broader at its eastern end. It is perhaps for this reason that the trail authorities decided to divide the trail into two as it approaches Dover – to cover in greater detail the Downs at this eastern extremity.

The better-known and more popular of the two paths – and the one described in detail in Part 4 of this book – heads north-east after Boughton Lees to travel via Canterbury to Dover; while the 24.3-mile (39.1km) alternative takes a more south-easterly direction to visit Wye and brush alongside Folkestone, before travelling north along the coastal cliffs to a reunion with the other trail and the end of the path.

The obvious question for Way walkers to ask, therefore, is which trail should you take? The National Trail website remains resolutely neutral on this matter, treating each of the two branches equally. (Indeed, if you study their website you would think that in order to complete the trail you need to do *both* routes! For example, throughout the website they describe the trail as being 153 miles long – which is about right only if you take both paths (though we actually think the total figure is nearer 155.9 miles/250.9km).

The reason we chose to describe the more northerly route via Canterbury in more detail in Part 4 in this book was in recognition of its greater popularity rather than through any aesthetic considerations. It can only be assumed that this path's popularity is largely due to the fame of Canterbury itself. For it must be said that while the path between Boughton Lees and Canterbury is wonderful, passing as it does through that most quintessential of Kentish sceneries, an undulating terrain of orchards and oast-houses, the path after Canterbury is, in our opinion, a little mundane. The southern route, on the other hand, is, we think, a prettier and more interesting walk overall, taking in the handsome village of Wye as well as some lovely, sumptuous landscapes on the way to the coast. This southern trail also finishes with an extensive stretch of coastal clifftop walking that provides, we think, a more suitably grand finale to the National Trail than the route from Canterbury to Dover which we are not huge fans of, dribbling as it does via road and field before finally limping to the coast.

Route outline

This southern path starts off mundanely enough with a level, unspectacular tramp through agricultural fields, though there is a pleasant little **café and farm shop at Perry Court Farm** (💻 perrycourt.farm; daily 8am-6pm).

Continuing through the fields and across the train tracks will bring you to **Wye** (Map A), a lovely and fairly large village that's home to a decent **café**, *Wye Coffee Shop* (☎ 01233-812452, 💻 wyecoffee.co.uk; food Mon-Fri 8am-4pm, Sat 9am-5pm, Sun 9am-4pm; WI-FI; 🐾), *Wye Bakery* (💻 wyebakery.com; Tue, Thur & Fri 8.30am-3pm, Sat to 12.30pm), a cash-only **Chinese restaurant and takeaway** (*Golden Wye*: ☎ 01233-811871; Sun-Mon & Wed-Thur noon-2pm & 5-10pm, Fri & Sat noon-2pm & 5-11pm) and a **post office** (Mon-Fri 9am-5.30pm, Sat 9am-12.30pm), all within a few metres of the trail, and just a few steps off the trail is a Co-op **supermarket** (daily 7am-10pm).

The trail also takes you past the front doors of a couple of decent pubs including the beautifully situated *Tickled Trout* (☎ 01233-812227, 💻 thetickledtrout.co.uk; food served summer daily noon-3pm & 5-8.30pm, Sat noon-8.30pm, Sun noon-4.30pm; winter hours variable so check; WI-FI; 🐾) and, on Church St, *The King's Head* (☎ 01233-812418, 💻 kingsheadwye.com; WI-FI; 🐾; food served Mon-Fri 8-11am, noon-3pm & 6-9pm, Sat 8am-9pm, Sun 8-10.30am, noon-4pm & 6-9pm). The King's Head also provides **B&B** (6D/1Tr, all en suite; 🛆; WI-FI; 🐾; from £34-44.50pp, sgl occ room rate).

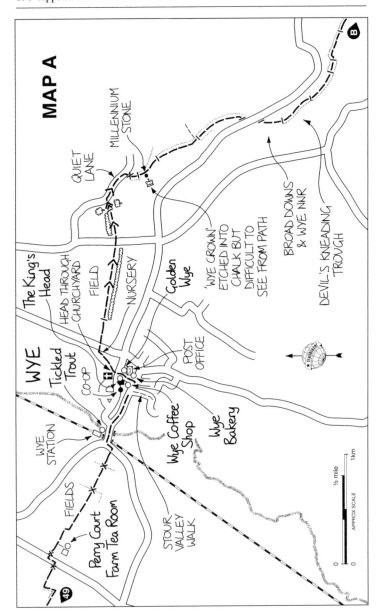

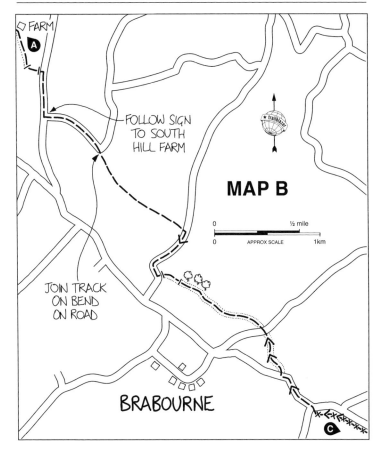

There are convenient **train services** (operated by South Eastern Railway; see box pp42-3) from Wye to Canterbury, Ashford International and London and **bus services** to Canterbury and Ashford; see pp45-8 for details.

It's after Wye that the scenery truly grows more majestic, reaching fairly spectacular heights at **Wye Crown**, a crown etched into the chalk on the hills overlooking the village, which was carved into the ground by local schoolchildren in 1902 to celebrate the accession of Edward VII to the throne. Further delights await just a few minutes further along at the **Devil's Kneading Trough**, a sheer-sided valley and part of Wye National Nature Reserve, which is home to no fewer than 21 different species of orchid.

From here the path takes you on some roadside rambling down to **Stowting** (Map C) and the secluded *Tiger Inn* (☎ 01303-862130, 💻 tigerinn.co.uk; food Wed-Sat noon-9pm, Sun noon-5pm). Note that the pub is closed on Mondays and Tuesdays other than on Bank Holiday Mondays. *(cont'd on p201)*

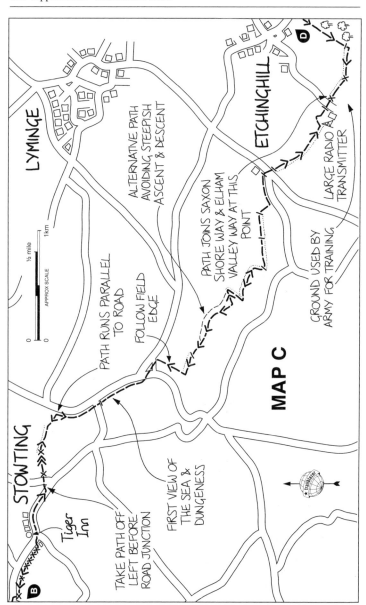

LYMINGE

ETCHINGHILL

STOWTING

Tiger Inn

B

D

MAP C

APPROX SCALE

½ mile

1km

ALTERNATIVE PATH AVOIDING STEEPISH ASCENT & DESCENT

PATH RUNS PARALLEL TO ROAD

FOLLOW FIELD EDGE

PATH JOINS SAXON SHORE WAY & ELHAM VALLEY WAY AT THIS POINT

GROUND USED BY ARMY FOR TRAINING

LARGE RADIO & TRANSMITTER

TAKE PATH OFF LEFT BEFORE ROAD JUNCTION

FIRST VIEW OF THE SEA & DUNGENESS

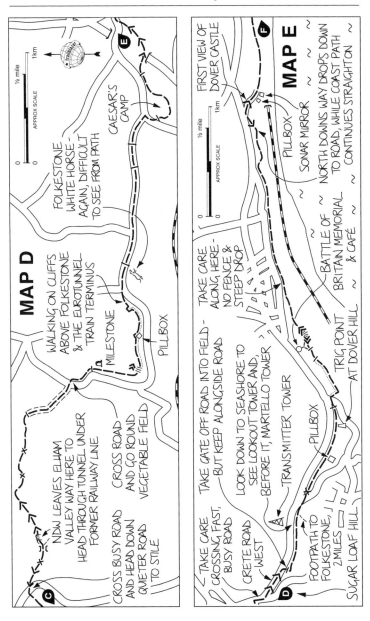

MAP D

WALKING ON CLIFFS
ABOVE FOLKESTONE
& THE EUROTUNNEL
TRAIN TERMINUS

MILESTONE

PILLBOX

CROSS ROAD
AND GO ROUND
VEGETABLE FIELD

CROSS BUSY ROAD
AND HEAD DOWN
QUIETER ROAD
TO STILE

NDW LEAVES ELHAM
VALLEY WAY HERE TO
HEAD THROUGH TUNNEL UNDER
FORMER RAILWAY LINE

FOLKESTONE
WHITE HORSE -
AGAIN, DIFFICULT
TO SEE FROM PATH

CAESAR'S
CAMP

APPROX SCALE

0   ½ mile   1 km

MAP E

FIRST VIEW OF
DOVER CASTLE

PILLBOX

SONAR MIRROR

NORTH DOWNS WAY DROPS DOWN
TO ROAD, WHILE COAST PATH
CONTINUES STRAIGHT ON

BATTLE OF
BRITAIN MEMORIAL
& CAFÉ

TRIG POINT
AT DOVER HILL

PILLBOX

TRANSMITTER TOWER

TAKE CARE
ALONG HERE -
NO FENCE &
STEEP DROP

LOOK DOWN TO SEASHORE TO
SEE LOOKOUT TOWER AND,
BEFORE IT, MARTELLO TOWER

TAKE GATE OFF ROAD INTO FIELD -
BUT KEEP ALONGSIDE ROAD

CRETE ROAD
WEST

TAKE CARE
CROSSING FAST,
BUSY ROAD

FOOTPATH TO
FOLKESTONE,
2 MILES

SUGAR LOAF HILL

APPROX SCALE

0   ½ mile   1 km

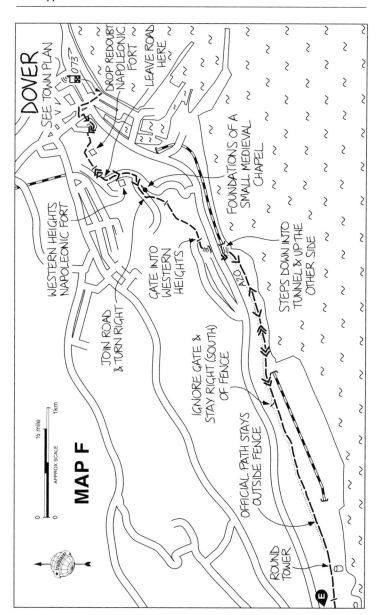

MAP F

APPROX SCALE

0   ½ mile
0   1km

DOVER

SEE TOWN PLAN

A2073

DROP REDOUBT NAPOLEONIC FORT

LEAVE ROAD HERE

WESTERN HEIGHTS NAPOLEONIC FORT

FOUNDATIONS OF A SMALL MEDIEVAL CHAPEL

GATE INTO WESTERN HEIGHTS

JOIN ROAD & TURN RIGHT

A20

STEPS DOWN INTO TUNNEL & UP THE OTHER SIDE

IGNORE GATE & STAY RIGHT (SOUTH) OF FENCE

OFFICIAL PATH STAYS OUTSIDE FENCE

ROUND TOWER

E

(cont'd from p197) It's a good place to rest before the tough haul back up to the crest of the Downs and your first view of the **English Channel** and, in the distance to your right, the thin spit of land of Dungeness, with the nuclear-power plant on its tail. You've got a lot of hard walking to do before you reach the shoreline, however, as the trail meanders through more farmland to the Folkestone Downs, an SSSI, and on around the outskirts of Folkestone itself, with the cacophony of the Eurotunnel train terminus immediately beneath you.

Folkestone itself can be reached from the trail via a footpath, though its a steep two-mile downhill trudge, which means of course an equally steep two-mile *uphill* trudge to return to the North Downs Way. Rather than head all that way, if it's just a bite to eat that you're after, we recommend keeping to the trail round the unusual cliff-edge mound hiding the remnants of **Folkestone Castle**, known locally if inaccurately as **Caesar's Camp** (Map D; the castle is believed to be Norman in origin, dating from approximately the 12th century), past its neighbour, the rutted, conical hill of **Sugar Loaf** next door (believed to have once been a pagan religious centre around 4000 years ago), to the **Battle of Britain Memorial** (Map E; ⌨ battleofbritainmemorial.org; memorial open 24 hours but indoor exhibition open daily Mar-Sep 10am-5pm, Oct-Feb to 4pm) at Capel-le-Ferne, with an interesting exhibition and a very good value *café* (same opening times as exhibition).

The clifftop walking begins in earnest now as, accompanied by the England Coast Path (which, curiously, often takes a different but parallel path to our own; why the two couldn't share the same path I have no idea), the North Downs Way soars above the Channel atop the famed **White Cliffs of Dover**. Look to your right and if the day is clear you should be able to discern the chalky undulations of the French coast across the Channel. It perhaps comes as little surprise, therefore, to find these last few miles spotted with various **pillboxes** and other fortifications. Most striking of all, perhaps, is the '**sonar mirror**', a large square concrete construction, concave on one side, that was built between the wars to act as an early warning system: the shape of the mirror allowing those who stand beneath it to detect the noise of approaching enemy planes from afar. Though several are still standing, they never actually saw active service – the radar was brought in soon after and proved a much more reliable and precise system.

After several exhilarating miles of this the path finally drops, heads inland and crosses the A20 via an underpass to negotiate the outskirts of Dover. What initially seems like an uninteresting route soon proves to be anything but as the trail leads you via the **foundations of a small medieval chapel** (Map F) built, possibly, by the Knights Templar, as well as two huge Napoleonic Forts, the second of which, the **Drop Redoubt**, is mightily impressive, particularly when viewed from above from the trail. From here it's a mere tumble down the hill to the town centre, from where you can turn left to the main square and the tourist office; or right towards the seafront and the official end of the North Downs Way.

It's a lovely ending, to a lovely, lovely walk.

APPENDIX B: TAKING A DOG

TAKING DOGS ALONG THE WAY

Many are the rewards that await those prepared to make the extra effort required to bring their best friend along the trail. But you shouldn't underestimate the amount of work involved. Indeed, just about every decision you make will be influenced by the fact that you've got a dog: how you plan to travel to the start of the trail, where you're going to stay, how far you're going to walk each day, where you're going to rest and where you're going to eat in the evening etc.

If you're sure your dog can cope with (and will enjoy) walking 10 miles or more a day for several days in a row, you need to start preparing accordingly. Extra thought needs to go into your itinerary. The best starting point is to study the town & village facilities table on pp28-9 (and the advice below), and plan where to stop and where to buy food.

Looking after your dog

To begin with, you need to make sure that your dog is fully **inoculated** against the usual doggy illnesses, and also up to date with regard to **worm pills** (eg Drontal) and **flea preventatives** such as Frontline – they are, after all, following in the pawprints of many a dog before them, some of whom may well have left fleas or other parasites on the trail that now lie in wait for their next meal to arrive. **Pet insurance** is also a very good idea; if you've already got insurance, do check that it will cover a trip such as this. On the subject of looking after your dog's health, perhaps the most important implement you can take with you is the **plastic tick remover**, available from vets for a couple of quid. These removers, while fiddly, help you to remove the tick safely (ie without leaving its head behind buried under the dog's skin). Being in unfamiliar territory also makes it more likely that you and your dog could become separated. All dogs now have to be **microchipped** but make sure your dog also has a **tag with your contact details on it** (a mobile phone number would be best if you are carrying one with you).

When to keep your dog on a lead

● **On cliff tops** It's a sad fact that, every year, a few dogs lose their lives falling over the edge of the cliffs. It usually occurs when they are chasing rabbits (which know where the cliff-edge is and are able, unlike your poor pooch, to stop in time). This point is particularly relevant if you opt for the Alternative Route (see Appendix A, pp195-201) which culminates in a lengthy stretch of cliff-top rambling before Dover.

● **When crossing farmland**, particularly in the lambing season (March to May) when your dog can scare the sheep, causing them to lose their young. Farmers are allowed by law to shoot at and kill any dogs that they consider are worrying their sheep. During lambing, most farmers would prefer it if you didn't take your dog at all. The exception is if your dog is being attacked by cows. Some years ago there were three deaths in the UK caused by walkers being trampled as they tried to rescue their dogs from the attentions of cattle. The advice in this instance is to let go of the lead, head speedily to a position of safety (usually the other side of the field gate or stile) and call your dog to you.

● **On National Trust land**, where it is compulsory to keep your dog on a lead.

● **Around ground-nesting birds** It's important to keep your dog under control when crossing an area where certain species of birds nest on the ground. Most dogs love foraging around in the woods but make sure you have permission to do so; some woods are used as 'nurseries' for game birds and dogs are only allowed through them if they are on a lead.

What to pack

You've probably already got a good idea of what to bring to keep your dog alive and happy, but the following is a checklist:

● **Food/water bowl** Foldable cloth bowls are popular with walkers, being light and taking up little room in the rucksack. You can get also get a water-bottle-and-bowl combination, where the bottle folds into a 'trough' from which the dog can drink.

● **Lead and collar** An extendable one is probably preferable for this sort of trip. Make sure both lead and collar are in good condition – you don't want either to snap on the trail, or you may end up carrying your dog through sheep fields until a replacement can be found.

● **Medication** You'll know if you need to bring any lotions or potions.

● **Bedding** A simple blanket may suffice, or you can opt for something more elaborate if you aren't carrying your own luggage.

● **Tick remover** See above.

● **Poo bags** Essential.

- **Hygiene wipes** For cleaning your dog after it's rolled in stuff.
- **A favourite toy** Helps prevent your dog from pining for the entire walk.
- **Food/water** Remember to bring treats as well as regular food to keep up the mutt's morale. That said, if your dog is anything like mine the chances are they'll spend most of the walk dining on rabbit droppings and sheep poo anyway.
- **Corkscrew stake** Available from camping or pet shops, this will help you to keep your dog secure in one place while you set up camp/doze.
- **Raingear** It can rain! • **Old towels** For drying your dog.

When it comes to packing, I always leave an exterior pocket of my rucksack empty so I can put used poo bags in there (for deposit at the first bin reached). I always like to keep all the dog's kit together and separate from the other luggage (usually inside a plastic bag inside my rucksack). I have also seen several dogs sporting their own 'doggy rucksack', so they can carry their own food, water, poo etc – which certainly reduces the burden on their owner!

Cleaning up after your dog

It is extremely important that dog owners behave in a responsible way when walking the path. Dog excrement should be cleaned up. In towns, villages and fields where animals graze or which will be cut for silage, hay etc, you need to pick up and bag the excrement.

Staying (and eating) with your dog

In this guide we have used the symbol 🐕 to denote where a place welcomes dogs. However, this always needs to be arranged in advance and some places may charge extra (the fee being anything from nothing to a whopping £50). Many B&B-style places have only one or two rooms suitable for people with dogs; hostels (both YHA and independent) do not permit them unless they are an assistance (guide) dog; smaller campsites tend to accept them, but some of the larger holiday parks do not – however, in either case it is likely the dog will have to be on a lead. Before you turn up always double check whether the place you would like to stay accepts dogs and whether there is space for them. When it comes to eating, some cafés accept dogs and most landlords allow dogs in at least a section of their pubs, though few restaurants do. Make sure you always ask first and ensure your dog is on a lead and secured to your table or a radiator so it doesn't run around.

Henry Stedman

APPENDIX C: GPS WAYPOINTS

Map	Waypoint	OS Grid ref	Description
1	001	N51° 12.771' W0° 47.621'	Start of NDW
2	002	N51° 13.007' W0° 44.421'	Bridge off road
3	003	N51° 13.236' W0° 42.944'	Turn-off to Seale
4	004	N51° 13.318' W0° 40.087'	The Good Intent at Puttenham
5	005	N51° 13.218' W0° 37.856'	Junction near Watts Gallery
6	006	N51° 13.503' W0° 34.603'	Turn-off after bridge to Guildford
7	007	N51° 13.490' W0° 31.779'	St Martha's Church
8	008	N51° 13.894' W0° 30.491'	Path to Countryside Centre, Newlands Cnr
9	009	N51° 13.833' W0° 27.918'	Hollister Cottage
9	010	N51° 13.757' W0° 27.547'	Turn-off to Shere
10	011	N51° 13.963' W0° 26.479'	First large concrete bowl
11	012	N51° 13.991' W0° 23.744'	Turn-off to the right off path
12	013	N51° 14.466' W0° 21.789'	Junction in Ranmore Common

Map	Waypoint	OS Grid ref	Description
13	014	N51° 15.180' W0° 19.372'	Underpass under A24
14	015	N51° 15.385' W0° 15.707'	Path leaves road north of Betchworth Stn
15	016	N51° 15.394' W0° 12.988'	Water tower
16	017	N51° 15.362' W0° 11.535'	Car park and snack bar
16	018	N51° 15.617' W0° 10.745'	Stonehenge-like slabs
17	019	N51° 15.902' W0° 09.185'	Quality Street, Merstham
18	020	N51° 16.058' W0° 06.050'	Whitehill Tower
19	021	N51° 15.658' W0° 05.061'	Finger post, Gravelly Hill
20	022	N51° 15.935' W0° 03.312'	Entrance to Marden Park & Church Woods
21	023	N51° 16.236' W0° 00.980'	Chalk Pit Lane to Oxted
22	024	N51° 17.098' E0° 01.477'	Mole End
23	025	N51° 17.050' E0° 03.886'	A233
23	026	N51° 17.539' E0° 05.003'	Gate by telegraph pole
24	027	N51° 18.111' E0° 06.054'	Stile after Melrose
25	028	N51° 18.702' E0° 07.697'	Turn-off to Knockholt Pound
26	029	N51° 18.785' E0° 11.273'	Otford Heritage Centre
27	030	N51° 18.761' E0° 13.844'	Turn-off to Kemsing
28	031	N51° 18.932' E0° 15.618'	Milestone
29	032	N51° 18.661' E0° 18.715'	Path behind some public bins
30	033	N51° 18.847' E0° 19.793'	Hognore Farmhouse
31	034	N51° 19.491' E0° 20.327'	Turn-off right down to Trosley Country Park
32	035	N51° 19.803' E0° 23.369'	Turn-off to Ryarsh
32	036	N51° 20.710' E0° 23.775'	Fork right over barrier
33	037	N51° 21.175' E0° 24.084'	Signpost to Sole Street Station
34	038	N51° 22.727' E0° 26.861'	Bridge over railway
35	039	N51° 22.861' E0° 28.140'	Speed memorial on A228
36	040	N51° 21.958' E0° 29.249'	Nashenden Farm
37	041	N51° 20.251' E0° 29.213'	Robin Hood pub
38	042	N51° 19.192' E0° 30.184'	Kit's Coty
38	043	N51° 18.895' E0° 30.892'	White Horse Stone
39	044	N51° 18.854' E0° 31.786'	Into woods after power lines
40	045	N51° 17.639' E0° 35.460'	Thurnham Castle
41	046	N51° 16.971' E0° 37.912'	Turn-off to viewpoint
42	047	N51° 16.092' E0° 38.611'	Join road in Hollingbourne
43	048	N51° 14.946' E0° 41.564'	Pilgrim's bench
44	049	N51° 14.647' E0° 43.249'	Lenham turn-off
45	050	N51° 14.213' E0° 45.057'	Sign to Highbourne Park
46	051	N51° 12.901' E0° 48.003'	Charing turn-off
47	052	N51° 12.722' E0° 48.448'	Lonebarn Farm

❏ **The first National Trail on Google Street View**
In 2016 Google announced that the North Downs Way was to become the first National Trail to feature on Google Street View. Volunteers and rangers were given heavy Google Trekker equipment – essentially a backpack fitted with a cluster of 15 lenses to record the entire length of the trail so that people at home could see what it's like to be on the trail from several different viewpoints – all without even leaving the comfort of their sofa at home. The backpack is said to weigh about 23kg (50lb) and volunteers were asked to take their time when recording the path to ensure the route is captured first time. In time it is hoped that all 15 trails will be captured and recorded in this way. See 🖥 nationaltrail .co.uk/north-downs-way/google-trekker.

Map	Waypoint	OS Grid ref	Description
48	053	N51° 11.796' E0° 50.950'	Dunn Street Farm Camping
49	054	N51° 11.472' E0° 54.121'	North Downs Way divides
50	055	N51° 11.773' E0° 54.566'	All Saints Church
51	056	N51° 13.272' E0° 55.942'	NDW milestone
52	057	N51° 14.682' E0° 57.755'	St Mary's, Chilham
53	058	N51° 15.826' E0° 59.862'	Under railway
54	059	N51° 15.975' E1° 00.681'	Road junction by Hatch Farm
55	060	N51° 16.874' E1° 03.821'	Take underpass to London Rd
56	061	N51° 16.743' E1° 04.858'	Canterbury Cathedral
57	062	N51° 15.357' E1° 08.076'	Roundabout at Patrixbourne
58	063	N51° 14.689' E1° 08.097'	Gate above A2
59	064	N51° 13.411' E1° 09.402'	Gate by drive to Ileden Farm
60	065	N51° 12.675' E1° 11.312'	Signpost in Womenswold
60	066	N51° 12.439' E1° 11.859'	Woolage Village
61	067	N51° 11.696' E1° 14.091'	Turn-off by pebbledash cottage
62	068	N51° 11.105' E1° 14.162'	Cross road in Shepherdswell
62	069	N51° 10.943' E1° 15.247'	Coldred Road
63	070	N51° 11.253' E1° 17.108'	Gate into overgrown churchyard
64	071	N51° 10.779' E1° 18.594'	Turn-off from Roman road
65	072	N51° 09.046' E1° 19.169'	Bridge over A2
66	073	N51° 07.333' E1° 18.916'	End of the NDW

Map key

		📖	Library/bookstore	●	Other
🛏	Where to stay	@	Internet	CP	Car park
O	Where to eat and drink	🏛	Museum/gallery	🚌	Bus station/stop
Δ	Campsite	✝	Church/cathedral	▭	Rail line & station
✉	Post Office	☏	Phone box	▦	Park
£	Bank/ATM	☒	Public toilet	📵 082	GPS waypoint
ⓘ	Tourist Information	☐	Building		

North Downs Way		Stile		Water	
Other path		Gate		Stream/river	
4 x 4 track		Cliffs		Trees/woodland	
Tarmac road		Bridge		Beach	
Steps		Fence		Lighthouse	
Slope		Wall		Golf course	
Steep slope		Hedge		32 Map continuation	

INDEX

Page references in **bold** type refer to maps

TRAILBLAZER TITLE LIST

Adventure Cycle-Touring Handbook
Adventure Motorcycling Handbook
Australia by Rail
Cleveland Way (British Walking Guide) – due 2018
Coast to Coast (British Walking Guide)
Cornwall Coast Path (British Walking Guide)
Cotswold Way (British Walking Guide)
The Cyclist's Anthology
Dales Way (British Walking Guide)
Dorset & Sth Devon Coast Path (British Walking Gde)
Exmoor & Nth Devon Coast Path (British Walking Gde)
Great Glen Way (British Walking Guide)
Hadrian's Wall Path (British Walking Guide)
Himalaya by Bike – a route and planning guide
Inca Trail, Cusco & Machu Picchu
Japan by Rail
Kilimanjaro – the trekking guide (includes Mt Meru)
Moroccan Atlas – The Trekking Guide
Morocco Overland (4x4/motorcycle/mountainbike)
Nepal Trekking & The Great Himalaya Trail
New Zealand – The Great Walks
North Downs Way (British Walking Guide)
Offa's Dyke Path (British Walking Guide)
Overlanders' Handbook – worldwide driving guide
Norfolk Coast Path & Peddars Way (British Walking Gde)
Pembrokeshire Coast Path (British Walking Guide)
Pennine Way (British Walking Guide)
Peru's Cordilleras Blanca & Huayhuash – Hiking/Biking
The Railway Anthology
The Ridgeway (British Walking Guide)
Sahara Overland – a route and planning guide
Scottish Highlands – Hillwalking Guide
Siberian BAM Guide – rail, rivers & road
The Silk Roads – a route and planning guide
Sinai – the trekking guide
South Downs Way (British Walking Guide)
Thames Path (British Walking Guide)
Tour du Mont Blanc
Trans-Canada Rail Guide
Trans-Siberian Handbook
Trekking in the Everest Region
The Walker's Anthology
The Walker's Anthology – further tales
The Walker's Haute Route – Mont Blanc to Matterhorn
West Highland Way (British Walking Guide)

For more information about Trailblazer and our
expanding range of guides, for guidebook updates or
for credit card mail order sales visit our website:

www.trailblazer-guides.com

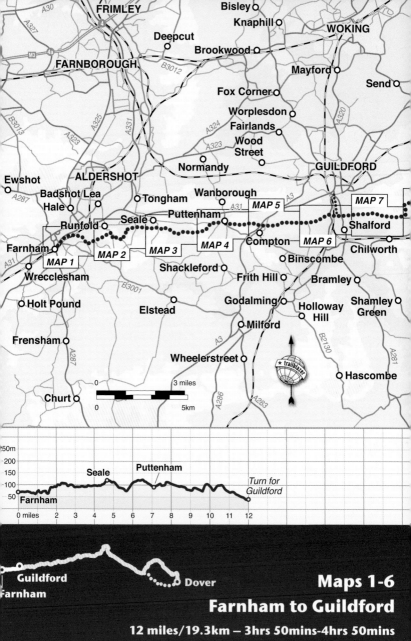

Maps 1-6

Farnham to Guildford

12 miles/19.3km – 3hrs 50mins-4hrs 50mins

NOTE: Add 20-30% to these times to allow for stops

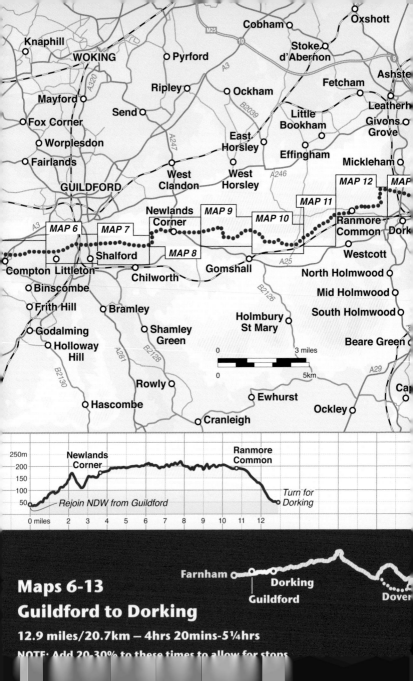

Knaphill · WOKING · Pyrford · Cobham · Oxshott · Stoke d'Abernon · Ashste

Mayford · Ripley · Ockham · Fetcham · Leatherh

Fox Corner · Send · Little Bookham · Givons Grove

Worplesdon · East Horsley · Effingham · Mickleham

Fairlands · West Clandon · West Horsley · A246

GUILDFORD

MAP 12 · **MAP**

Newlands Corner · **MAP 9** · **MAP 11** · Ranmore Common · Dork

MAP 6 · **MAP 7** · **MAP 10** · Westcott

Compton · Littleton · Shalford · **MAP 8** · Gomshall · North Holmwood

Binscombe · Chilworth · Mid Holmwood

Frith Hill · Bramley · Holmbury St Mary · South Holmwood

Godalming · Shamley Green · Beare Green

Holloway Hill · Rowly · Ewhurst · Capel

Hascombe · Cranleigh · Ockley

0 ——— 3 miles
0 ——— 5km

Elevation profile

250m · 200 · 150 · 100 · 50

Newlands Corner · Ranmore Common

Rejoin NDW from Guildford · Turn for Dorking

0 miles · 2 · 3 · 4 · 5 · 6 · 7 · 8 · 9 · 10 · 11 · 12

Farnham · Dorking · Dover

Guildford

Maps 6-13
Guildford to Dorking

12.9 miles/20.7km – 4hrs 20mins-5¼hrs

NOTE: Add 20-30% to these times to allow for stops

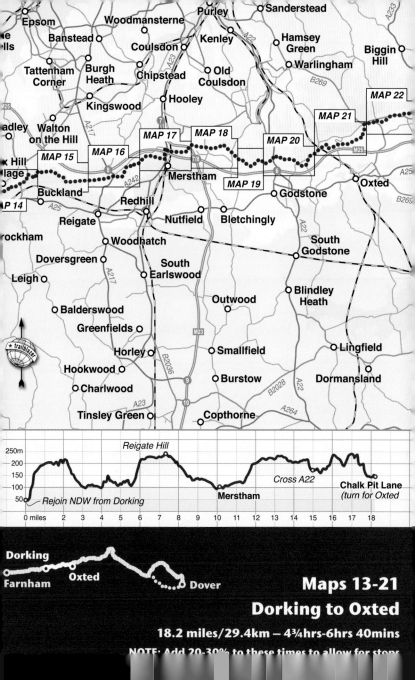

Epsom
Woodmansterne
Purley
Sanderstead
Banstead
Coulsdon
Kenley
Hamsey
Green
Biggin
Hill
Tattenham
Corner
Burgh
Heath
Chipstead
Old
Coulsdon
Warlingham
Kingswood
Hooley
MAP 22
MAP 21
Walton
on the Hill
MAP 15
MAP 16
MAP 17
MAP 18
MAP 20
Oxted
x Hill
lage
Buckland
Merstham
MAP 19
Redhill
Godstone
Reigate
Nutfield
Bletchingly
rockham
Woodhatch
South
Godstone
Doversgreen
South
Earlswood
South
Godstone
Leigh
Blindley
Heath
Baldersswood
Outwood
Greenfields
trailblazer
Horley
Smallfield
Lingfield
Hookwood
Burstow
Dormansland
Charlwood
Tinsley Green
Copthorne

Reigate Hill

250m
200
150
100
50

Rejoin NDW from Dorking

Merstham

Cross A22

Chalk Pit Lane
(turn for Oxted

0 miles 2 3 4 5 6 7 8 9 10 11 12 13 14 15 16 17 18

Dorking
Oxted
Farnham
Dover

Maps 13-21
Dorking to Oxted
18.2 miles/29.4km – 4¾hrs-6hrs 40mins
NOTE: Add 20-30% to these times to allow for stops

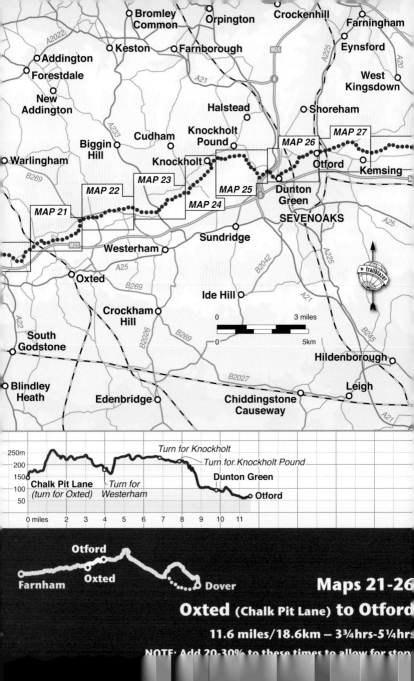

Bromley Common
Orpington
Crockenhill
Farningham
Keston
Farnborough
Eynsford
Addington
West Kingsdown
Forestdale
New Addington
Halstead
Shoreham
MAP 27
Cudham
Knockholt Pound
MAP 26
Warlingham
Biggin Hill
Knockholt
Otford
Kemsing
MAP 22
MAP 23
MAP 25
Dunton Green
MAP 21
MAP 24
SEVENOAKS
Westerham
Sundridge
Oxted
Ide Hill
Crockham Hill
South Godstone
Hildenborough
Blindley Heath
Edenbridge
Chiddingstone Causeway
Leigh

0   3 miles
0   5km

250m
200
150
100
50

Turn for Knockholt
Turn for Knockholt Pound
Dunton Green
Chalk Pit Lane
(turn for Oxted)
Turn for Westerham
Otford

0 miles   2   3   4   5   6   7   8   9   10   11

Farnham
Oxted
Otford
Dover

Maps 21-26

Oxted (Chalk Pit Lane) to Otford

11.6 miles/18.6km — 3¾hrs-5¼hrs

NOTE: Add 20-30% to these times to allow for stop

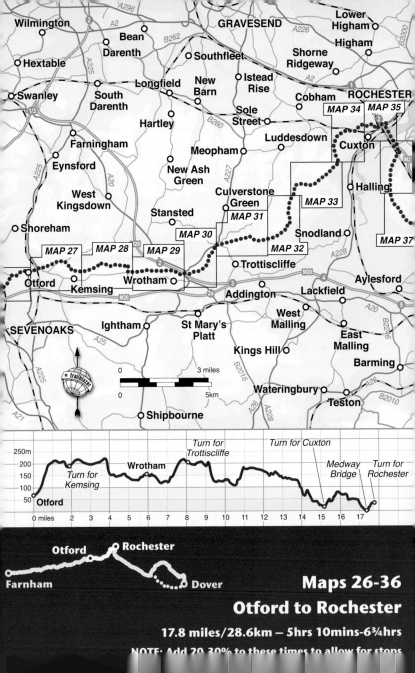

A296 · A2 · GRAVESEND · A226 · Lower Higham · B2000

Wilmington · Bean · Darenth · B262 · Southfleet · Higham · Shorne Ridgeway · A2

Hextable · Longfield · New Barn · Istead Rise · Cobham · ROCHESTER

Swanley · South Darenth · A225 · Sole Street · MAP 34 · MAP 35

A20 · Hartley · B260 · Luddesdown · Cuxton · M2

Farningham · Meopham · A227 · Halling

Eynsford · New Ash Green · Culverstone Green · MAP 33

West Kingsdown · Stansted · MAP 31 · Snodland

Shoreham · MAP 30 · MAP 32 · MAP 37

MAP 27 · MAP 28 · MAP 29 · M20 · Trottiscliffe · Aylesford

Otford · Kemsing · Wrotham · Addington · Lackfield · A20

SEVENOAKS · Ightham · St Mary's Platt · West Malling · East Malling · Barming

Kings Hill · B2016 · Wateringbury · A26 · Teston · B2010

0   3 miles
0   5km

Shipbourne

250m
200
150
100
50

Turn for Trottiscliffe · Turn for Cuxton · Medway Bridge · Turn for Rochester

Turn for Kemsing · Wrotham

Otford

0 miles 2 3 4 5 6 7 8 9 10 11 12 13 14 15 16 17

Otford · Rochester

Farnham · Dover

Maps 26-36

Otford to Rochester

17.8 miles/28.6km – 5hrs 10mins-6¾hrs

NOTE: Add 20-30% to these times to allow for stops

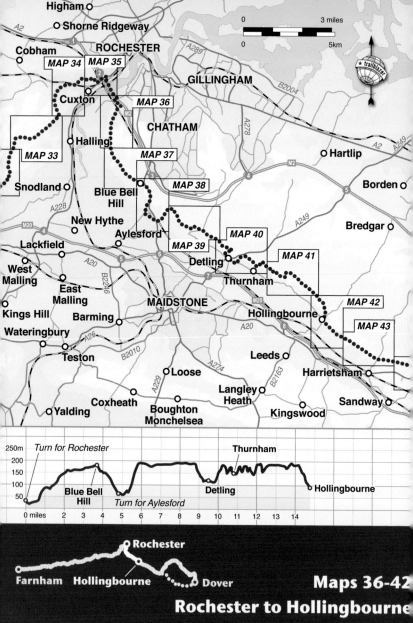

Maps 36-42

Rochester to Hollingbourne

14.8 miles/23.8km – 4hrs 35mins-6hrs 5mins

NOTE: Add 20-30% to these times to allow for stop

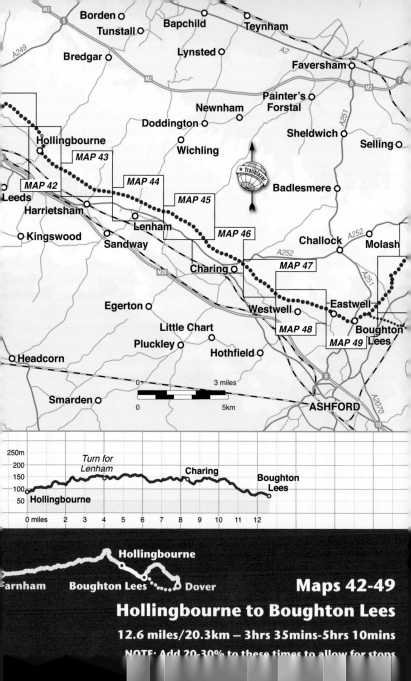

Borden ○
Tunstall ○
Bredgar ○
Hollingbourne
MAP 43
MAP 42
Leeds
Harrietsham
○ Kingswood
Sandway
Lenham
MAP 44
Egerton ○
Little Chart
Pluckley ○
○ Headcorn
Smarden ○

Bapchild ○
Lynsted ○
Newnham ○
Doddington ○
Wichling
MAP 45
MAP 46
Charing ○
Hothfield ○

Teynham ○
Faversham ○
Painter's ○
Forstal
Sheldwich ○
Selling ○
Badlesmere ○
Challock ○
Molash
MAP 47
Westwell ○
Eastwell
Boughton
Lees
MAP 48
MAP 49
ASHFORD

0   3 miles
0   5km

250m
200
150
100
50

*Turn for
Lenham*   Charing

Hollingbourne   Boughton
                                                    Lees

0 miles   2   3   4   5   6   7   8   9   10   11   12

Hollingbourne

Farnham   Boughton Lees ····· Dover

Maps 42-49

Hollingbourne to Boughton Lees

12.6 miles/20.3km — 3hrs 35mins-5hrs 10mins

NOTE: Add 20-30% to these times to allow for stops

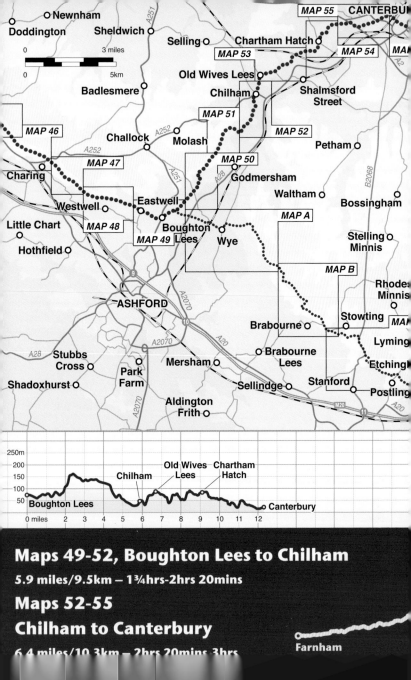

MAP 55   CANTERBU

Newnham

Doddington

Sheldwich

Selling

Chartham Hatch

MAP 53

MAP 54   MA

Old Wives Lees

Chilham

Shalmsford Street

Badlesmere

MAP 51

MAP 52

Petham

MAP 46

Challock

Molash

MAP 50

A252

Godmersham

Charing

MAP 47

Waltham

Bossingham

Eastwell

MAP A

Westwell

Boughton Lees

Wye

Stelling Minnis

Little Chart

MAP 48

MAP 49

MAP B

Rhode Minnis

Hothfield

ASHFORD

Brabourne

Stowting

MA

Lyming

Stubbs Cross

Park Farm

Mersham

Brabourne Lees

Etching

Shadoxhurst

Sellindge

Stanford

Postling

Aldington Frith

Maps 49–52, Boughton Lees to Chilham
5.9 miles/9.5km — 1¾hrs-2hrs 20mins

Maps 52–55

Chilham to Canterbury

6.4 miles/10.3km – 2hrs 20mins-3hrs

Farnham

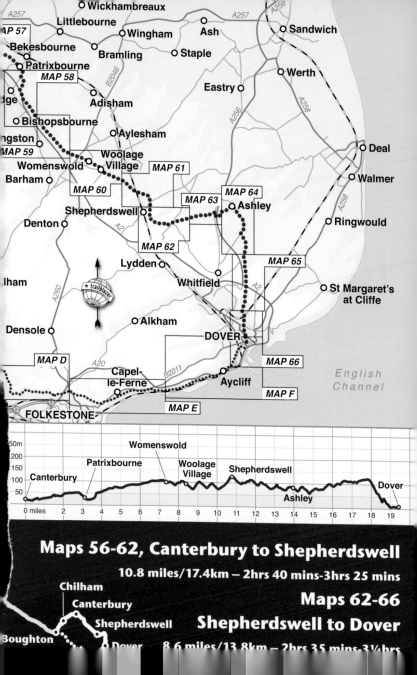

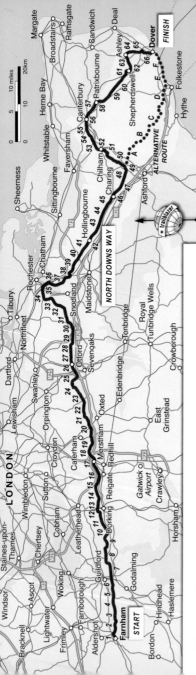

North Downs Way FARNHAM – DOVER via CANTERBURY